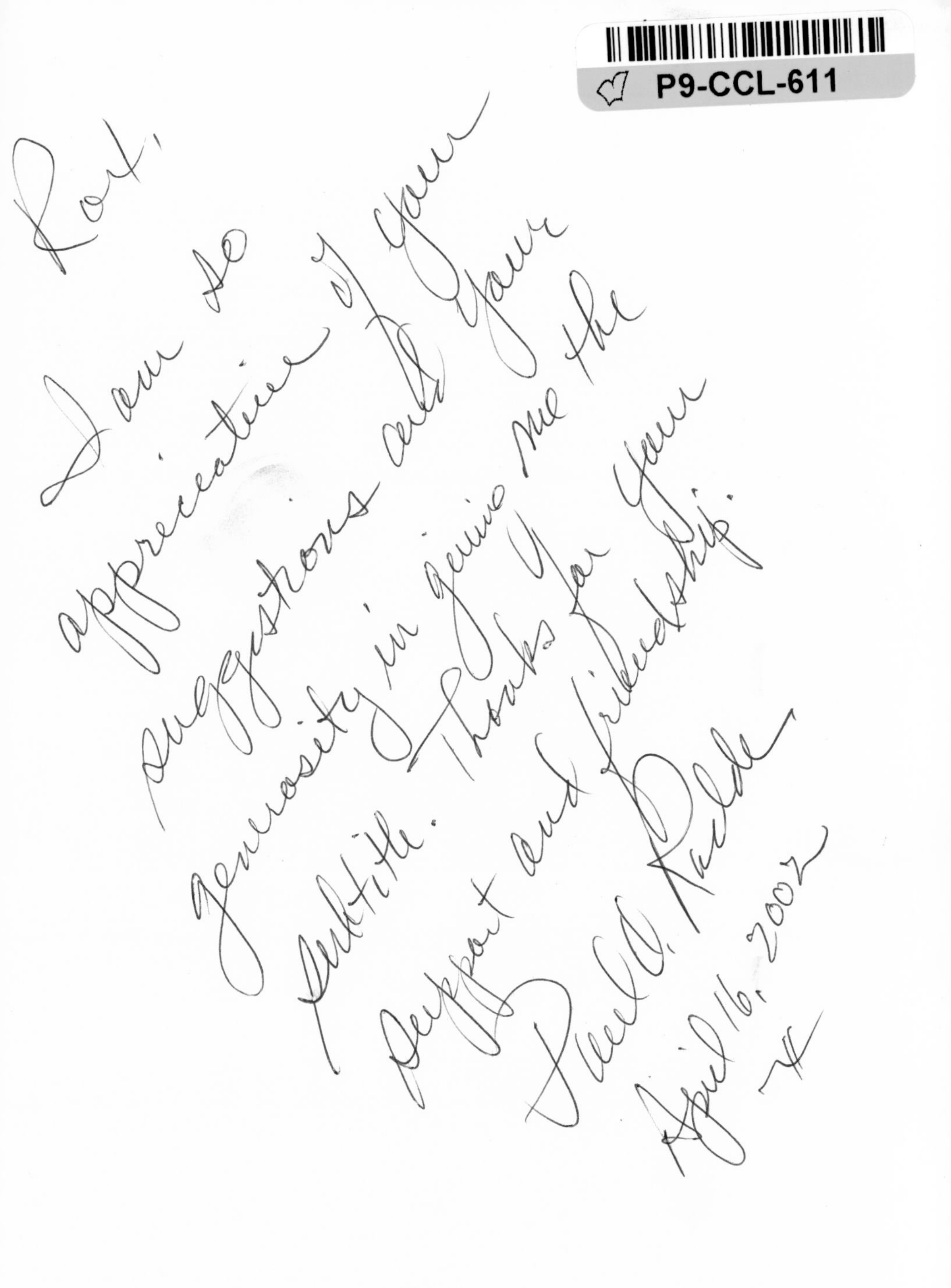

Ron,
I am so appreciative of your suggestions and your generosity in giving me the subtitle. Thanks for your support and friendship.
Paul O. Radde
April 16, 2002

Exercises to Access Thrival Instantly: The Sweetness of Self-Acceptance

You may be in a hurry to begin thriving. So, here are two of the quickest exercises that can get you into the thriving state immediately.

Having The Wind Knocked Out of You
You have probably found yourself doubled over, lying on the floor, gasping for breath. A sibling may have punched you in the "bread basket," or you ran into an immovable object and had the wind knocked out of you. The feeling of imminent collapse, even suffocation, is scary. For a few brief moments you experienced some of the challenges an asthmatic routinely faces for days on end – *Will I be able to draw another breath?* Wheeze…wheeze…wheeze. It is traumatic.

Chronic Defense Reinforced Against Trauma
Once you have been caved in, a physical whack may no longer be required to keep you cringing. You may begin bracing yourself for future contact. An insult, a put-down, slur, insinuation, threat, unkind word can feel like a punch in the stomach.

You flex your midsection in order to withstand the onslaught. What then happens over time is that your bracing yourself in anticipation, in self-defense, makes you tight all the time. However, your awareness may be so low that you are not even aware of your chronic tension.

How Do You Get the Wind Knocked Into You?
You can engage in practices to release, dissolve, and counter the effects that come from having the wind knocked out of you. But first, become aware of the tightness around your zyphoid appendix. That is the little *tailbone-like* structure that extends down from the middle-front of your rib cage. If

you are always on alert for the next punch to your midsection, physical or emotional, that defensive armor plating can keep you from living with any degree of joy.

Exercise One

1. Release Tension
Think about how an individual may settle into an easy chair at home to celebrate a success, such as reaching a goal. Lip-smacking contentment comes to mind. Certainly taking one or more full, deep breaths, even sighs, marks the moment. Chronic tension may be released briefly during this interlude, the ban on deep enjoyment lifted due to reaching a goal.

Try sighing to yourself right now. Sighing stretches out or expands your constricted solar plexus. Do you sense how it involves a fuller inhalation than normal? Followed by a shrugging off of tension?

2. Dissolve Tension
When you act upon the good feelings you generated through a *success,* you may feel invulnerable, and invincible. Your inner conversation says, "I have earned the right to be unassailable in this organization (relationship, family, community). I am *not liable to doubt, attack, or question* for the time being. During this time I value and treasure myself. I feel worthy, deserving, justified." And you may allow your solar plexus to melt and release tension from the inside out, becoming buttery rather than case-hardened.

With your enjoyment of success may come a tincture of love and appreciation for yourself. As solar plexus tension subsides, there is a tranquilizing effect on chronically tense stomach muscles. A feeling of well-being emerges. You emanate a warm glow in your belly. With the added touch of breathing freely, expansively, and openly, your heart naturally opens and you feel the buoyancy and lightness of thriving.

3. Counter Tension

This may be the least effective of the three approaches, for essentially you will be taking an adversarial approach to your own tension. That may invite more eventual resistance. But it can still bring short-term benefits. Countering your tension may result in fatiguing the chronically tense muscles, wearing them down until they cannot reassert themselves. Running, singing, bicycling, yoga, deep breathing, rapid fire breathing, may each and all exhaust the chronic tension for a period of time, a "grace period."

Those who rev themselves up not only are rewarded by an immediate endorphin rush, but may also experience the calm of a relaxed solar plexus, and the opening of their heart. The peace, calm, and serenity they attain constitute an implicit self-acceptance. However, to sustain that *high*, you will want to make your self-acceptance more explicit.

Here is yet another way of looking at the practices that relax the solar plexus.

Intentional

1. Physical – countering tightness, expanding the habitually constricted musculature of your solar plexus, opening it up with a full breath, deriving well-being.
2. Attitudinal – release, a sense of receptivity to relaxation, to not having to maintain constant defensiveness. A recent success is not required to attain this release, but it may provide the occasion and rationale with which to practice releasing.
3. Invoking – dissolve, seek your *inner beloved*, focus directly on your own practices in nurturing yourself through meditation, prayer, contemplation with willingness and determination.

Serendipitous

4. Spontaneous – disposed, open to the possibility, your feeling of self-acceptance just happens. You are comfortable, and in that comfort discover a serenity, warmth, and inner glow.

Exercise Two

Sing

Considered by itself, singing is one of the most spirit-lifting activities. Even the Bible says that *singing is seven times praying*. Sound vibrates throughout your being, providing a harmonious wave throughout your body. That alone provides release of tension. This basic attunement within yourself requires that you breathe deeply, that you support yourself with your breath, and that you express yourself as you let out this sound.

Use Your Discretion!

This is the main and underlying advisement with which you should consider anything you read here. You will still be required to exercise discernment and discretion in what you do as a result of reading this book, and in how you do it. You have to exercise skilled trust of yourself in utilizing intuition, gut feel, a strong sense of urgency, or an internal nudge as your prompt for action. You are ultimately the one who will live the results. Exercise your choice wisely.

For those of you who realize that the transition to thriving will take a bit more than these exercises, please continue on and read the book….

Use a highlighter throughout so that you can then flip through the pages and give yourself a lift reading your favorite tips, techniques & quotes.

Thrival Systems® is a registered service mark #1101750 of Dr. Paul O. Radde, first filed with the U.S. Patent and Trademark Office on January 14, 1977, as International class 041, and U.S. class 107: "conducting educational and training services, namely conducting lectures and workshops in self-management skills, knowledge, attitudes to attain a level of existence beyond survival." The offering of representations of thrival as speech, lecture, or seminar topic or content is restricted to the author and to registered associates of The Thrival Institute™.

Innertude® is a registered service mark #1963263 of the Dr. Paul O. Radde, first filed with the U.S. Patent and Trademark Office on March 29, 1995, as Type 041, "educational services, namely conducting conferences, workshops, seminars and classes in the field of inspiration."

The Thrival Institute™ is a subdivision of Thrival Systems® dedicated to research, assessment, conferences, and dissemination of information on eusthenics, the science of thriving. The Institute maintains the validity and authenticity of what is represented to the public as "thrival," in the venues outlined by class 041 of International trademark registry, in order to maintain the integrity of the word and meaning of thrival. Training, assessment and certification of Thrival Associates is conducted through the Thrival Institue™.

How to Have

Thrival!

An Above Average Day Every Day

Dr. Paul O. Radde

Path Lighter Press
Austin, Texas

Thrival! How to Have an Above Average Day Every Day

Thrival Systems®
1500 Riverside Drive, Suite 810
Austin, TX 78741
Website: thrival.com; e-mail:PRadde@thrival.com
(800) 966-8333, (512) 441-0833
Cover art and design by Michele Vrentas
Front cover photo © Karen Keeney
Back cover photo © Scott Warner

The author of this book does not dispense medical advice nor prescribe the use of any technique as a form of treatment for physical or mental problems without the advice of a physician either directly or indirectly. In the event you use any of the information in this book neither the author nor the publisher can assume any responsibility for your actions. The intent of the author is only to offer information of a general nature to help you in your quest for personal growth.

First printing, April, 2002
ISBN 0-9025872-1-4
Librarians contact Paul@thrival.com for cataloguing data.
Printed in USA

Futures Personal Growth Positive Psychology 1. Success, Psychological Aspects 2.Leadership

Thrival !

How to Have an Above Average Day Every Day

Part I. Defining Thriving and Thrival — Page

Books by Dr. Paul O. Radde

Supervising: A Guide for All Levels. San Diego, CA: University Associates,1981.Revised and republished as:

The Supervisor/Manager's Desk Top Guide. Austin, Tx.: Pathlighter Press, 2002

The Supervision Decision: An Employee Guide to Choosing and Moving Into a Supervisory Position. Austin, Tx.: Learning Concepts, 1981. Consolidated and republished as:

The Supervision Transition! An Employee Guide to Choosing and Moving Into a Supervisory Position. Fort Washington, MD: Thriving Publications, 1990.

Dr. Paul O. Radde Websites

I. **Thrival.com** contains many products and links to recommended products. This is the main website with contact information for the author's speaking, coaching, and consultative services. Paul@thrival.com

II. **ThrivalCoach.com** contains information regarding Dr. Radde's executive and professional coaching as well as management and organizational development consulting..

Foreword

When I first saw Paul Radde ten years ago, he was standing barefoot in a large bucket of ice water in front of a few hundred aspiring and professional speakers giving a presentation titled "Get Real and Get Rich." He was demonstrating a technique he uses for getting in touch with his thriving innards.

What stood out for me about Paul's presentation was that he was going way beyond speaking about life. He was actually ***living*** his life in front of us. He was showing us one of the countless ways he reaches and sustains a state of thrival, even as he shared his wonderful ideas with us.

As an "expert" on speaking, who has always valued and coached being real, I was finally experiencing a professional speaker who had gone all the way! He was literally vibrating authenticity, so much so that we all sat shivering with him in our seats.

I am excited to report that Paul has found a way to translate into writing his capacity to live and thrive, and to demonstrate it in front of groups. If you are prepared to receive him and engage him in the chapters that follow, you will not only resonate with his thrival experience, you will experience your own life energy flowing through you, as you sit reading and reflecting on his words.

Since, as Paul makes clear, thriving is not about *doing*, but rather about *being*. I encourage you to let him guide you toward the new frontier within yourself as you let his words enter your willingness.

You will discover beyond any doubt that true success is nothing but a certain feeling. And once you tap into those times you had that certain feeling, Paul will help you reenter it at will until your feeling of success becomes a locked-in state of well-being.

All the tips, techniques, skills and research of Paul's extraordinary and achievable life flowed from him onto these pages. And they are about to flow from these pages into your heart, mind, and soul. I invite you to live them and breathe them, and be well.

Lee Glickstein

Author of *Be Heard Now....*
Founder, Speakers Circles International

To

Denise Cavanaugh, and John P. "Jack" Clark

With Great Appreciation for Their Support

Acknowledgements

This book had gone through some 17 writings from 1976 to 2002. Consequently, I have involved and am indebted to many who have been supportive during that time period. With concern for those whom I may overlook, I wish to acknowledge and thank:

Elliot and Vera Aronson provided the group experience that led to my thriving in April, 1972, in Austin, Texas. Ray Bard, Larry Nolan Davis, Dick Casper, Marthanne Luzader, and Anne Durrum Robinson provided early discussion and support.

Naomi Monat opened the U.S. Chamber of Commerce Leadership Development Institute to the first Thrival™ workshop. Dr. Kathleen Sullivan, Notre Dame Alumni & Continuing Education Office provided a platform for continuing development .

John and Ana Koehne and Priscilla and Tarn-Tarn Singh-Friedberg provided and early writer's retreat and discussion. Readers and those who offered constructive comment include: Hunt Anderson, Maggie Bedrosian, Frank and Ramah Briganti, Robert Caspers, Kay Christopher, Dr. Ed Cronin, Ben Dean, Ramona DiDomenico, Roxanne Emmerich, Tim and Lindye Finn, Richard D. "Nick" Grant, Brenda Hayden, Patricia Loyd, Mary Marcdante, Ron and Mary Nahser, Anita Narvarte-Kitchens, Lee Neiderman, Kevin O'Sullivan, James M. Radde, S.J., Roger A. Revell, Ben Rodriguez, Al Seibert, Kathy Dougherty-Worner, Jane Wise, and Mary Zeigenhagen. Nelin Hudani provided rich learning in the completion stages.

Corey at Bailey's Crossroads Staples, Erin at Office Depot, and Pam at Buffalo Gallery, provided support along the way. Ruth Ann Wood, and Linda Wolfe Keister edited early drafts.

Main credit goes to my main editor, Leslie Stephen, who smoothed out the wrinkles, and to Jamie Fuller, an exquisite copy editor. Michelle Vrentas designed the cover. Karen Keeney provided the cover photo and witty comment throughout.

Part I

Defining Thriving and Thrival

Chapter 1
Life Can Be Better

All animals except man know that
the ultimate of life is to enjoy it.
Samuel Butler

Life can be better. You can love your life right where you are. That's correct. Right where you are. No more waiting for magical, seemingly impossible circumstances, conditions, or qualifications.

You can live better on a daily basis and enjoy your life to the fullest. You can learn to thrive on a daily basis. **Thriving is *not* about making *you* better. You are enough to begin with. Thriving is about making *your life* better.**

Circumstances change, for example. And the impact of those circumstances on you changes. One key to improving your life and thriving comes with adopting an inner stance that will sustain the resilience within you. You can be buoyant no matter what is going on around you. You can take a stance in yourself to live luxuriantly and to love your life.

Survive/Survival; Thrive/Thrival

The word "survive" relates to "survival," just as the word "thrive" relates to "thrival." Engaging in specific practices that make up the process of thriving will take you to the goal of thrival, just as past practices that made up the process of surviving have ensured your continued survival. Now it is time to move on beyond mere survival. Thrival moves us beyond survival.

Thrival is a new challenge, hope, and promise to the human species. It is a new goal to be sought after by our population just as survival has been the major goal of civilization up until now. By thriving moment to moment, you find enthusiasm in everyday work and living.

Up Until Now: Survival; From Now On: Thrival

Most of us are familiar with survival striving. The context in which most of humanity has lived up until now has been framed against a background of survival mentality, mindset, and lifestyle. Most of us have had neither the prolonged experience of thriving nor adequate circumstances to support and sustain the thriving experience.

"Thrival" does not yet enjoy widespread usage. When questioned about the word in 1976, Webster's Dictionary replied that "it is an interesting word. Please keep us informed of continued usage."

It is over 25 years since that letter, and internet searches show increasing awareness and use of the word "thrival." But few use or define thrival with the fullness of benefit it can bring to us as a species.

Not currently in dictionaries, "thrival" is a natural extension of the verb "to thrive, to grasp, to prosper." When thrival refers to a goal to be sought after, a state of being, it is a noun. But when thrival is used as a descriptor such as in reference to a *thrival skill*, then it is an adjective.

Thrival (thriv'l) n.

1. The act, state, or fact of prospering or flourishing in spite of or irrespective of circumstances.

Thrival: A Flagship Approach

"Thrival" is an umbrella term that comprehends the major movement of the entire personal growth, health, and wellness industry. It represents the potential for expansion of consciousness beyond the survival mindset among a large part of our population, moving toward the thrival mindset and mentality of abundance, confidence, and love. This is where we are going as a species, an inner journey with major implications for how we will live.

We are all headed toward thrival, whether we recognize it or not. Many approaches are advancing that cause, even when the approach does not comprehend the full implications of its trajectory.

The Flow State: So Near Yet So Far

Many who study states of awareness are within a hair's breadth of thrival, yet they do not comprehend the fullness of what they describe. For example, people confuse thriving with the "flow state" field-researched internationally and introduced by Dr. Mihalyi Csikszentmihalyi.

He details numerous observations of behaviors that indicate the thriving state, yet he does not distinguish the flow state from the thriving state. Dr. Csikszentmihalyi's flow state occurs when one is engaged in or highly focused and involved in a *goal-oriented activity*. Time may seem to slow down, or to fly by, one is so captivated by the interaction.

Thrival Is Distinct from the Flow State

Thriving, by contrast, is ***not limited to doing***, i.e., to goal-oriented activity, striving for progress, or to a work in progress. And that is a major difference.

You do not have to be "on task" to thrive. You can simply luxuriate in the glow of your own presence. For thriving is not about doing, but rather about being.

Thriving Is About Living Fully, Not Economic Status

Many writers, seminar presenters, columnists, and others have used the terms "surviving" and "thriving" to indicate contrast or progression, as in "thrive, don't just survive." But they are almost always referring to external economic circumstances. Their popular usage still refers to "diminishing the fears associated with survival by doing well in the new economy." Their contrast of the terms has little or nothing to do with inner fulfillment.

In this book, thriving is meant to be more than "relaxed survival" or "enduring existence." It is actually a great leap beyond survival, not simply a slight gradation or improvement. Thriving is a next level, living large.

It means that people "have it made" in an inner sense even when outside circumstances are trying. They can persist and elevate their inner standard of living with ease or effortlessness. Life can be on an ongoing roll, even when external circumstances are most difficult and unforgiving.

You will become aware of your future in the yet-to-be-discovered-and-explored opportunities for thriving in your own life. You will revel in the boundless possibilities open to you. This is your introduction to the new frontier within yourself.

Your new frontier is you. But rather than buying a fast car for a modern land rush, you only need to stake a claim and take full responsibility for your life. That will require your fully immersing yourself in managing your life.

Happiness...can grow in any soil, live in any condition.
It defies environment. It comes from within;
It is the revelation of the depths of the inner life as
Light and heat proclaim the sun from which they radiate.
Happiness consists not of having, but of being;
Not of possessing, but of enjoying.
It is the warm glow of a heart at peace with itself...
Happiness is the soul's joy in the possession of the intangible...
Happiness is paradoxical because it may coexist with trial, sorrow and poverty.
It is the gladness of the heart, rising superior to all conditions...

William George Jordan

Joy Is Your Birthright

This can mean living on a higher level of consciousness. Recognizing your internal options can free you to return to a joy that is your birthright.

Not sure if you are ready for that just yet? No rush. You can begin at your own rate and pace.

Living on a higher level of consciousness and enjoyment does not depend upon elevation in economic class, promotion, retirement, relationship. Your work begins within, and your results are not dependent upon circumstances.

The essence of thriving is the ability to persevere and maximize the moment, irrespective of what is going on around you. Unlimited joy, peace of mind, and serenity await you once you gain a mastery over yourself in order to put yourself in a sustainable balance and state of being. You can learn how to manage and to support a more complete presence, fuller awareness, and deeply seated appreciation.

Thriving Essentially "Is" the Feeling of Success

We are all meant to experience the lightness, buoyancy, peace of mind, deep connection, and exuberance for life that so often are the very feelings that accompany success. That feeling of success can be retained and sustained through changing circumstances and adversarial confrontations. But first you will want to get into the thriving state.

In the long run, no one but you really makes your life better. How you manage yourself determines whether you will thrive or just get by. Boosting your life to a "better" level is neither automatic nor a free ride. There are always dues to be paid. So, if you are like most of us, you have issues to deal with regarding your current self-image and personality. You probably have some issues to address on your way to thriving.

If there are shortcuts to thriving, one could come in the form of an early realization, full acceptance, even reverence, of who you are. Then you can enjoy the fruits of that realization immediately. But generally before thriving becomes second nature to you, you will need to become practiced at self-monitoring and self-management skills.

The particular guidelines set out in later chapters consider major approaches and typical paths. Individual journeys to get into the thrival state will vary in length over diverse personal terrain. Take a shortcut if you find one. And be prepared to discover your own unique path and portal.

Spelling Out the Tacit Dimension of Thriving

Most of us "know more than we can say." But, we can work on saying more about what we know. Even so, our experience is going to limp a little in any telling or description. You not only had to be there, but to be in that state or experience.

It would have been best if you had been in my skin for that experience. You weren't. So, a major enterprise in relating a thriving experience is in drawing sufficient parallels and comparisons so that you can understand it in terms of similarities with your own experience.

The tacit dimension of an experience is said to be similar to the portion of an iceberg that remains submerged and unseen. As more and more of the thriving experience is articulated, more of the experience is exposed. The tacit, known, yet unarticulated, becomes known and articulated.

As we break new ground toward thriving, you have the potential to contribute to others' thriving. As you begin to home in on the experience for yourself, you benefit others by detailing and articulating your approach, what works for you, and your experience of thriving.

For the moment, in order to recognize the challenge of relating your meaningful experiences, recall your last truly delightful experience. Then attempt to explain it so that a listener can understand and arrive at some semblance of that experience for oneself. This will help you to understand the challenge in helping you to capture the essence of what thriving truly is, through words.

Years of reflection, inquiry, and synthesis have gone into:

1. posing and translating my experience for you in terms that you already have experienced, and then in
2. detailing the known guidelines or portals of entry to gain access to the thriving state.

And it all began in a weekend workshop.

The Author's Personal History with Thriving
My own initial experience with thriving as a distinctive and extraordinary state of being went on for fifteen weeks from mid-April into late August of 1972. During that period, I was a graduate student in counseling psychology at the University of Texas at Austin. For that time, I truly lived the "richest experience" of my life.

I experienced high positive energy, personal presence, and bliss. I was in a highly sensitized state of awareness. I was paying attention and responding for the first time to my own sense of connectedness.

When I first began to really relish every moment of my life, I thought that what I had discovered for myself was simply a natural next step from my earlier, more restrained lifestyle. At the time I thought this new way of feeling, acting, and being was the normal progression that everyone experienced when he or she stepped beyond where I had been.

For some, perhaps my experience of thriving sounds much like their average day. For me, it was a satisfying, fulfilling, full level above my former lifestyle. And I initially just rose into it like a diver rising to the surface.

Graduate school in counseling psychology had its good moments, most of them in extracurricular activity. I had been involved in student activities, and at one point turned down a run for student body president. But thriving resulted from my dealing with issues I had with myself.

For some time I had carried a major burden of guilt regarding my mother's death. When I was nine months old, she died of complications due to the still birth of my brother. Uninformed of the still birth, I took responsibility for her death until I was told at twenty-seven. I bore guilt for having killed her. Even when I found out that I was not responsible, this guilt had become such a part of my daily existence that I continued to carry it. And I stifled any sense of joy.

I was concerned that I could be a danger to others, that deep down I might be malicious. After all, if you can kill your own mother, what else might you be capable of? Given that belief and concern, I kept a tight rein on myself.

The experience that led to thriving came from my trying to help out a friend who was stuck on a personal issue. But rather than take my advice, he told me that the fact that I cared enough to be concerned meant more to him than the specific advice I was offering. Anything additional was superfluous.

While reviewing that experience the next day, I suddenly realized that I was really not malicious. When that discovery finally hit home, enough pent-up inhibition released to launch me into my thriving state.

It was like finally bringing all of myself to the table. I involved myself more directly with people, coming on straight, saying what was on my mind, and maintaining good posture.

I responded to where people were coming from without evasiveness, facing compliment and complaint equally. I stopped my own distracting head tilting or brow wrinkling. Rather, I would level with people, look them straight in the eye, and state my truth with caring and tact.

Approach-Approach v. Approach-Avoidance

As part of my newfound directness, there was nothing I ran away from, nothing that invoked fear. I faced everything in an approach-approach mode, not my prior approach-avoidance mode. I met all challenges head on and relished them.

My life was finely tuned. I breathed deeply and fully, with flared nostrils – no Breathe Right® strip needed. I ate just the right amount of food and slept about 5 hours of really deep sleep a night. Then I would wake up rested and raring to go. I faced the day without dread.

Whenever I momentarily fell out of the thriving state, I could recover the lightness, grounding, centeredness, expansiveness, even euphoria by simply taking a deep full breath into the front of my solar plexus. That reconnected me.

I felt that I had finally arrived as a person. More than the acceptance I felt for myself, I just felt so good that I thought I had broken through to a transformation level that several of my more positive friends had been enjoying all along.

I immediately set out to tell them of my breakthrough. However, as I relayed my experience to friends and colleagues, it became obvious that they did not know what I was talking about.

For example, I was eager to let my friend Bill know that I had finally arrived at his level of personal acceptance and commensurate good humor. Bill always seemed to have a smile on his face. It took only a minute to tell him that I finally felt like I was in a better place, one I thought he had been in all along.

I felt so content with myself, and so energized. I considered myself on an entirely new level of enjoyment. And I was glad to be finally joining him, able to match his ebullient mood. At least I would not be dragging him down.

Sharing or Scaring with the News

Bill's reaction was totally unanticipated. His eyes glazed over. He whirled around and walked away without a word. At that moment, I was simply dumbstruck.

What I made out of Bill's behavior, was that he was probably not self-accepting after all. He had taken my intended compliment as a confrontation. While he had always shown that congenial, hail-fellow-well-met, gregarious, Irish-American exterior, that was apparently only a thinly disguised veneer, one that I had unwittingly misread.

The Fall from Grace

Over the last weeks of my sustained run of thriving, several issues arose and one close relationship cratered. What then seemed like events of major life importance all piled on in one great crescendo. For example, the person who created the field I wanted to enter, my major advisor, was down on my case.

Shortly thereafter, I woke up one day and had lost my key to getting back into thriving. I could no longer access my thriving state. Suddenly I was separated by a plate glass window, now living on the margins outside this wonderful state of being.

Taking the Vow

At that time, I made what I call my "Scarlet O'Hara vow." Remember Scarlet's scene in *Gone with the Wind*? She was clawing for roots with her bare hands out in the turnip fields at her plantation, Tara. The Civil War was over and there was nothing to eat. She vowed with upraised fist, "as God is my witness, I will never go hungry again."

My personal vow to myself was that I would get back into the thriving state. And when I did get back in, I vowed I would know **each step of the way** so that I could get it back when I wanted.

At the very least I wanted to be able to "find the way in" to thriving at will and then be able to live there the thriving state more. And, best-case scenario, I wanted to find ways to bolster my thrival connection, to lock into the thriving state.

Entry has certainly been more possible. I have yet to lock into my thrival connection permanently. That work remains to be done. And you can join me in the quest.

My Vow to You

In writing this book over the past 26 years, a major intention was to be able to share with you, my reader, specific guidelines on how to get into the thriving state. I wanted to lay down a trail of breadcrumbs with which you could easily find your way. I wanted to spell it out so that ultimately you could get there on your own, manage your own thriving, reliably, whenever you wished.

That is what this book is all about…a reliable trail through three rules and seven guidelines to thriving. That search has propelled me through 18 writings of an ever-evolving work.

Thriving: Not a Commonplace Experience

Through all my explorations into methods for regaining thrival since 1972, whether doing speeches, psychotherapy, conducting training groups, organizational consulting, or just hanging out with friends, I am convinced that the thriving experience is not commonplace. At least it has not been something that people talk about without prompting.

Very few people seem to be living in a thriving space, or letting on that they are, if indeed they are. A very small number, about one per cent of my thrival speech and workshop audience report that they are in the thriving state most of the time.

Doing the Numbers on the Percentage of Thrivers: 1%

Initially, I estimated that about 5 percent of the population was thriving regularly. However, I have since **revised my estimate downward to about 1 percent of the population who thrive regularly, or fewer.** Those are the few who currently **derive the richest experience of, and full enjoyment from, their lives.**

I am, however, hopeful and convinced that many have experienced the thriving state. Yet for them thriving constituted **an exceptional state of well-being**, one that few expected could become a regular part of their daily life by choice. The don't see thriving as viable, possible.

Committed Seekers: 35%
My guesstimate is that some 35 percent of the population, have had undeniable experiences of thriving. And they want more! They are searching and personally committed to get it back. But they do not know whether there is a clear path or approach to thriving, let alone where to look. Answering their search is part of the reason for this book. They [you] are the readers for whom this book was written.

Going About Their Daily Lives: 40%
Yet another 30 to 40 percent of the population can tap into or recall a thriving experience. But they have not put energy into seeking to thrive directly. Their involvement with other matters may leave them short of the body-mind-spirit resources, or even "time," to actively pursue thriving.

Think Thriving Is Forbidden Fruit: 24%
The remaining 20 percent seriously doubt that they deserve or are supposed to feel this good during this lifetime for an extended period of time. Isn't this what the *hereafter* is supposed to be about?

The specific directions presented here are offered as current state-of-the-art thrival guidelines and approaches placed in narrative and exercises that will provide the understanding, skill, and commitment required for you to ***reach and return to the thriving state: thrival.***

You can gain a greater aptitude and capacity for thriving by utilizing the tips, techniques, tools, skills, attitude, and knowledge you will gain here to assist you in accessing the thriving state. You will learn life management skills together with seven guidelines to your thriving state.

The Work of This Book Is:

1. To make you aware of the opportunity to live in a thriving state that is natural and effortless, together with the
2. Specific means to access that state of being, while at the same time
3. Making you aware of the great discipline of focus, balance, and will power to access and sustain your thriving state.

Remember that thriving is your natural state. So, once you truly align your intention and attitude to allow yourself to love your life and thrive, you will marvel at the ease and effortlessness of your life.

The Road Ahead

This book provides the tips, techniques, and skills that can lead to thriving. It describes specific steps and guidelines by which to approach thriving. It offers specific perspective and approaches to help you in anticipating and working through the process of transition from survival mentality to thrival lifestyle. And it offers incentives, encouragement, clarity, and guidance about your exploration.

Gaining Reliable Access

One challenge in my search was to find ways to internally organize myself in order to access thriving more. How could I get myself back into thriving? Much happened in the first 19 years to make me aware that the transition that thriving requires is not a simple flip of a light switch. More later….

Different people will require individualized and unique guidance to reach thriving. So, to accommodate the likely variety of journeys, this book lays out several non-linear approaches. And there may be certain incantations required as well. You will be breaking through an eons-long survival trance state that has captured us all.

Because Survival Is Just Not Enough Anymore

So far almost all of human history has been motivated by the basic desire to endure, to survive, to postpone death. But neither survival nor mere existence is enough anymore. The mentality and lifestyle standard is being raised to thrival.

You can learn to thrive from what you have already done, from your own personal thrival experiences. You can also go deeply within to release yourself back to your natural, essential self. And there, with full appreciation of who you are, you can release your energy and thrive. And you can also learn from other people's experiences.

My Wish for You: To Feel What It Is to Thrive!

When Steve Young, quarterback of the San Francisco 49ers' was interviewed after his first Super Bowl win, he said, "This is so wonderful. I wish you all could feel this." ***This*** refers to his feeling of ecstasy for his accomplishment.

Steve succinctly expressed my desire – that you feel how wonderful it is to thrive. For even though you and I will not be quarterbacking the Super Bowl, we can still thrive no matter what our profession, age, station, or place in life. You can learn to love your life right where you are. Do you want to thrive? Or merely exist? As Robert Frost challenges:

I bid you to a one-man revolution,
The only revolution that is coming

Chapter 2

The Thrill of Thriving: Life as Good as It Gets

Now most of us have experienced from time to time a period of supreme aliveness. I know that at such times when everything is right within me, when my body is well and my thoughts are in tune with the world, my spirit soars with the joy of living. Every sense organ in me is wide open to drink in the impressions of all that I see and feel and hear. And at such times, I actually feel intoxicated with the ecstasy of just being alive. No task is too difficult; no hurdle too high.

Halbert Dunn, High Level Wellness

The focus of this book is on this exceptional state of well-being called thriving.. Thriving is an experience of lightness, expansiveness, and exceptional well-being; the precise exceptional moments of well-being that many people say make life worth living. Yet, the thriving state exceeds the typical daily experience of most people So, this book is dedicated to providing you with the means to having more of those magical moments of pure presence that add zest to life, and put a thrill in your solar plexus.

Yet accessing that thriving state of well-being depends upon connecting with a place within yourself, rather than depending upon any overt action you might take. If you come from your deep fire, you are in closer contact with your enthusiasm, exuberance, and tingling moments. So, we will explore and familiarize ourselves with that place.

The Origins of the Thrill

When I was a child, I rode "shotgun" in the right front seat of the car. And most highways would have uneven patches of pavement. When the car hit a sudden rise in the road it tended to lift off and float for a moment before returning to the pavement. In those brief moments, I used to get what was called a "thrill" from that lift and float. The thrill was the feeling of lightness, buoyancy, weightlessness.

On occasion, when I rode on a Ferris wheel at an amusement park, I would get that same feeling, only more sustained. As my seat circled over the top and began to glide down, I again felt that lightness of being, that thrill.

When I first experienced thriving, one consistent part of the experience was that feeling of a thrill in my sternum and solar plexus. And then I found I was able to prompt that feeling with my breath. With a good expansive breath into my solar plexus and belly, I could connect with that feeling. Then, continuing to hold the focus, I could expand that feeling, making it spread throughout my body.

A giddy feeling was now spreading throughout my body, giving me a thrill all over. That thrill is like a little tickle or tremor, at once sensuous and delightful. And I can often sustain it with more full breaths. Each breath generates another flush of delightful sensations.

Several of the early positive psychology studies find subjects reporting a thrill when they are given little gifts or unexpected surprises. It is more than the hair on the back of their necks standing up and goose bumps breaking out. It becomes a little wave of joy that pulses throughout.

This phenomenon already has practices in several cultures. For example, the Cajuns in Louisiana talk of the practice of "lagniappe," or giving a little extra. Grocers in my home town in the fifties used to provide treats such as a few candy bars as a bonus for paying the monthly tab for the groceries. In Spanish, the word *pilon* refers to adding a little extra.

The term "thrill" comes from ***being run through by a sword.*** In fact, a thrill is a little bit like a penetration. But it is more subtle, more like a drop of rain on a still pond. The ripples emanate out from the point of entry. The thrill enters like silent laughter and spreads throughout the body if you allow it or give it even the slightest encouragement.

Many see it as a giddiness, the stuff of childish experience. And they stop it immediately, or wait for it to subside. When you stop it from pulsing through your body, you miss a great deal of enjoyment.

> One who is happy is fulfilling
> the purpose of existence.
>
> Dostoevsky

Getting *That Feeling* Again

So far, descriptions of thriving given by others have been readily recognizable among those who have experienced thriving and discussed the experience. The feelings experienced while thriving may be prove to be quite varied, but so far there is a great deal of similarity. Here are several:

For some this thriving feeling is **the release** they experience when they put their feet up after a long day, marking a precious moment of well-being, peace, and equanimity.

For others, their **inner sense of satisfaction** shows up in a little Cheshire cat grin that can break out at the corners of the mouth. This is **a feeling of contentment** rather than an expression of smugness.

An athlete might put on her "game face," which **belies the welling excitement** but confirms the **grounding and inner confidence** she brings to the contest. She is well within herself.

Someone else might stimulate a whiff of menthol coolness in His air passages. Once expanded each breath may become more robust, expansive, relaxed, and soothing.

Other People's Descriptions of Thriving

Still others have described their own experience of thriving in sound bites such as *"feeling really together, lightness, satisfaction, contentment, humor, high self-esteem, connectedness, and wisdom."* Others crystallize their experience as *"the ultimate in psychological well-being, limitless pleasure, repossessing myself, cherishing what is inside, a new quality of existence, finding my core energy, multi-dimensional maturity, coming home to my true deep self, upbeat, joy indefinable,... living juicy."*

Thriving is an enviable state to be in. Imagine no longer tensing yourself up, or making yourself vulnerable to the indiscriminate or whimsical judgments of boss, associates, family, or friends. Would that be a relief?

The Richest Experience of Your Life

Thriving is about maximizing the moment and having **the richest experience of your life**. That means that whatever you are feeling or experiencing, you will feel it fully, deeply, profoundly. That is the goal in thriving, to have the richest experience of your life, full and unfiltered.

Feeling great may begin with enjoying incoming sensations. But you have to allow yourself that ease to begin with. And that means loving your life right where you are. You may be in the midst of the morning sprint to get the kids to child care. How can you enjoy that to the fullest?

When you tap into that thriving level of experience, your spirit soars. You feel a profound simplicity and depth in your being. You become whole, unconflicted. Each breath is an inspiration and a discovery. You can suck the juice right out of that moment.

Feelings, glimmers, and pulsings arise like an effervescence and grab your attention with special intensity. You release and ride a groundswell of energy that comes from within. As you begin to bask in the glow of your own presence, you discover the peacefulness that comes with self-realization.

The beginning of wisdom is
the definition of terms.
Socrates

Thriving Defined
The Merriam Webster Collegiate Dictionary, tenth edition, characterizes "thriving" as marked

- *by success or prosperity,*
- *by growing vigorously [flourishing],*
- *gaining in wealth and possessions.*

Thriving Sound Bite: It's "That Feeling" of Success
For years I have attempted to hone down and synthesize the definition of thrival. Attention spans and media exposure demand the elevator speech, the 5 o'clock news sound bite description of thrival. When you are on a ski lift, you don't have much time. The same with a marketing phone call. Make it quick or forget it.

Thriving tends to resonate most with people's experience when referred to as **the feeling that often accompanies success: lightness, expansiveness, buoyancy, and even euphoria.** Most people I have asked tend to equate the feeling that accompanies success with thriving.

When they reach whatever point constitutes success for them, they expect to have *that feeling* or it makes the effort empty and ultimately disappointing. The people with whom I spoke also assumed that they had to achieve a definite goal or outcome in order to "be successful" and to get that accompanying feeling. They were from the "doing" school of thought.

The successful person is described as one who is:
thoughtful and peaceful;
full of love, joy, fun;
full of bliss, harmony, ease;
who is carefree, spontaneous, even outrageous;
who knows he or she has endless choices,
endless possibilities;
who believes in lots of laughter, serenity, and
effortlessness.

Daniel Jingwa
Blue Sky Thinking

You can access that thriving feeling without great strain or difficult projects. In fact, thriving is effortless. It is your natural state. So, the thrill of success can come to you as your emerging essence, from the inside out, rather than as the result of a compelling act from the outside in.

Thriving, as presented here, means:

- *relishing your life,*
- *enjoying each moment,*
- *living where your spirit soars,*
- *flourishing under life's major pressures,*
- *rekindling the connection with your deep fire.*

The Thriving Experience Described

We begin with a description of this form of living. Tie it into your own experience.

It's an inner peace. Externally I'm not affected. It's like being at one with your element in spite of how that sounds. I don't have to prove anything to anyone. My mere existence has importance. I don't need approval. You don't need anyone to make you feel how good you are.

When I get up in the morning I like what I see in the mirror. That's thriving. That person has value – the ability to accomplish something. Even walking out the door has value, working in the garden. For example, I might be working in my garden, and when I finish what I am doing, I can look at the flowers, and I have a sense about the job I've done. I don't need someone to drive up and approve.

People told me for years that I couldn't do things. At Notre Dame when I entered as a freshman, I weighed 133 pounds. Ara Parseghian was afraid to let me play. By the time I graduated, I had bulked up to a full 155 pounds. People told me I was too small, too short, that I couldn't handle the punishment. I had to learn to thrive within. It is a sense of confidence about who you are!

Joe Theisman, Super Bowl-winning quarterback for the Washington Redskins in a July 25, 1992 interview.

In thriving, you find and feel the value in everything you do. Joe also distinguished thriving from both

- being in the zone and
- the ecstatic state of being at one with everything.

Thriving Is Distinct from Being in the *Zone*

Of the zone, he said, "There are some days when I would throw a pass and it would bounce right off the receiver's numbers, and he would still pull it down. On days like that I knew that things would go right."

Being in the zone is frequently about an altered state of consciousness that promotes exceptional performance. Often there is extraordinary focus, or an expansion or anomaly of perception. For Ted Williams, it meant that he could see the stitches on the baseball as it headed toward the plate. A basketball player might start shooting the lights out while the basket looks as wide as the Grand Canyon and there is no missing.

Thriving Is on a Progression to Ecstasy

So, while thriving can include ecstasy, that heightened state may not be sustainable. The feeling of deep union with the universe seems more like an ecstatic state, somewhat above thriving, and not as sustainable. Joe said, "When I went under center for the last snap of the Super Bowl, I was 33 years old, and I had just attained my lifetime dream. Even though I was completely exhausted, I felt this warm flush of energy pour through my body, and I felt at one with everything."

This is that "on top of the world feeling" sports announcers comment about at the conclusion of a major sporting event. Those who themselves have been champions say something to the winners like, "Have you got 'that feeling'?" And they follow it up with the advice to "enjoy it as long as you can. It doesn't last."

Coley O'Brien quarterbacked Notre Dame to a 51-0 drubbing of Southern California to conclude the 1966 National Championship season. The victory was far beyond everyone's wildest expectations. And Coley reports riding the wave of that feeling for months.

Thriving at the White House

The chairperson of one White House gala had a personal epiphany of thriving with a satisfying release that occurred just one week before the event. Feeling empowered, she was now less guilt prone in relationships, more sure of herself, totally present in the moment. And it was with this empowered "high" that she approached this major special event of her life.

When the event came, she was comfortable letting her mother and her date entertain each other. She went through the entire evening very much engaged, present, and involved in effectively troubleshooting the proceedings, while also transcending the event. At times she even thought of herself observing the event like a fly on the wall.

The evening was not without its crises. First there was the confrontation at the White House gates when she discovered that in her rush she had forgotten her security pass. But she calmly talked her way past the White House guards. Later inside the White House, she could watch herself greeting people, feeling great, ticking off the arrangements one by one, and keeping one presidential candidate sequestered in a side room when he tried to crash the event.

Throughout the evening, she kept her presence of mind and her good humor. She thoroughly enjoyed herself and was fully present, not missing one moment, even though she bore the major responsibility for the success of the evening.

When she first got into thriving, the week before the event, Patricia said that it felt a little like a time when she had a fever and felt a bit giddy. Having associated that feeling with an illness, she was surprised that it actually turned out to be a very solid internal state, once she became comfortable and let the giddiness settle in and stay.

Thriving Is *Not* about Being Happy All the Time

If your pet is run over, you are not going to feel happy. That would be denying the natural feelings of loss and grieving. To deny deep losses leads to physical symptoms, even illness.

Part of living is to experience a full range of feelings. Some are wake-up calls. Others may put stretch marks on your self-image, or you may be left searching for an immediate response. But you will experience feelings that expand you. And there is little likelihood these experiences will be happy.

Feelings are neither good nor bad. They just are. However, what you do with them, how you might act on them or not act, is your responsibility. You can do whatever you want, and you will also face the consequences.

Thriving itself is more about having the richest experience of your life. An experience can be rich, profound, and poignant without being pleasant. Richness, depth, profundity all take precedence over pleasure.

Choosing Also Involves Losing

If you want to have the richest experience of your life, not only do you have to experience the loss and go through the grieving process, you also have to face it directly, and embrace it.

Today, with such a proliferation of choices, people feel they have less latitude to make mistakes. They should choose well. They may have a self-demand to choose well. The variety of options dictates that they not screw up. So they cut themselves less slack, and may even lose morale or feel overwhelmed by this abundance.

You may remember Robin Williams playing a Russian defector seeking asylum in New York City in *Moscow on the Hudson*. When confronted with an entire supermarket shelf replete with a huge selection of coffees, he was overwhelmed at the abundance of choices, and promptly fainted. In Moscow he would have been lucky to have had one brand of coffee to buy.

Loss will always be a part of choosing and living. When you choose one option, you lose the others. So thriving is not just about being happy, but rather about having the richest experience of your life.

Thriving!

No matter what your circumstances, no matter how seemingly out of your control:

When you commit to thriving, you experience a release of tension that allows you to float free and buoyant in situations that you have always found burdensome. You let go of imagined needs and false responsibilities.

Of course, a lifetime of fear does not dissolve overnight. But you can reprogram your own constrictive practices, perspectives, and fears that you learned from those who were fearful and who sought to avoid feeling. To replace your fears requires:

a. a conscious dismantling of practices of distrust, followed then by
b. a selective reassembling of practices for skilled trust of yourself.

You build these new practices through your conscious intention. Each one of us can recapture a sense of self that is filled with joy simply by discovering, uncovering, and exploring the fullness of our daily experience.

When you accept yourself fully and directly, you can move beyond addiction, dependency, and craving. There is no more need to look outside, for what you seek is already available here within you. You are enough right now, no matter what. And you are also emerging.

Just for the price of your next breath, you can release yourself from constriction and heaviness, enter fully into this moment, and thrive.

Like a mist rising over the water, you can float lightly and freely above what formerly had been oppressive and draining to you. Unburdened by tightness and self-distraction, you know you are indisputably present. You feel a supreme self-confidence in all that you do.

Your "release" provides you with an abundance of energy that allows you to focus your attention and energy freely and fully on whatever you choose to do. At work or play, you become focused, conscious, and connected within yourself. And as you connect within, you make more contact with others.
You move more directly and deeply into relationships with others when you first trust and deepen your experience with yourself. You develop a reverence for your own presence. As you accept yourself, you develop, in turn, a deep reverence and respect for others.

Recognizing in others what you deeply revere in yourself provides a sense of peace. The more deeply you realize and regard yourself and others, the more peaceful a core you will develop.

From this peaceful core, then, emerges the best you have to offer, your personal best, every moment of every day. What you do in your thriving state can be creative and filled with wonder. You can relish your life each and every moment.

Prior needs, addictions, preoccupations with image, appearance, and approval from others are dissolved by the deep satisfaction of connection with your true inner core.

At the same time you need to stabilize and steady yourself to maintain your course no matter what undercurrents are at play or what gusts are blowing. Establish your own grounding, set your tie lines to center yourself, and find your inner stillness. You can be both buoyant and contained, flexible and grounded, resilient and firm.
You appreciate the delicate nature of balance points and forces. Your predisposition toward what you take in and what you do quite literally foretells your openness to picking your way across the highest points of your peak experiences.

You begin to differentiate your true self as quite distinct from others even while you feel more truly interconnected with them. You are free, yet interdependent. You are less influenced by implications, inferences, and compulsions. You are sensitive to and guided by your own inner wisdom.

You are Thriving!

Benefits of Thriving

From this thriving state, the richness of your natural self will stream from you to impact your:

- personal health with an improved immune system,
- relationships with authenticity, integrity, dignity, and congruence,
- professional performance, based on self-respect,

- creativity with a psychologically safe environment, both inside and outside for productivity,
- resonance with the release and focus of energy,
- initiative with an impelling force from within.

This is your life in balance. This is the "place" at which the air bubble of balance is perfectly stabilized between the two middle calibrations on the carpenter's level. This is a place for our peaceful core. Up until now, few have had the time or inclination or the tips, tools, and techniques for maintaining this degree of inner focus, responsibility, and balance. Now we do.

How Good Can It Get?

- What is your sense about how good life can be?

- Does it come primarily from the example of parents, peers, or other role models?

- Does it come from disappointment?

- Have you accepted the acrimony and skepticism of others regarding what life quality is possible?

- Does that make it easier for you to give up hoping for a richer experience of life?

Happiness is the journey, the goal to be obtained.
We have to find happiness within
as part of grasping life.

Chapter 3

Entering the Thrival Era

Origins of the Survival Mentality

For most of human history, a major portion of daily energy went into sheer survival, continuing life, deterring the grim reaper. Survival was the major goal.

Out of our survival era grew the survival mentality, a mindset that today pervades our daily lifestyle and beliefs. Survival, in its most bland portrayal, is a matter of keeping on, enduring, persevering against circumstances.

Most of us recognize immediately that we have moved beyond survival in basic necessities and fundamental economy. We have already met our basic survival needs of food, shelter, clothing, safety, and security. And even though we might experience momentary shortages or threats, we are now able to focus beyond mere survival concerns.

Up Until Now, Survival Is All We Have Known

Survival has been both the trip and the vehicle so far. Survival was the lifelong experience and motivator for most of our ancestors, and defines our experience as a species. And it unfolded in two long eras of our history up until now.

What you will see is that our history divides up neatly into two survival eras, accounting for most of human history, and most recently the beginning of the thrival era. The first two divisions chronicle our survival past, the staging area for our thrival future. In his book, Breakpoint and Beyond. George Ainsworth-Land neatly partitioned the survival era of history into two distinct stages.

We have moved past the immediate threat of nuclear annihilation, though we have yet to solve problems and threats associated with nuclear weaponry. And we have in place a level of commerce, a climate of global cooperation, and foundational skills and infrastructures as a platform to support the launch into this new era of thrival.

The Beginning of the Thrival Era

Now, survival is no longer enough, and for the first time we are beginning to move beyond survival as a mode of life.

We are truly at the beginning of the second major epoch in all of human history.

But where do we go from here? We are no longer so engaged in just making a living. We can focus on higher aspirations, on the meaning of our life, and on how to enrich it. What are our higher needs? How do we satisfy our needs for meaning, enrichment, and fulfillment? And how do we improve on our daily lives right now?

Toward Thrival

Survival is no longer enough. ***Thrival*** is the goal, the state of peace of mind, high vitality, focused performance, and well-being that constitutes an ongoing, wished-for outcome. Now you can choose it, attain it, and even sustain it.

Thrival is the new goal we are moving toward as a species. It is time to develop the tools, techniques, and practices each of us requires to thrive on a daily basis, so that you can develop your own personal Thrival System®.

Proactive Conscious Evolution

As a species we are currently in the very early stages of this new phase of human existence, in which we can how determine how we will live in the future. ***We can choose***

whether and how we wish to evolve, consciously, as a species. We can choose and craft our evolution to determine.

Cause for hope has never been greater. This can be the most remarkable advance ever. We have overcome material want and constraints and have sufficient food, shelter, and clothing to survive. We have more than a sustainable future if we take care of our internal *invironment*, as well as the external environment.

The Problem of the Penumbra

You will recall from seventh grade natural science class that the penumbra is the shaded boundary area between shadow and light, as when a cloud shades the sun, or a full moon casts a shadow. And we are in that penumbra of history at this very moment.

May you be born in interesting times.
Chinese curse

Most of us discover patterns in our own lives long after the events have occurred that made no particular sense to us at the time. We discover these trends and patterns when we look back on our lives through the rearview mirror of memory. With the perspective of a backward glance over a broader span of time, we discover the outline of growth, challenges, and meaning for our lives.

It may seem pretentious to suggest just how special this current time is in all of human history. But this is not like the first-time grandparent showing off his grandbaby as the "best ever." We don't really have to be chauvinistic about the times in which we live. The pace of change alone exacts a toll almost daily. But what if something truly special, transformational, and pivotal is happening right now?

Thrival Is a New Goal for Each One of Us

We Have the Universe of Thrival Experiences to Explore
Now, at the dawn of a new era in history, we are moving on to thrival concerns, mindset, mentality, and lifestyle. Of what will it consist? And how can we discover it in all its fullness while transitioning out of our survival-oriented past?

It calls for a major expansion of concept and consciousness. It is a lot to comprehend. It will require our embracing thrival. So, first we will take at look at just how this is happening right now in history.

Always Possible, Now More Probable
In fact, thrival has always been attainable from the beginning of the species. It was always in the realm of human possibility. The sublime experiences that could trigger this feeling have always been with us. Was a full moon on a starlit night any less wondrous in 350 B.C.? It was probably even better without current-day pollution in the atmosphere.

Of course, no one can tell what similar experiences of self-realization and self-acceptance have meant to people over the ages. It is possible that people may have been more centered, grounded, self-accepting and self-realizing in other cultures in simpler, less distracting times.

Changing conditions over recent centuries, such as leisure, have cleared the time for focusing on thriving, a recent phenomenon for a large part of the population. Those who thrived before did so pretty much on their own unless they had supportive communities. So, while thriving may have been an ideal goal for many, it is not impossible. You can choose to thrive.

Why Now?
This major transformation is not occurring just as a matter of our earthly odometer clicking over to 2000, a nice round number. Few theorists consider our civilization to be calendar driven to begin with, especially since other cultures have different calendars. But this current tsunami of change has been building through the centuries.

Era I: Survival
13,000 B.C. - 6000 B.C., A Time of "Doing"
The first phase of recorded history found the human species engaged in hunting and gathering while living in small groupings or bands that survived by continual activity, by ***doing***. They used their wits and ingenuity in killing animals and their perseverance in grubbing for roots, fruits, and berries.

God and nature were then perceived as one and the same entity, and they were both considered "the enemy," due to the imminent threat that nature posed to survival. A change in weather could endanger the group's food supply by driving herds to distant grazing grounds. A drought parching the soil would cut their food supply.

Survival was the main motivator throughout this epoch of human history as it would be in the second survival era as well. Survival was the driving force in daily living, the continual preoccupation couched in getting enough to eat.

However, people did not pause to reflect on their being driven to survive. Like the fish being the last to know it is in water, survival was simply a fact of life, part of the context of the times. External circumstances compelled action on their parts. They were in perpetual motion, doing, doing, doing, to stay alive.

Era II: Survival

6000 B.C. to 2000 A.D. A Time of "Having"

According to George Ainsworth-Land, the second epoch began with the domestication of animals – pigs and dogs first, and eventually the horse – and the cultivation of crops. In this era, it became important to possess and defend land or property on which crops were cultivated or animals raised. Where formerly nomadic mobility and conservatism were important to sustaining life, now nobility and preservation of property, "having and holding" were important.

People banded together for protection, commerce, and community. They protected themselves from the enemy, the *other*, incoming hordes who could enslave, kill, or drive them from their land. Much effort was spent in possession and defense of property, life, and livelihood.

City, state, and national forms of government grew out of this phase. Basic infrastructures, monetary systems, roads, food supply lines, linked up to support large civilizations. Life span varied according to hygiene and effective defense, while quality of life improved even in the survival milieu.

Over time, the concept of the enemy as "the other" congealed around the Cold War conflict between the United States and the Soviet Union. It reached its high point when President Reagan referred to the Soviet Union as "the evil empire."

The dissolution of this phase of history became evident on November 9, 1989, with the fall of the Berlin Wall. And while this was not necessarily "the" turning point of the end of an 8,000 year phase of human history, it was a defining moment. The symbolic value was such that it marked the end of that era. The fall of the USSR two years later seemed little more than an obvious ramification, an afterthought.

With the fall of the wall came the end of the specter of major external enemies threatening us with weapons of mass destruction, an imminent threat from without. This signified a major and irreversible change in a history of survival by moving us forward markedly and conclusively into the next phase of history, the thrival phase.

The fall of the wall compressed a time line of change into a single event. So, even while this major change became obvious in 1989 and 1991, we round the numbers off to 2000.

Era III: Thrival

2,000 A.D. A Time of "Being"

Today we are drawn together in large and dense urban populations as part of an immense infrastructure that marks the interdependence of a global village. The global brain is in evidence through the Internet, satellites, and wireless communication. The world economy reverberates from micro-adjustments in local economies now around the world. Peacekeeping, proactive negotiation, and military presence replace all-out warfare. And we monitor threats to the environment to assure a sustainable future.

Now that nature is understood and poses less frequent or immediate threat, now that there is no longer a major continuous threat from a nation of similar strength, we have first and foremost to consider the issues that arise from our own unknown, disowned, denied, and feared aspects. And even while terrorism, nuclear arsenals, and narco-trafficking pose threats and concerns to our lives and the stability of our governments, the new *enemy* of this era is the "shadow side" within each one of us, the unknown, the denied aspects.

This shadow side has already gone on display, in vivid relief. Now that the press no longer follows a code of silence regarding the private lives of public officials, gaffes, foibles, and missteps draw more attention to public servants than good works. The flawed aspects of a former president were prominently displayed. And scandal still holds attention from an increasingly jaded public that expresses relief at examining the flaws of others.

"There But for the Grace of God Go I"

The public humiliation of others does not lead to introspection and familiarization with one's own shadow but serves as a welcome distraction, a reprieve from that admission. Yet it is still our individual work to embrace and illuminate those feared and disowned aspects of ourselves, to enlighten ourselves on this part of ourselves.

The work each one of us has to do in order to take ownership of and illuminate our darker aspects speaks to a revolution in consciousness, and of a progression in emotional maturity. In it, we shed and move past limiting stages, forms, and relationships of the past.

The New Motivation Is Toward Thrival, to Thrive

Now for the first time in history, the new motive and driving force is to thrive, not just survive. Now that the Berlin Wall is down, we have only the walls within us and between us to deal with. We have to discover, reconnect with, and restore our own lost and disowned parts.

More than witnesses to an historical event, we are witnessing a transformation with far-reaching ramifications for relationships, quality of life, and a sense of serenity and peace. It can effect a shift and transition within each one of us over time.

We each have to take deliberate steps toward thriving on a daily basis. For an increasing number, the idea of "having an above average day, every day" is more acceptable and readily attainable.

What Distinguishes Thriving from Surviving?
Essentially what separates someone operating in a survival mode from one who is operating in a thrival mode is the attitude, centering, and sense of presence with which that individual approaches a situation.

For example, many who have handled responsibilities similar to those described in the earlier White House incident report that they hold their breath and literally breathe shallowly throughout an entire conference, just hoping nothing will go wrong. They are employing a survival mode. By the end of the event, the only enjoyment they get is the relief that it is finally over and they scraped through without a reprimand.

Had they been operating in a thrival mode, they would have been breathing fully, enthusiastically breathing in the spirit, rekindling their deep embers. They would have been conscious, present, and enjoying the event throughout. As it was, they were uptight and gasping for air. What will it take to move from survival mindset and mode of living, to thrival mindset and lifestyle?

Major Point About Change:

Things Change. People Transition.

Generally, in spite of all the talk about the changes thrust upon us, people do not make abrupt changes in their major and habitual life practices. One exception would be alterations in behavior brought about by extreme trauma or a stroke. And very few can resolve and successfully go "cold turkey" on prior habits, practices, or addictions. Few can turn around long-established patterns of behavior in an instant.

Things change. Ideas change. Like a light switch, they can go from "off" to "on." But people require a period to transition that looks more like a roller coaster. Ups and downs are expected, with forward progress in the form of a trend toward upward evolution over time.

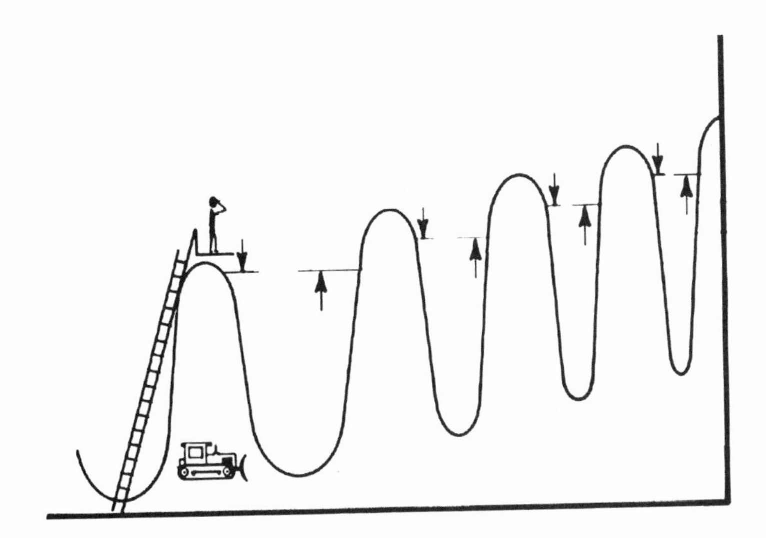

A shift of this depth requires a long period of adjustment. As you aspire to thrive on a day-to-day basis, you need to bear in mind that the transition you will undergo has this roller coaster shape. For just when you think you are secure in an exceptional state of well-being, some unforeseen factor or habitual practice will whack you out of it. But each of these seeming backward slides can also be a learning opportunity for moving forward to establish thriving more prominently as your lifestyle.

At best, you will require a period of adjustment in moving toward thriving on a daily basis. You have to decontaminate your psyche from the fear, distrust, self-condemnation, self-doubt, shame, and self-sabotage that you have observed in others and adopted for yourself. These are the ***bliss busters***™ that you will confront during our transition.

In the Penumbra

We are all in the penumbra, the light area of a shadow, moving into the light of a new era. That is what makes it so unsettling. Great disruption comes with this major upheaval in civilization's underpinnings. Many clutch more fervently and desperately at their power and domination of others. They assume that they have some form of control.

As the transition begins, it has already been marked with holdovers from our earlier survival eras: ethnic cleansing, border disputes, major atrocities, and a rising tide of our own shadow side manifesting in urban violence, school shootings, terrorism, and supremacist movements. Resistance to change is always most fierce at first. And those who hold to a survival mindset will be most threatened.

Turning the Corner Toward the Possibility of Thriving

The main transition point, and the first step, required for you to enter this thrival mindset, is

- *to recognize or*
- *take the chance, that thriving is possible.*

Only then can you begin accessing the part of yourself that is deeply and assuredly self-accepting, the part that cannot be distracted or overwhelmed by circumstances.

The basic premise of this book is that thriving is possible. And given that assumption, you will be interested to pursue the thrival practices.

> **n.b. Is Thriving Really Possible?**
> The first question you want to ask about thriving is, "Is it possible?" If your answer is no, then everything from here on would be a waste of your time.

On the Other Hand

You may find, on further deliberation, that you personally do not think it possible to thrive on a daily basis. If good feelings and good times don't last in your world, then you have to contend with limitations from your own entrenched survival mindset. That mindset probably diminishes your quality of life on a daily basis. You can make such decisions about your quality of life every day, or lay your foundation now for the future at a whole new level.

Three Types of Goals: Real, Ideal, Illusion

1. Real: A real goal is one that is readily attainable. Real may include substandard, standard, and exceptional performance. For example, as a salesperson, you may have exceeded your quota 80% of the time…and you can do it again. The fact is that you *have already attained* that particular goal, so it does not constitute an unfamiliar stretch for you. And even if it were an exceptional performance, you have already done it, so it is likely you can repeat it. The means are within your grasp.

2. Ideal: An ideal goal is one that you have not attained yet but that is doable, attainable, feasible. It is within the realm of the possible for you. You simply may not have the means, practice, or knack at present. You may even set focus on "that distant star" or "set your bar high" as an incentive to perform above your usual standard. You will have to consider your human dimension, i.e. what is possible for you.

It Is Possible to Thrive All or Most of the Time!

Until 1956, a four-minute mile was considered an ideal. Once broken, it has been exceeded hundreds of times, with high school runners among that number. Is what you consider an ideal goal within your realm of the possible?

3. Illusion: An illusion is unattainable, impossible, out of reach. Most people confuse ideal goals with illusions. However, you can make both a real and an ideal goal impossible. All you have to do is shorten or lengthen the time element so that accomplishment is not possible. Shorten the time for completion of a project, and it can become impossible.

This book will assist in the process of finding your way back to, restoring yourself to this natural state. For most, thrival will be an ideal goal. For a lucky few it will be a real goal just for the choosing, without a lengthy up and down transition.

Observing Breakthroughs

Every two years now, aspiring athletes watch the Olympians as new records are set and great moves are made. Often, these new moves have not been witnessed before. They can happen in any performance art: ballet or basketball. They inspire wonder and awe in the spectator.

Once they witness them, even skeptics can no longer maintain that these superb athletic moves are impossible. They have just seen it happen, or will have it replayed instantly and for all time on video.

Three questions arise within the mind of each spectator interested in duplicating these feats:

1. *Possible? Do I want to do that?*

2. *Probable? How much of that can I do?*

3. *Repeatable? How would I do that again and again, day after day?*

So it will be with thriving: Once you recall your own personal basis in experience, you will no longer be concerned that it is possible. You will already have it on good authority, your own.

Do you have to experience thriving to believe it?

Or,

Do you have to believe in thriving before you experience it?

Thriving Brings Inner Stability
Thriving provides grounding amidst the turbulence of our times and work. Thriving provides a deep anchor in your self. The more deeply you can anchor within yourself, the more you can withstand the turbulence around you.

This is the what most are seeking, the endpoint – greater realization of themselves moment by moment, the richest experience of their lives. You can attain this sustainable state of consciousness called thrival.

It's the System
The tips, tools, techniques, and skills for thriving are not a totally new minting of approaches and concepts. In fact, you will find you are familiar with much of what helps to constitute the thriving state. However, thrival sets the goal and a new context within which these personal growth and development concepts relate and operate more effectively.

You will find a full spectrum of resources and considerations to explore with confidence. ***What is new, distinct, and essential to this approach is the full range of thriving practices possible in the broader context of thrival, together with the comprehensive, systematic approach of Thrival Systems®.***

Check It All Out
This is a mind-body-spirit approach. You are encouraged to become familiar with the entire approach rather than stopping before getting the entire picture.

Add Your Discoveries to Help Others to Thrive
One person might be able to access thriving through breathing, while another might require more varied and extensive work. If you discover your own distinct and unique approach to thriving, that adds to the body of best practices that you read here.

Please share that information with future readers at DrPradde@aol.com, or Paul@thrival.com. Place a wider range of access routes at everyone's disposal. Readers will have the opportunity to contribute their own personal discoveries and insights in the footnotes in the later printings.

Chapter 4

The Yearning We Don't Talk About

To be nobody-but-yourself – in a world which is doing its best, night and day, to make you everybody else – means to fight the hardest battle which any human being can fight; and never stop fighting.

e. e. cummings

The Compelling Track So Many Are on Is a Distraction

"Who Wants to Be A Millionaire?" I have been asking members of my speech and seminar audiences, "Who actually wants to be a millionaire?" When hands go up, I ask what they would do with the money. I get a range of energetic applications from paying off bills, sending the grandkids to college, going to exotic places. But very few have thought through the ramifications of this windfall. No one seems to have given any thought to the changes such a massive infusion would require.

No one seems to be focused on the feeling they imagine would follow their good fortune. And having that feeling is really what makes it all worthwhile. People have to change inside and out to accommodate this abundance. The expectation of great gain and benefit and resultant happiness from material items ends up being an illusion.

Lottery winners have found that within a year they are no happier than they were before they won. People have a misconception about money. After a while, the emptiness comes back. How many suits can you wear? How many cars can you drive at one time?

Once you get past poverty [survival level conditions], money doesn't buy happiness. You achieve a level of wealth, and you need to re-juice the joy. Once you reach a level, there is a striving for a higher level, more, in order to regain that little internal boost.

Obtaining a level of success finds us comparing [ourselves] with those on the next highest rung. Comparisons can kill satisfaction by creating higher striving.

1998 NBC program on "Happiness" with John Stoessle

Extreme Wealth Does Not Guarantee Satisfaction

In the NBC program on "Greed" that followed, Ted Turner observed that he was not satisfied even with extreme wealth. In that program, Turner commented that when the list of the world's top 10 wealthiest came out, he figured that each person on it looked to see his relative position. And, subsequently, he himself wished to better his position on that list. Turner admitted that he is in it for the game, to win. This is an example of how *compulsive striving kills* thriving, by making self-worth and peace of mind dependent upon external circumstances.

People suffer needlessly
while failing to realize
the universe of enjoyment
within them.

A Return to One's Natural Self

One description or explanation of the meaning of life and people that makes sense to me is that each of us has a natural self that is our own best person. Interference with the original innocence of this natural self can begin as early as the womb when the interposition of fear and constriction can predispose a fetus to take on a persona that does not reflect the fullness of who it really is. This is like an early or original separation from what it was created to be.

This early loss of congruence and integrity can then become magnified over a lifetime. If the trend of the persona holds sway, the individual becomes more and more separated from his true self. And that separation brings not only a great degree of internal conflict, chronic stress, and wear and tear; it also brings an immense sadness and longing to be reunited with one's true self.

Incongruence Withers the Soul

During the time the individual is separate and apart from his natural self, his soul withers at worst, but certainly does little flourishing. He lacks nourishment from the vitality and presence of his own spirit. For example, he may make a career choice that is not in alignment with his deeper nature. She may marry someone for all the wrong reasons and find herself unfulfilled. Often the core reason for such decisions is tied to a need for approval, livelihood, or some other term that originates as a primitive concern for survival.

Melting the Crust over the Soul

Often a crust can develop, the result of a hardening of the persona to the detriment of the person. This *Scrooge-like* denial of the self is also a denial of joy and requires rebirth to tap into the wellsprings of joy. For some, rebirth begins with tears that melt the crust over the soul and allow it to breathe and be revitalized.

We are meant to live life in an effortless fashion, with real ease. But often our survival aspect, that is, our persona/ego aspect is so false and off center for who we truly are, that living in the posture required by the posing persona is a continuing and confining stretch for the natural self.

The natural self is by definition at ease and free of wear and tear. The natural self is freed of its adversarial aspects. Major conflicts are resolved. Strain is reduced. The heart pumps at a lower rate, without resistance, creating an unrestricted flow throughout the body. The mind is more at ease. The brain is not on constant alert for threat, so it is not putting out an array of ultimately debilitating chemicals.

Peeling the Onion

We each have the choice to peel our way through the onion that shrouds our better self. We can do that with intention and firm resolution to get back to that peaceful core, with weeping and with joy.

The sanctuary of the natural innocent in each one of us is the core of our individual being. How many ways there are to focus on that center and make that trip I do not know. But I do know that several of those trips can be made on the way to thriving.

"Thrival" is in all actuality the state of grace, a natural and higher state of consciousness in perfect mind-body-spirit harmony with our higher self. So, as I describe the desire for thriving further, I hope that you find some value in considering whether to have a go at it for yourself.

Many of us are made aware of deeper, more satisfying, fulfilling, and meaningful aspects to life through perceptions that may be fleeting or resident for a short time in our psyche. It is difficult to deny that you have had these poignant moments. But if you don't know how to get them back, and if daily living provides little space for you to "act or feel like that," then your interest and time in pursuit of your true self may seem like a poor investment.

The Longing We Don't Talk About

You have had your own memorable thriving experiences at some point in your life. And what you do recognize as a result of your experience is the existence of a higher or deeper place within yourself that is eminently more satisfying than your daily existence and lifestyle.

The desire to thrive is inherent in each one of us. Even if you have not spelled it out as a distinct, discernible state of existence and one of your goals, you want more of it. However, you may not know a way to get it back, or to get back to it.

Fully 99 percent of our population does not know how to thrive. If they have had the experience, which most have, they dismiss it as something that happens to them. It is circumstantial. Without the right conditions, they don't stand a chance, so they think. So, lacking the conditions, they lack hope.

Many have grown weary of trying to reach that place in themselves without a clue of how to get there. For them it is easier to abandon the quest as futile, rather than persevere into frustration and eventually exasperation. So, rather than trying to get that thriving place back, many will quietly give up the quest.

Others keep on plugging away, determined to get that feeling along with their next success. And if that feeling of lightness, buoyancy, even euphoria does not accompany their success, they will feel cheated once again. But, when "that feeling" does accompany their success, they feel vindicated for their efforts. That is really what they were going for anyway – the success was just the condition placed to release the feeling.

Striving for the Golden Apple

This striving mode recalls the story of the princess on *Glass Mountain* who held the golden apple, the reward to any knight who could ride his horse all the way to the top. Once there, she would bestow the reward on him.

Many think that thriving requires the determination to climb Glass Mountain. Still others think it requires the patience of Job, an enduring patience to await their next "once in a blue moon" episode of thriving.

Well, such effort or striving can throw them off balance. Their *trying* keeps them off balance. But patience may provide one parameter of balance within.

Furthermore, when they have that focus and feeling, the golden apple, even the slightest change of circumstance can knock them right out of the thriving state.

Kurt, a salesman, had already made three sales by mid-afternoon. When I asked him how he felt, he said, *"Right now, I'm on top of the world." And then without hesitation, he volunteered, "But that feeling will be gone before morning."* Many people have had, and can identify, their ebullient, thriving moments. Meanwhile, most do not have a clue how to hold onto that feeling.

One executive described the thriving feeling that accompanies her success and the subsequent loss. *"It's like you are riding high, cresting on a wave," she said. "At some point, someone takes the wave right out from under you. You crash. Although sometimes I create my own crash just to avoid the tension of when it will happen."*

Thriving Can Exist Irrespective of Circumstances

Thriving does not depend upon externals for its occurrence or its continuance. However, externals can certainly support your thriving, provide a challenge to your thriving, or knock you out of it. However, learning how to hold on to that feeling and state of being is part of the process of thriving.

The thrival state seems to meet the criteria for what we want from ourselves:

- the richest experience of our lives minute by minute
- meaningful moments with a sense of poignancy
- higher energy
- reduced strain, conflict, and energy drains
- igniting ablaze with the cool flame of serenity
- being centered and grounded in oneself, unshaken by circumstances.

Hanging On to That Feeling

According to my own experience, as well as the thriving experiences of others, slipping into that state of well-being has been only one part of the mystery to them. Their next concern then becomes how to hold on to that feeling.

An executive at the World Bank knew exactly what I was talking about when I brought up the topic of thriving. He remarked, "I had a period of six months after being diagnosed with Lou Gehrig's disease. During that time I had a sense of presence and feeling of peace that was incredible. I was determined to hold on to that feeling. But, when a second physician gave his 'second opinion' six months later – that it was obviously a misdiagnosis, for there was no sign of the disease -- I also lost that feeling and have been unable to regain it. And I really wanted to hold on to it."

Several weeks later, I spoke with him again and told him that my assessment was that he had essentially healed himself.

There was no misdiagnosis at all. The enhancement in his immune system from thriving erased all signs of disease. One of his friends had told him the same thing.

You realize, of course, that this was our opinion. No scientific protocol was used to arrive at this conclusion. But I am convinced that thriving empowers the immune system.

He, like many others, has had the experience of peak presence, lightness, buoyancy, expansiveness, even euphoria, that each one of us wants more of. We want to thrive, and we want to hold on to that feeling. Yet few know how to get it, let alone how to get it back.

This book is designed as a guide for those who want to learn to get into the thriving state, and to get it back when they lose it. For the state is really the experience of your higher self, your natural self, the person you are meant to be. The Garden of Eden is within.

Heaven On Earth

And all the commensurate rewards come along with your working your way through your own artificially erected barriers to the core of your joy. God did not make any junk when he created each one of us. If there is any junk in us, it is what we each have consumed, made of ourselves, done to ourselves. And we can undo it, release it, let it go.

If we have played god ourselves and replaced our naturally gifted self with an ego-laden persona, then we have created ourselves in our own image and likeness. Often that has been in an image and likeness that we have thought acceptable to others. Or it was an image and likeness that we thought could survive. So, we have created our own idol for others to worship. And in doing so, we have denied to ourselves and to others the greatest gift of all…the presence of our true selves.

When you are in touch with and living your true, whole, presence you do not run indiscriminately fully exposed and expressing. The naked truth often ignores the context in which it is expressed and can trigger extreme and potentially damaging reactions from others. You are compassionate with others. You are discrete.

Part of the continuing requirements for functioning in the so-called real world is to maintain a level of discernment and discretion in all that you do. It is still advisable to carry yourself in a way that those with whom you deal can appreciate and relate to.

Then There's the Classic Search for the "Good Life"

The quest for a better life is not a new one to the human species. Creative solutions to age-old problems and innovations have eased our daily burden. However, the focus has most often been on our externals and material well-being. The focus of thriving is on our internal well-being.

Over the ages, philosophers have discussed and sought insight into what makes for the ideal life. In this book, this psychologist undertakes the exploration of what it takes to be at one's best, how people can thrive on a daily basis.

This is not New Age psycho-babble, a fashion-driven gambit. This is a continuation of that very classic search for the "good life," knowledge and wisdom that philosophers have pursued for ages, **the search for living life better on a daily basis and enjoying your life to the fullest.**

Research Psychology Gets into the Act As Well

In the past, psychology has limited itself to how people were deficient, broken or derailed. Research psychologists know little about what truly helps people to flourish. The field of psychology itself has only recently begun to adopt a positive focus apart from treating deficits and pathology.

Psychology is now looking at how to develop strengths in the individual, as well as skills for increasing "subjective well-being." That impetus that psychology is taking toward the positive is due in large part to Dr. Martin Seligman, already well known for his writings on learned helplessness and optimism.

Open Questions to Pursue

So many questions are open to inquiry in positive psychology, especially given the virgin soil being tilled. For example, what enables happiness? What makes one moment better than another? What leads to well-being, positive individuals, and thriving communities? How can people's lives be most worth living? What does it take to craft a work setting that supports the greatest satisfaction and fulfillment for the employees?

Put simply: **What would you require to have an "above average" day, every day, beginning now and carrying into the future?**

Once the entire background is laid out, you will find a full spectrum of resources and considerations that anyone seeking to access the thriving state can explore with confidence.

Is it your goal to thrive?

Chapter 5

To Thrive: Now a Choice and Challenge

You. Yes, You. You Can Learn to Thrive
To begin with, you can learn to thrive. Thriving is a new item on the behavioral menu. Ultimately, and even today, you can thrive all or most of the time. This book is designed to start that process, consciously and explicitly, to help you to thrive when you choose.

Thriving Is Not Just for Plants and Animals Anymore
Plants, animals, and insects thrive. So do bacteria and mushrooms. There are specific definable conditions under which these thriving creatures multiply, expand, and continue to utilize resources on a sustainable basis to prosper and flourish Why not people? And why not now?

Up until now little attention or concern has been paid to thriving for people. Only on the hospital charts of the newborn infant is "failure to thrive" a concern and a diagnostic category. According to mylifepath.com, "failure to thrive is a condition in which your baby stops growing or loses weight, specifically dropping below the third percentile in weight." This standard is most common during a child's first three years, but of particular concern during the first year.

And while this failure-to-thrive category can also be adjusted and applied in diagnosing adults, it is seldom used. Once a person is launched in life, there are so many indicators of basic health, we tend not to have clear standards for thriving.

Been There. Done That.

Everyone has had his own memorable thriving experiences. People who have been there, the thrival state, and done that, thrived, need to learn how to hold onto thriving, or how to get it back. *What they recognize as a result of their experience is the existence of a higher or deeper place within themselves that is eminently more satisfying than their daily lifestyle.* However, not knowing a way to get it back, or get back to it, they tend to lose hope.

The Choice to Thrive Is Yours

Thrival is a potent new choice and aspiration. The world has sought what Dr. Peter Ellyard, Australian futurist calls ***thrivability***. Peter works more in the macro-approach for society in general. Thrival.com describes thrival as that "inner joy that defies circumstances," a feeling I associate with living on a higher level of existence.

Your results in thriving may depend upon gaining a new mastery over yourself in order to put yourself in a sustainable balance and state of being that affords you presence, fuller awareness, and deep-seated self-appreciation.

The essence of thriving is the ability to persevere and maximize the moment, irrespective of what is going on around you.

To Thrive is Now a Conscious Choice

You alone are in a position to enjoy your life to the fullest.

1. **Everything you need to thrive is already within you.** Because thriving is your natural state of being, you were born with all the essentials you require, ready to have the richest experience of your life.

Joy indeed is your birthright and predisposition.

Life can be so much better. But getting "better" depends entirely on you. Essentially, you make your life better. You have the unimpeded task of working at it, facing fears, going through pain, and adjusting your attitude and skills. Then thriving becomes more likely, effortless, even second nature.

2. **Everything that keeps you from thriving is also within you.** Thriving is your natural state. You were born to thrive. So, you are not plowing virgin territory. You are pursuing your birthright. You simply have to establish that you deserve it, be open to it, and then work for it. Your work includes overcoming obstacles and internal barriers, most of which you have adopted within yourself.

Human Environment Hothouse Control Unlikely

You will probably never live in the controlled conditions of a biosphere, space station, or underwater sea laboratory. And you cannot realistically expect to control your environment or circumstances.

And, while some people might limit human contact as one way of establishing more predictability and control in their lives, their introverted lifestyle would not suffice for the majority who are more extroverted, outgoing, and willing to adjust socially.

Thrival Was Formerly Thought to Be an Illusion

Perhaps that accounts for the people who have already felt and experienced thriving, yet are currently not in the thriving state. Few have struck on the right balance for themselves, found their own system for thriving, their thrival system®. Many do not know it is possible, yet remain hopeful. Still others have no clue, or think it inappropriate. In the midst of these different "takes" on thriving, the message of this book is that **thriving is now a choice.**

If you are going to thrive, the only person you can adjust is you. That's the good news. You are in charge of that. And, since everything that keeps you from thriving is within you, that means you simply have to change your inner game. And that involves assuming full responsibility for yourself, immersing yourself fully in your own life.

3. **Self-improvement is not required to thrive.** The striving for self-improvement can widen the breach between who you are, your natural self, and that "improved" or "perfect" version of yourself who you think you must become in order to be acceptable. Your internal demand and resulting tension alone can distract you from accepting yourself. However, explicit self-acceptance is one part of the price of admission to the thriving state.

Instant gratification takes too long.

Carrie Fisher

Choice and Willingness and Predisposition

You can choose to live a life in deep satisfaction and fulfillment. You can learn to increase exceptional moments of well-being in your life and bask in the glow of your arising, evolving presence, over and over again. Now, this wonder-filled confluence of body-mind-spirit unity, the thriving state, this feeling of subjective well-being, of having it all together,… is a choice!

The more you become attuned to what arises within you, the more you will self-realize your pure presence. It is in you and nowhere else. Face it. Embrace it. Respect it as an emerging aspect of yourself. Experience it as fully as you are able. Allow it to arise and to subside without holding on. Make room for your next experience.

Do you make space for energy to arise within you? Or, fearing you cannot take the voltage, do you tend to avoid or diminish the charge? That, of course leaves you fearful for the next surge of energy. Unless you are holding a live wire from a power line, chances are that you can, and should, trust the energy that flows through you, and that provides the basis of your experiences.

Consider what reservations or concerns you may have about the energy and effervescence that can arise within you. You may not be allowing sufficient space for your own inner fireworks displays.

Please Note - Self-Improvement Can Impair Thriving !

This is a book about self-realization, not self-improvement. Accept that you are basically complete, sufficient, and enough right now, to begin with. If you simply appreciated your self alone, you would accept yourself without qualification or condition. You have an original innocence, a true self, and inner wisdom that you can access at any given moment. But, to do so, you may need to slow down and catch up with yourself in order to fully appreciate who you are.

Your uniqueness alone is cause for celebration. But first you have to get yourself together.

This book is by no means the last word on thriving. It is meant to be an introduction to your present possibilities and your future way of life. Much in the future will turn on your conscious choice. The frontier to this inner discovery is wide open and uncharted. The new frontier is you.

What you allow to enter your conscious awareness may depend upon where you have tuned your internal dial to begin with.

Why Us?

How is it that it is we who are the ones challenged to take the greatest step forward in all of human history? Timing is everything. A confluence of forces makes it possible. And there are close to one-half billion people at the socio-economic level of middle class and above, who would be directly affected. So we, you and I, are the first to really be able to make the choice and take the challenge toward thriving, then pursue it with commitment and persistence.

No Sweat, No Challenge

The following story is one I made up in order to make a point about taking advantage of the choices before us. Imagine the following scenario as a metaphor for where we are as a people right now in history.

Once upon a time, a physical therapist was traveling through a small southwestern town surrounded by red bluffs, the place where tumbleweeds roll down main street in a high wind. After he ate lunch at a café, he took a short stroll around town. He found the shady central plaza where the men assembled at noon around dominoes and checkers played at tables. Some of the heaviest interest was in a hotly contested checkers game concluding between a man in a wheelchair and a bearded man who stood over the table throughout the entire game. He said standing gave him perspective.

Thinking that he might be able to provide some assistance, the therapist inquired what had happened that the wheel chair-bound player did not walk. "Oh, that's Ralph," responded a store clerk named Dave. "He's here every noon." "Well, what happened to him? Why is he in a wheel-chair?" the therapist said, probing.

"When he was a baby, Ralph didn't seem to have much interest in walking. Oh, he could stand okay. Even stood there unassisted. But when it came to taking steps, he never did. Different medical people checked him over, even took him to the Mayo Clinic in Phoenix. But no one could find any problem - neurological, muscular, or other. Eventually they concluded that he simply chose not to walk." And to this day, friend and neighbor alike declare this a waste of a basic capability that was never exercised. But they accept him the way he is.

Ralph's story counters the assumption that each one of us is attracted to grow through normal increments in development, such as crawl – stand – walk. Most of us emulate our elders and try to become like them. That only seems natural, unless each one of us were ignorant of our very real options and possibilities.

Honoring Our Ancestors by Continuing the Journey

Have you ever thought what your ancestors went through to get you where you are today? All of human history has led to your being in the socioeconomic situation you are in today. The blood, sweat, sacrifice, and hopes of your ancestors were invested in more than just staying alive. They have freed you from the dogged days in which all your effort would have gone into simply enduring, staying alive, postponing death. Our ancestors have propped us up higher on the tree of civilization than any prior generation

They, like modern-day immigrants and parents, sought to make life better for their children. Now that you have come to this point of fruition, their fondest dreams can be realized. So, it seems that even if you don't venture forth for yourself, you owe a debt of gratitude for what all those who came before you did for you. And the effort of a civilization needs to be honored by each one of us actively seeking to thrive.

In Transition Toward Thriving

We have carried the survival mindset and mentality with us. It resides in our cells and tissue. It takes only the slightest threat to rearm all of our concerns and reactivate our ego and defense system. It will take time and determination for the walls within to erode and topple. We have to be patient with ourselves.

We need to evolve a new consciousness that is more self-observant and self-forgiving, rather than self-judging, doubting, and punitive. It will take time to rewire our nervous system and to expunge survival beliefs from our system. We need to begin with personal decontamination of survival beliefs, attitudes, assumptions, and practices. That requires keeping a journal of self-observation, monitoring, and self-management.

True Appreciation Requires Moving Forward

Our ancestors' hopes and dreams ride on each one of us to take the ***best next step possible***, to live a life worth living. Through their work to survive, they have put us in a position to take the thrival challenge and thrive on a daily basis. They provided us a more stable launching pad from which to go even higher because of them. They have built us a high-water platform, given us a branch high enough on the tree of civilization, that we each can learn to flap our wings and fly toward a broader horizon. Or, like Ralph, we can choose not to take the steps onto the higher ground of thriving practices.

Ralph's folly demonstrates that developing your own capabilities to your best advantage just makes good sense. It is a no-brainer. So is making the transition from a survival lifestyle to a thriving lifestyle. Not to move forward is **as preposterous** as Ralph's not learning to walk.

The Challenge You Face

You are now looking ahead to a future in which you are capable of thriving. You could continue as you are in a semi-survival mode without ruffling anyone's expectations at all. You can choose not to pursue thriving and no one will be the wiser. However, you will know. And you can thrive even if it is beyond your immediate expectations. However, you will have to seek it actively. No one can get it for you. It is your choice to make.

Part II

Getting Started on Your Path to Thriving

Opening your life up to access the joy that is your birthright requires a basic adjustment in disposition, attitude and focus. Thriving takes discipline. It requires:

1. *opening yourself up to the possibility of thriving,*
2. *making up your mind to thrive, and then*
3. *taking action.*

This section is about beginning your transition.

In many respects, you will be doing nothing more than recovering your natural self. So much of thriving requires your dispelling the cultural trance people have been in for much of our history as a species. Most of us start from a position of subtle fragmentation, one that is captured in the following quote:

> *I'm lost.*
> *I've gone to look for myself.*
> *If I should get back before I return,*
> *Please ask me to wait.*

Have you ever felt this way? Do you recognize where this person is coming from? Have you felt a little split off from yourself, separated, remote from your deeper, original, more natural self? Are you on a quest to find your natural self?

Opening yourself to the practice of thriving returns you to your neutral space where you are neither ingratiating, nor intimidating of others. You are at once "well" and "well within" yourself.

The following section sets out the initial steps in this longer journey back to your self. It uses as the vehicle the knowledge, skills, and attitude required to thrive and also for your return to your natural self, the self you are when you are at your best, the person you were born to be.

Transforming
Habitual
Response Into An
Invigorating
Vital
Applied
Lifestyle

Chapter 6

First Actions Toward Thriving

To consciously choose thrival, after thousands of years of life in a survival mode, it is essential to define clearly how we can evolve as a people. And that task cannot be explained in a slogan or bumper sticker nor achieved frivolously. This is where the work begins.

I. A Major Transition Tool: Keeping a Journal

Few people face the prospect of major change without having concerns, so even if you have someone with whom you can work out every stage of your transition to a thriving lifestyle, a journal is an indispensable tool to utilize, and one of the first steps toward thriving on a sustainable basis.

It is important to engage your journal from the very beginning – starting now, to flush out your reactions and duly note them. They will provide a useful and continuing resource and reference point to guide you on your way.

Everything You Choose Goes Inside

The journal allows for totally confidential conversations with yourself. It also provides a more permanent record of your thoughts, goals, fantasies, perceptions, dreams, puzzlements, doodles, passions, interactions, feelings, feared scenarios, emotions, peak experiences, poems, magic moments; than does your own memory. Use the journal as a zip drive for your memory.

Confidentiality Is Essential

Everything is fair game for your journal. However, ultimately you will find time and space constraints. You should plan to keep your journal in a place that is totally private. In no way should you compromise the complete, and unassailable privacy of your journal. The moment you are reluctant to write anything down for fear of discovery by someone else, you begin to compromise the integrity of the work you can do in a journal.

Tell Yourself the Truth

Most of us learn at an early age to say what is expected of us, rather than to have a clean, clear connection within. In order to establish that connection, you need to remove distract-ions. So, an important rule is not to lie to yourself. The journal should assist you in discovering more truth and clarity about yourself, and telling yourself more of that truth.

I have had clients who could not count on keeping their journals private either at work or at home. So they used their bank safety deposit box. During the week, they would go into one of the private rooms by the vault and make their entries. While this seems extreme, the need for confi-dentiality is essential if you are going to bring up your truth and communicate it to yourself.

Writing in the Journal

Generally, I recommend you keep your journal in longhand. There is something visceral about using your own penman-ship, having your own lines and squiggles coming out the end of your writing instrument. It says something about you to yourself, about your mental state and clarity at the time. It can also be stabilizing just to be making the letters rather than typing them into a computer. That means finding the appropriate type of journal itself.

Types of Journals

Most bookstores have bound journals with blank pages, often at prices of $15.00 on up. This may be due to the quality of paper, but it is still a hefty price. And if you were to go to an arts and crafts fair, you could find journals with beautifully crafted covers. For others a simple spiral bound notebook similar to a college class notebook will suffice.

Get something that will hold a minimum of 6 months of entries to begin with, and a binding that can tolerate a lot of page turning. You want to keep and refer back to this document for a long time. This is your personal archive and archival memory.

How Often Do You Make Entries?
My coaching and therapy clients are encouraged to write a minimum of 20 minutes twice a week. That is what I recommend. Keep the journal by your bed, with a flashlight, in order to write down your dreams in detail, without fully waking either yourself or your sleep partner.

Specialized Journals
There are a number of journals for various and avowed purposes. I advocate an open-ended entry in order to leave yourself open to listening from deeply within. Formats can be distracting for our purposes. And several questions posed within this book do provide some impetus for getting your journal started.

Ira Progoff was the early promoter of journaling. His book, *At a Journal Workshop*, is a classic. *The Artist's Way: A Spiritual Path to Higher Creativity,* by Julia Cameron, is an approach to writing and creativity that suggests that you write for the first 20 minutes immediately after getting up. There are numerous groups throughout the country that use that approach. You may find that discipline helpful.

II. Meeting Resistance to Thriving
As part of your transition to a thrival lifestyle and mindset, resistance will definitely precede, accompany, or follow your moving toward thriving. Some fierce resistance will arise

later, but some of the early internal nay-saying can start immediately. That is resistance you walked in with. And it can be especially severe at first, testing your resolve.

When you bargain with
the devil that impedes you,
in exchange for
continuing existence at the survival level,
that devil is your ego.

Patricia Long

Vive Le Response!

Shortly, you will run into a variety of responses toward your own thriving. These will be solely of your own making. Maybe some of that response is arising already. The initial wave may arise in resistance to things said here in the text. The more you feel of whatever response, the greater the indication of particular buttons being pressed. Those buttons will give you indications of your areas of greatest resistance, and also of the pathways that need clearing.

Become aware of what hits you and presses your buttons. Take note and you can raise your personal learning curve on what it will take for you to thrive. f we are going to do anything of value here, to get down to a level of belief, value, and practices that touch on what is already blocking you from bliss, you are going to have your hackles raised and resist some of what you read. Note it. Acknowledge it. And you will make sense of it later on, in review.

Check the Readiness Scale

Each one of us already has a tendency, a wish, and a desire deep within to feel better, to have a better life. Don't you? Yet there is a reluctance to act on that desire. It is almost as if pleasure were a forbidden fruit. So, you go after it secretly.

But it doesn't have to be that way. The choice is really up to you.

Be explicit and direct about what you want. Begin with a check of your predisposition or readiness to feel better on a sustainable basis. Check where you stand on the Readiness Scale below.

This Is Not a Good Time in My Life

- ❑ Pay attention right now to any conflict you are experiencing. Write it down in the margins. Is this something you want to deal with? You may not be ready. Or, you may not have time right now. That's okay. You will pick up this book when you are ready, in your own good time.

I'll Go As Far As I Can. Maybe Later I'll Get on With It.

- ❑ You may want to start the process but believe that when you confront difficult issues and fears, you will veer off the path. You may get so far along and feel as if you are not deserving, or think that you are going against the way things are supposed to be. That may be another way of recognizing that you are not fully ready right now. Maybe later.

I'm in It for the Long Haul

- ❑ If you simply do not know how to get yourself into an above average day, then hang on and keep reading. You are eager to learn the tips, techniques, skills, and support to ease into a higher level of living and lifestyle. Several of these you may already know. Others you will discover. Still others will be covered here and in other sources I recommend. As we move forward, you will also be reframing much of what you already know, to accommodate, reconfigure, and promote a better way of living.

III. Basic Elements of any Behavior Change

Fake It Till You Make It

You will hear people being encouraged to "fake it till they make it." This is one approach to making changes and evolving into congruence between what you intend to do and how you act.

Short of a stroke, trauma, or brain injury, there are two basic ways to truly make major adjustments in your behavior:

> 1. Change your surface behaviors and the core belief is affected.
> 2. Change your core belief and the surface behaviors change.

A. **Change what you do, and a new belief can emerge.** As you adopt new ways of acting, you groove your nervous system with new synapses. The entire interplay of elements in your body-mind-spirit is affected. At first your actions might feel strange, awkward, dissonant, and unusual. Over time, as you become more accustomed to the new way of acting, you may also feel some dissonance or incongruence with your belief system. So you begin to adjust your belief system to include your new behavior. For example, with prejudice, interacting with, even becoming interdependent with, someone toward whom you are prejudiced can result in a change of view to accommodate your experience and reduce dissonance.

B. Change your belief, and new behavior is likely to result.

Your belief system gives rise to your values, assumptions, emotions, and attitudes. The belief system is at the core, while values and attitudes emanate from, or are derived from, the basic core belief. So a change in belief should result in the choice of new behaviors. However, it may be the case that time is required to acquire those new behaviors. Until that time, intention lies in wait for appropriate means of expression.

How Can You Open Up to Abundance?

What follows are several questions. Consider each one in turn here or in your journal. Each has its place in helping you discover your predisposition to thriving. Write down your first reaction without editing. Put down any sketchy notes that come to mind as your quick reaction. There are no right answers. You can add more detail later.

1. How good are you willing to feel?

If you equate thriving with a constant fever pitch of energy, with chronic peak performance, extreme edge activity, orgasmic output, reconsider: no individual could sustain that level or pitch. It's simply impossible for the human body to sustain such a state. Wear and tear would get to you.

Downtime, respite, time to recoup and recover, is a necessary part of living. Part of what makes thriving possible and sustainable is a process of continual replenishment. ***Remember that thrival is a sustainable state and level of living just slightly below continual euphoria and extreme activity in both pace and intensity.*** After your neurons fire to send messages of even the most pleasant stimuli, they require time to recuperate before they are set to fire again. Unrelenting intensity does not necessarily translate into enjoyment.

Now consider how good you are truly willing to feel. Most people will respond with "oohs" and "aahs." Right now you have a real choice, a chance to choose, to plan how you will feel and enjoy your life. Choose wisely.

Chocolate is one of the ways you know that ecstasy is available on a daily basis.

Geneen Roth

What does it take to raise the bar on your enjoyment? Suppose that you love chocolate [fill in your favorite food] and you could never get enough of it. Then suddenly, you are offered the opportunity to have a vat of chocolate cooled to 78 degrees Fahrenheit placed totally at your disposal. For just this once, you could taste the chocolate through all the pores of your body. Would you want to roll in it, immerse yourself in it, soak in it? How could you taste it most fully?

How Much Happiness Can Your Heart Stand?

Numerous individuals think that their heart would give out if they felt "too good." There are others who think that there is a predetermined life ratio of good days to bad days, and they have to earn the good days. If they get ahead on their quota of good days, then that will trigger a run of bad days or bad weather.

Willy Stargill was interviewed in the locker room immediately after the Pittsburgh Pirates won the World Series. His comment was, "I feel so good, I'm afraid my heart is going to give out."

So go ahead, respond to the question that follows:
2. How much happiness can your heart stand?

Not to have lived fully is to have denied yourself, those near you, and all of humankind, the benefits that you derive from yourself and for yourself when you are living fully.

"Great, I'll take expansiveness and reverie, invigoration and keen vitality," you respond. "Just keep it coming." Now consider the question that follows:
3. For how "long" are you willing to feel good?

Perhaps it brings you up short to hear this question posed right after considering *how good you want to feel*. The question of "how long" can throw a wet blanket over this opportunity to feel as good as you wish to.

Many of us have not considered how long, only how high. This tells me that most people assume it is not possible to sustain that thriving feeling for long. Their belief is that feeling good, even simple satisfaction, is not sustainable, no matter how good. It will not last. So why bother?

There seem to be two fundamental blockages to thriving to begin with:

i. Accessibility: Feeling good is difficult.

ii. Sustainability: The belief that the feeling won't last for long.

To consider taking this serious leap forward for ourselves and for humankind, we have to be able to look beyond feeling good in the moment to sustaining that feeling. And that gives rise to the next question:

4. Could you live day after day feeling this good?

If you are like most, this question will challenge your assumptions about what life is supposed to be like. It delves into your basic belief system. Is continual struggle essential to your mindset about life? Remember that these questions are intended to reveal your predisposition to the possibility of thriving, to see whether you are receptive to that possibility to begin with.

This can save you time and investment as well. You may tell yourself that you indeed want to thrive, but when you seriously stop to consider it, you don't think it is in the cards for you this lifetime.

We create prisons of our own making,
and then beat at the bars.
Benjamin Franklin Purdy

The prisoner was in solitary for over four months when suddenly his cell door opened. Morning sunlight flooded in, warming the floor where he had slept and shivered. But this is not the way it is supposed to be on the inside. Besides, there was a draft as the fresh air poured in and replaced the stench of humid stale air. So the prisoner, on his own, pulled the door shut until he heard the familiar and reassuring click. He had become his own jailer. This is what his life was supposed to be like.

Aim Low

If you find that you are cautious or reticent, consider the following. The claim that you can thrive all or most of the time may seem overblown to you, so aim lower.

5. Would you like to have more above-average days?

How many?

6. How much of an above-average day can you stand?

7. What would it take for you to have more above-average days?

8. How good are you supposed to feel? Deserve to feel?

If you began with the bar pushed up very high, you may have to stretch your expectations to warm up to these choices about making your life better on a daily basis. So start on a modified track and give yourself time to consider. I have posed this last question to audiences. After the presentation, there are always several participants who wait for the crowd to subside and then come up one by one and whisper in my ear, "How good am I supposed to feel?" as if I held the answer.

IV. Take a Self-Reliant, Inside-Out Approach Thriving

What is required to thrive in all circumstances, is an approach to thriving from the "inside-out." And that starts by clearing the internal underbrush of your belief system that says no such state of being can long exist within you.

Then, you move forward in learning the skills, techniques, tips, tools, processes, attitude, and practices that will help you to maintain an inner balance and guidance system that keeps you on balance no matter what is going on around you.

You have to look to what it takes to create that blue sky environment inside. You already know that no one can control your environment, if you are to have any degree of freedom. So you cannot expect to thrive through an "outside-in" approach in which the environment or circumstances create an irresistible thriving climate.

You are enough right now, no matter what. The sooner you realize that, the sooner you will begin to make your days better days, and thrive. You will begin to experience more satisfaction.

Within

Now you can be without, and you can be within,
But if you are only without,
Then you are really without.
And if you are only within,
Then we are all without your within.

So first be within and without, so that
We will not be without your within,
And you will not be without.

Paul O. Radde

The Surest Approach is to Thrive within Yourself
You understand that only you ultimately determine if you will thrive. It may be easier to thrive in the company of a thriving partner, group, or community. But as soon as your companions change, you will no longer have the support you may have been relying upon to thrive.

So thriving is presented in such a way that you can get into the thriving space ***no matter what is happening around you***. To prepare yourself to "sit at the thriving table" of joy and richness in your own experience, these instructions are presented in such a way that you can get into thriving all on your own, even when your circumstances do not seem favorable or supportive.

Assume You Are "On Your Own"

If you have to move forward alone on your own, if that is the only way you can proceed toward thrival, then go for it. At some point you will have to be self-reliant anyway. Conditions will be challenging for you. If you can thrive on your own in hostile circumstances, then certainly you can get into thriving with others who are supportive. Meanwhile, you can learn to monitor, self-manage, and conduct your life in a manner that promotes your thriving all or most of the time

Be prepared to thrive in anywhere. That applies to those who do not have a support community, those who travel frequently, those whose spouse and family are not yet clued in, and those who live alone. Even a practicing recluse or hermit can focus on developing an inner game and capacity for coping vibrantly with circumstances. And....

Don't Go It Alone Unless You Have To. But Go!

This book emphasizes your being able to thrive all by yourself, with no support from anyone. However, that is not what I advocate. Personally, I suggest that you get the support and challenge of someone significant to you, someone who is also searching for the thriving state. That is a preferable way to work on thriving together, partnering, or affiliated.

As much as is discrete and possible, share what you know when asked by spouse, colleagues, and family in getting into thriving. Bring them along gently if they are interested. But first, be solid in your own knowledge, skills, and attitude. Don't overreach before you are firmly grounded and thriving. Keep your own counsel to gain stability. The more you can stand alone, the better you can encourage, support, and provide a role model for others.

Partner or Team Up with Significant Others

Partner whenever possible. Of course you will have to revert to your own personal pathway some of the time. But, there is no reason you cannot share the road or the journey. Smooth your path by partnering. It is preferable to have those close to you moving forward on the path toward thriving, to hurdle any obstacles before you. So, first consider partnering or teaming up with several people for mutual support.

Significant Others Can Make a Significant Difference
Most of us are reluctant to take on activities that are opposed, challenged, or thwarted by those close to us. For that reason, I strongly advocate that couples gain exposure to these thrival concepts and move forward together.

That means you and your spouse or companion would attend introductory courses or seminar sessions together, read books, or use other media. Partnering works best, especially in these pioneering times so you don't have to go it alone.

General Reader Advisory: Buy In. Don't Browse.
For years I have read accounts by journalists who report on various experiential workshops they had observed skeptically. But they had not participated in, so they only observed the interactions. Typically, they expressed cynicism about what was going on, showing no understanding of the process.

In order to gain the authority of your own personal basis in experience of the thriving state, you will have to dive in and participate. Thriving is not a spectator sport. You get nothing from it unless you temper your own internal experience. Then, and only then, can you begin to appreciate the full breadth and nuance involved in thriving.

Look at your intention, initiative, and intensity. But also be discerning. Buying into thriving practices means learning how it works and then actually applying it in your life. You will want to do more than flip through the pages.

Chapter 7

Opening Yourself Up to Thriving

Neighborhood children dress up in costumes and go out trick or treating on Halloween. They carry shopping bags to collect their treats. At their third stop, they knock at the door and are greeted by a friendly old man who offers each child a bicycle. But the children look dejected and downcast. They didn't bring bags large enough for the bicycles. And each one passes up the generous offer.

Have you ever been left holding the bag, unable to get it open far enough to hold what you most wanted? Is the "bag" you? Have you been unable to get yourself open sufficiently to enjoy what is inside you? Have you passed up great offers, even gifts, because you were not ready to open up and let in a compliment, or an offer of assistance, acknowledgment, or friendship? That's like going to a pool party without a swimming suit. You can't fully participate. Yet the party is life and it is going on now, and so are the treats. You have to be prepared to open up to the abundance around you right here and now.

If you miss your extraordinary moments of exceptional well-being, everyone is the poorer, for you have less to give. We are interdependent, recognize it or not. As one of us grows, we all grow. Pay attention to life around you and see this sense of human possibility being stretched before your very eyes as standards rise and records fall.

The Challenge

The main challenge for each of us is to undertake gladly to have the fullest, richest experience of our life. That is why we must be open to the next level of living—thriving.

Questions to Consider

Do you deserve to thrive?

If you didn't answer this question affirmatively, you have to deal with your own internal resistance or a subtle sabotage of your thriving. Then, how can you replicate the *thriving experience?* You have to make room for the experience in your life. Open up.

Keeping a Lid on Your Life

What do you do with moments of major enthusiasm and enjoyment? Do you fear appearing irrational? Or are you simply protecting yourself from possible disappointment?

There is a way to experience ups and downs that does not set you up for a "Wile E. Coyote" drop off a cliff. You have to remain well within yourself, be aware of your awareness, and not be dependent upon external circumstances.

I am aware of my own fear of losing control, or opening the drapes and letting life shine in. Often releasing energy to areas of constriction long sealed with residual trauma leads to the facing and embracing of fears and the streaming of tears.

You have to recognize that you are a work in progress. There will always be more you can do to increase your congruence, authenticity, integrity, spontaneity, and freshness. But what will it take to become open to all that arises within you in the first place?

Each breath, and the enthusiasm with which you take it, is an immediate test of how much of life you will let in, or a testimony of the wonder of the life you let in, and experience, and acknowledge. When you are not open, not predisposed, you miss the best of your life. Then those precious moments are gone forever.

Everyone loses sometime. But when you do not open to life, to having an above average day, to thriving; then we all lose.

The Surge From Within

Start to tune into your impelling experiences. Impelling energy is a surge from within. Consider experiencing the surges in your own body. In Washington, D.C. every Fourth of July, the fireworks are set off on the reflecting pool between the Lincoln Memorial and the Washington Monument. The display is dazzling. For 20-30 minutes of fireworks, hundreds of thousands crowd the nearby lawns and anchor their boats out in the Potomac River.

Here in this open space, the rockets can rise and burst, spewing out massive displays of geometrics, mandalas, spirals, and weeping willow sprays in the sky. The key here is having an open space to be filled. Do you have space in yourself for new illuminations to arise? It is uniquely yours to have and enjoy.

Incidentally, your not having a rich experience and enjoying it results in a loss for you. It simply goes to waste. ***For no one benefits from the experience you deny yourself.*** When I live my life richly, it is an experience that can redound to the benefit of others. At the very least it means less static in the atmosphere, a clearer, cleaner sense about me, a higher resonance to emanate out from me, more to share at no cost to anyone else.

Impelling Energy – The Flow of Grace
It is your immediate loss when you restrict your own inner space, for then you suppress your own internal light show.

You have to release the resistance and re-open your inner space, and make room for ecstasy. Resistance has to find a victim to suffer for what it denies the body.
Patricia Loyd

Our impelling energy is much like a fireworks display. It arises within us, and seeks sufficient space to expand, illuminating with full brilliance. Relaxing your musculature and taking deep breaths expands and clears that space within you. It also helps to get rid of leftover toxins and waste materials. Each breath acts like an eraser on a chalkboard, clearing the slate of past experience, making room for what arises next.

The natural unrestricted movement of impelling energy can be seen as the flow of grace. But when you are fearful, envious, self-restricting, then you are lacking in the faith or confidence to open up to this flow of grace.

Get Beyond Any Hype: Be Sure to Verify
If you continually seek an improved lifestyle, higher state of consciousness, greater enlightenment, peak performance, positive living, you have probably had many writers promise more than has been delivered. You no doubt have invested money and energy on journeys that have yet to materialize.

Your Persistence is Admirable
Yet, look at you. You are still shopping for new ideas, skills, tools, tips, and techniques to make your life better. Give yourself credit for your persistence and hopefulness. I congratulate you and applaud your determination.

Are you still fueled in your quest by an intense desire and continuing hope that there is more to life than you are experiencing now? I hope to re-ignite and fuel your hope, and to further your journey by providing new guidance and additional steps as part of the entire "how."

As you pursue what for you is a "better" way of life, you need to know that no one has examined thriving from all perspectives. No one can. Only you can do that for your life anyway. That will be your personal matter – to expand the search and adapt it to your situation and personality.

"Get It Down to Get It Done." Block Out Time Now
You have to begin to block out time for your transition right now. You have to make room in your schedule or routine for the changeover.

What is required in order for you to immerse yourself? You, of course, pick your level and degree of involvement. But if you are going to get back to your own future, you may need to achieve a level of thrust and momentum that you can get only by concentrated focus on what is required to elevate your standard of living on a daily basis.

Children may be able to add new activities to their lives without giving it a second thought. You may be able to jam another shirt or dress into your closet without wrinkling it totally. But you don't have the luxury of taking on a new approach to your life without making room for new practices. Just learning to floss your teeth probably took a lot of effort. Learning to thrive will take a more concentrated effort still.

Remember, you are a unique person,
Created to fill a very specific place in the world.
Don't measure yourself against others.
Rather, trust your inner spirit.

It is your uniqueness, background, experiences, attitude, temperament, disposition, capability, discipline, and felt desire that will in large part determine your success in improving your lifestyle. It is still my intent to provide you the essential perspective, building blocks, and tools to thrive. Yet you are ultimately responsible for where you take yourself in the course of your thrival journey.

Observe Your Inner Kaleidoscope

Your thriving is unique to you alone. If you look through a fine kaleidoscope that presents an array of colors in a configuration with many points, you know how difficult it is to hand the scope over to someone else so that they can see exactly what you are looking at. And, in this case you are only looking at something outside yourself, something explicit, measurable, an object that could feasibly be photographed. Internally, you are much more complex. And much of what emerges within you in thriving is not accessible to anyone but yourself. If you don't get it, no one gets it. The beauty of your experience is all for you and you alone.

Those who would
bring life to a stop and
end change
would finish life.

If things did not change or shift, life would be a one-shot Polaroid®. You and I would be stuck, jammed up with a single focus or a "one-slide" awareness. Or, you would have to manage your awareness like a TV set that provides superimposed and overlapping images from multiple channels all at the same time, from overly discrete to muddled. It would be a blur.

At the Same Time, You Can't Surf in the Basement

Let's play with imagery for a few moments:
At the beach, the prospect of hanging ten over the edge of a surfboard and feeling the warm sunshine on your body and the surge of the waves beneath the board is exhilarating. Now switch the location to your basement.

Picture for a moment the prospect of riding the waves on the surfboard in your basement. Not only do you need room for the water to rise and surge, once you get on the board, you also have to deal with a very low ceiling and overhanging pipes. You cannot stand up to your full height and enjoy the ride for fear of gashing open your skull on a low overhang. You begin with very severe limitations, having to be extremely cautious and hunkering down to be safe. That is not much of a ride. But inside you, there is plenty of space to explore your inner frontier.

Chapter 8

Benchmark Your Thriving Experiences

Learning from Your Special Moments

You have had extraordinary moments of exceptional well-being, those precious moments of feeling deep contentment. And, the impressions of those experiences are deeply implanted in your memory. So, by recalling those impressions, you can provide memories that allow you to actually re-enter the thriving state. The richness of memory provides your recall.

It is time to stake a claim to your own high ground of experience and begin to live there. You have already proved to yourself that you are able to attain the thrival level of experience.

You can learn from those experiences. There is sufficient mental-emotional imprint of that occasion to harvest it for what you can learn from it and repeat. Give yourself the opportunity to see what your body-mind-spirit brings to the surface. Learn from your afterimage.

Just as certain smells or surroundings remind you of what went on there in an earlier time, your sense-memory recall engenders a fuller experiencing. Sense-memory recall can return you to a variety of mental and emotional states. In this case, you retrace your memory…and you are there once again in your mind's eye. That recall can then serve as a benchmark for accessing the thriving state over and over.

Your prior thriving experiences can provide an immediate, even permanent, bridge back into thriving. Use vivid recall of your experience in a quiet time when you can do so undisturbed. Take it seriously. Don't slough off this opportunity. Give your self time to once again experience the full range of response that constituted your thriving moments.

Clear the Trail You Have Already Been Down

Vivid recall can establish a point of reference for re-grooving your neural pathways. With it, you can more easily access the next level and lifestyle. Bring back your memory in detail. There is a place inside each one of us that is not being sufficiently connected or inhabited.

> Rediscover that place inside that holds the
> unconditional love for self, and
> ... share that freely with others.
> Mitch Axelrod

One method of furthering this recall experience is to establish a baseline for thriving by noting this exercise in your journal. Document your insights and the path you craft toward mastery of thrival. This may be as simple as clearing brush as you find your way on the trail again. In other cases, you may find heavy tree trunks have crashed across your route and have blocked access. Short of heavy lifting or using a chain saw, you will make no headway. So first explore your recall. Here is the exercise.

Directions

Undertake this exercise when you have a minimum of 15-20 minutes to relax fully, to focus, and get into it. Being rushed, or doing this exercise just because you want to read through this chapter, will not work. If you don't have the time, mark this page and come back when you do have time. Also, do this recall exercise only when you have the willingness to explore. Find a place free of disruptions. Hold your calls. Turn off your cell phone and beeper. Then begin your recall.

Loosen any tight-fitting, constrictive clothing. Find a comfortable chair that supports your spine and allows your feet to touch the floor. Put your hands in your lap or on your knees rather than propping them up on the arm of the chair. Elevating your shoulders maintains stress. Relax and drop your shoulders.

Pay attention to any sounds in the room. Anticipate potential intrusions on your silence, and let them be. Then focus on your breathing. None of us lives in a distraction-free world, so learn to relax beyond distractions as a way of improving your concentration and relaxation. Any time that your attention is drawn away, use that distraction as a basis for focusing even more keenly within yourself.

Begin to breathe through your nostrils, high up into your shoulders, almost as if you had shoulder pads for lungs. Inhale without straining. Hold in your breath briefly. Then expel all the air through your nose or your mouth after each breath.

Hold your breath out for a moment. Then, move your breathing down, inhale, and fill out the area defined by your rib cage. Fill the entire area, including the back of your rib cage. Expel all the air, and then fill out the small of your back, and breathe forward into your diaphragm. Take your time. There is no rush.

Now breathe down into your pelvis without straining. At any point that you find strain, release the pressure of your breath and breathe only to that place at which the strain begins. Then return your breathing to your normal and natural place and rhythm.

Once you are relaxed and ready, recall a time when you were truly "on beam" and thriving. If anyone had asked you if you were being "your own best person," you could have responded with no hesitation that this is truly who you are at this moment. This is the richest experience of your life. This moment captures your essence. It is the essential you. Take some time to recapture that experience fully.

Now pay attention to how you got to this experience in the first place.

What in particular had you done that contributed to the special nature of this moment?

Recall the context and the circumstances. What importance or meaning had you assigned to these?

Had you met some precondition or qualification?

Was your extraordinary moment of well-being pretty much a surprise, or were you openly seeking it?

Was someone else involved? If so, how?

How did you initially organize yourself to enter and participate in that thriving state? How did you predispose yourself to thrive?

What brought about your feeling of success and peace of mind? What conditions did you first have to meet so that you qualified to allow yourself that level of well being?

What was the definable process you went through?

Recall the colors, smells, sensations, the ambiance that comes to mind.

How long did you thrive?

What ended your feeling of thriving?

Help Your Process Along with Self-Acceptance

Basically thriving is a state of being that can also be brought about through an act of self-acceptance, a gift from you to you requiring no particular accomplishment. You can prime your own pump, release personal benevolence, and be self-nurturing.

Now, fill in as many details as you can explore from your experience. Do not rush. Then, once you are complete on this part of the exercise, continue with the directions below:

Take a deep breath and let out all the air. While exhaling, recall a time recently when things were hectic, chaotic, and out of control. Immerse yourself in that experience and get a sense of how you felt. Allow no more than 30 seconds for this.

Then, take a deep breath, and come back to your recollection of your thriving experience, of being on beam, and being your own best person. Get a sense of what you knew how to do at that time, what you allowed yourself to do, that made your thriving experience more likely.

Consider specifically what contributed to your thriving state. The more you can focus on your internal state, the more likely you are to glean specific strengths that will assist you in thriving tomorrow and in the future.

You already know a great deal about thriving. You just have to remember how much you already know. And you have yourself together. You only need to realize how together, and just how you are together.

Carry Over Your Extraordinary Moment of Well-Being
It is important that this exercise have some carryover effect in your life. This little mental alarm clock is a way of predisposing yourself to extend your recall experience, applying the feeling by handing it off to yourself within a short time frame.

Planning: Pick out a specific time or situation within the next 8 hours during which you will consciously choose to pause and recall the thriving state. Envision that time, occasion, or relationship in your mind's eye right now. Project your feelings of thriving into that situation. Give yourself permission to slow down enough to get firmly in place. Once you are clear on this, move to the next part of the exercise.

When you are ready, breathe in the energy that is around you. Breathe it into your right leg and foot. Let out all the air. Then breathe it into your left arm and hand. Draw it into the entire trunk of your body. Breathe it into your neck and head. Draw it into your left leg and left foot. Breathe it into your right arm and hand.

Bring yourself back into full awareness of your surroundings. Open your eyes, if you closed them. Then, keeping yourself in silence, write down in 1-5 words in the center of the oblong figure below a crystallization of your thriving experience.

Directions for Charting Your Recall
Chart out certain aspects of this experience on the figure below:

On the arrows leading into the oblong from the extreme left side of the page, write down specific skills, insights, and feelings that contributed to your thriving state. And on the arrows leading away from the oblong, write down any specific additional applications you have for thriving in the future, based on the specific strengths you discovered that you already have.

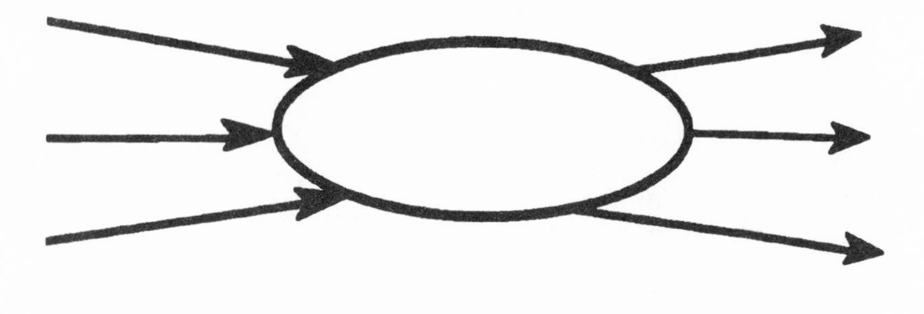

Strengths For Thriving **Future Applications**

Figure 8-1

Partner Up

You can benefit greatly from this exercise by reviewing your thriving recall with one other person, or within a team or support group. It helps to have someone objective to talk with about your experience.

An objective third party can help to underline for you what is an important strength in thriving. You may then discover and determine additional factors that contributed to your thriving. Pairing up and airing your experience gives you that opportunity. Your partner can be a close associate, colleague, friend, or someone whom you have just met.

See if your partner can spot strengths in your recall of thriving that you have taken for granted or consider a given. Ask that person to play devil's advocate to assist you

in fleshing out specific additional factors that contributed to your thriving in your recall situation.

If you do not have someone present and available right now, write down the details of your recall in your journal. Then, when you do have someone available to listen and reflect on the strengths implicit in what is heard, see what they can add to your own discoveries of thriving knowledge, skills, and attitudes that you already employ.

If possible, find someone who can be a part of your ongoing support system so that that person can start with you at the beginning of your transition.

List below additional skills and strengths that you have for thriving:

- o
- o
- o

Now, once again, reconfirm precisely when you will make a special point of recalling your thriving experience and reconnecting with your own best self. Pick a specific time. Set an alarm or buzzer to remind you. As soon as possible, test your ability to return to the thriving state in practical everyday circumstances.

Thriving Is an Inner Joy That Defies Circumstances

Unlike the "flow" experience that we clearly requires each individual's fascination of being on task, on a mission, or moving toward a pre-determined goal; thriving does not depend upon exterior circumstances. In fact, you have heard it described as an inner joy that *defies circumstances*. It's your inner stance that counts, not outer circumstances.

Often individuals will recall an experience in which they were recognized, promoted, loved by, totally enraptured with…, and those circumstances subsequently resulted in their having extraordinary moments and the feeling of success. However, the problem with depending upon circumstances becomes obvious when circumstances change. If circumstances can take you up, they can also shoot you down.

You can, of course, have an intense experience of near rapture and euphoria that you may attribute in large part to external circumstances. But when the smoke clears, the experiences, skills, and attitudes you look to and rely upon to sustain that thriving experience and the eventual mastery of thriving, are those skills in which the source of the thriving experience comes from within you.

So, how do you get your inner game together in such a way that you can overcome circumstances or thrive in spite of circumstances? You will want to look at what knowledge, skills, and attitudes you can control yourself. Therefore, you can carry them over and apply them toward future thriving.

Look How Much You Already Can Do for Yourself

Revisit for a moment just how you recalled your thriving experience. There was nothing in the directions provided that you could not do for yourself. You did it all for yourself.

Did you enter the hectic and chaotic part of the directions? Easily move from the centered-ness of thriving, to chaos, and then return to the thriving state? Then you have already demonstrated to yourself, by these simple activities, that you can choose to get into the thriving state.

You did it, or came close, through your recall experience. You also have shown yourself that you can choose to leave that thriving state and go into the experience of being hectic, ungrounded, and chaotic. Then, when you choose, you can come back to the thriving experience.

However, about 2-4% of participants do get stuck in the chaos and are momentarily unable to get back to the thriving state. If that includes you, just accept it for now.

You now know that thriving is a choice, your choice. You can get into thriving, intentionally leave the thriving state, then return to it, just by choosing to do so. And you can do that by and for yourself.

Do You Want to Thrive More of the Time?

You have just experienced how you can re-enter the thriving state through recall, just one of several strategies for gaining access. With simple, uncomplicated directions you recalled and experienced thriving for yourself. So, why don't you thrive more? This may sound like a no-brainer type of question. Who wouldn't want to thrive more of the time, living at the next level?

Pay special attention to your responses. Write them in your journal. At first blush, when faced with this question, individuals come up with a good reason *why not*: "*It would take too much time. I don't know how. It's too hard.*" There are a myriad of reasons.

In a pinch, any excuse will work, no matter how weak. Excuses demonstrate hesitance or unwillingness to take ownership and proceed forward on the path toward thriving.

Raising Your Voltage

Each of us knows generative, high-voltage personalities. They not only light up a room, they also demonstrate a level of energy that is contagious. One feels buoyed up in their presence. They pulsate waves of well-being.

This phenomenon involves a carrying capacity of energy, an unrestricted flow that is not considered common to most people. Thriving involves the same circuitry for high positive energy in the nervous system and body. It is just more efficient.

However, there must be something different in the brain, for the resulting higher state emits beneficial brain chemistry that supports a level of joy. It seems as if when your carrying capacity and energy go up, you handle a broader bandwidth. There is less resistance. You have a more efficient state of being with less commensurate wear and tear. This is a more refined level of functioning.

You may sense a little tentativeness in your approach to thriving. But you will not necessarily be reflective or self-conscious about what is happening to you? Who wants to be reflective when you are finding such contentment. When you are flowing with the current, you take your full measure of enjoyment.

Becoming more systematic about restoring the thriving experience comes later when you lose it and want it back. You can always think about establishing your Thrival System® later, but be sure to utilize what you already know from your experience.

Reorganize Yourself on Several Levels: Learn Every Step
If you aspire to a more refined level of being, you will want to consciously develop a greater carrying capacity aerobically, psycho-neurologically, and mentally. There will be some people who are naturals at this. But they will be the exception.

The main thing is that you are responsible for you, getting yourself what you need. To be self-sufficient in thriving, you will want to know every step along the way so that you can monitor, manage, and coach yourself along the path.

At times you will wonder about whether this state can be sustained. It feels like a precarious balance to maintain, like keeping a ping pong ball perched on the top of a jet of water. Who could get that right the first time? You will need practice.

Thriving seems so unusual, yet feels so good and natural. You have to reconnect and then recapture the connections frequently to restore easy access. That reopens the trail and grooves the pathways in the brain. Your circuit breakers may click in several times. You may even feel overwhelmed. But you have to keep throwing your own internal breaker back on to power up toward thriving.

Releasing Energy

To begin with, you will want to ease any constriction and increase your general flow of energy and enthusiasm. We each have 100 percent of our energy all the time. That is really a truism isn't it? It is contained within us, and expended by us in various ways. The question is how that energy then gets distributed, diminished, diverted, shut down, or placed in conflict with our natural flow and involvement. A certain percentage is devoted to internal resistance, conflict, and inhibition. And that fights our natural flow.

Keeping Fit

Everyone has a different life experience, temperament, bone structure, and body type. However, being fit and maintaining proper nutrition and weight are likely to increase your chances of thriving. I find that being on the lean side makes me more finely tuned and acutely aware of my inner linkage. And eating lightly, staying *just a little hungry*, helps me to monitor my feelings much better. Find out what works for you.

You Blaze Your Own Trail

Remember that this is not a well-traveled road. You are unique. And this time and this context are unique. You have to find your own special pathway and blaze your own trail. You have to monitor and manage your own trip. And that means experimenting with yourself to see what makes a difference for you.

The journal helps here as well. Write down different factors in your daily life that can help you to home in on what helps you to thrive. That is precisely what you need to know, to get down your basics, your fundamentals of thriving.

As you develop new thriving practices in your life, you get a new bundling of nerves around your thriving experience, activities, feelings. And, of course, the more recent your last thriving experience, the less you may have to reach, or rely on tricks and techniques to get your entire unified entity of body-mind-spirit tuned to your thriving frequency.

You are accessing your natural state, so you should have a high degree of recognition when you home in on your thrival station. You may have been attuning to the distractions from your natural state for so long that distractions have become normal for you. You may have to reclaim your natural state from your state of being perennially distracted and entranced.

Thriving generates a full range of transformation, a re-organization from within. Once you are in the thriving state, you will not have to individually note and target specific activities in order to convert them over to thriving activities. But you will have to become the change you want in the world.

What you do now occurs in the thriving context that is your life. Everything is done from that perspective. That is the slant. You naturally adapt. And things fall into place. This is, once again, your natural state. There is nothing more you need do to be here. You are home.

You will find yourself doing things differently, living differently. When you come from your natural state, you are coming from a purer source. The channels are deeper, smoother, and not constricted by self-defeating and self-diminishing practices.

Releasing the floodgates of your own energy fills you completely and naturally with a level that is supportive, invigorating, and replenishing. Inhibitions dissolve. In their stead is this warmth and compassion that begins inside and spills over in interaction with others and for others. And with it comes the utterance of a great "Ahhhhhhhhh!"

You may need to boost your aerobic condition to a level at which you can function more efficiently. Deep breathing, and the resulting hyper-oxygenation, can be a cleansing agent that clears the mind and provides smoother mental functioning. Increase your blood's capacity to carry oxygen and open your body and mind to increased functioning. You will deal more with breathing when we get to the doorways to the thriving state.

Summary

This chapter presented you with a very straightforward recall exercise as a way of getting you back into the thriving state. Even if you did not lock into that exceptional state of well-being, you can learn from what you recaptured, especially the feelings, skills, and disposition to enter that state.

You have 100 percent of your energy at all times.
Your assignment is to learn to release it.

You may also want to regenerate the internal carrying capacity of your entire aerobic, neurological, cardiovascular, and skeletal-muscular systems. The journal serves to build a foundation and to anchor your experience of thriving.

Chapter 9

Five Things That You Can Control in Your Life

"The stoics understood over two millennia ago that 'we control nothing beyond ourselves; everything external is outside our powers. Only our own efforts and reactions can be pure.'"

David VonDrehle, The Washington Post, Oct. 1, 2000, pp. 1-2

You may find it helpful to know what you really can control in your life. Five things that fit that criterion are your:

1. *Practices – What you do*
2. *Intake – What you take into yourself*
3. *Attitude – How you approach life*
4. *Thinking – How you focus your mental energy*
5. *Energy and Resonance – What you emanate, give off*

This is your main menu of choices in your life. Look it over and choose wisely. Knowing what you can control may help you put in focus what you can really make happen, as well as what is out of your control. This can assist you in avoiding energy drains, futile effort, exasperation, frustration, or victim hood.

1. Practices – What You Do

You have choices through your day regarding what you do: the time you go to bed and arise, whether you brush your teeth well, the clothing you wear, whether to have a balanced breakfast, and so forth.

There are things you know how to do but have yet to start. There are things you have yet to learn, things you ought to do more of, and those you would do well to stop. But they all get boiled down to practices: operations, skills put into practice, habits, all of which make up what you do in life. You can choose what you put into action. You can learn more practices and improve upon those you currently have. And then you can change them completely.

Practices make up the social order, the observable actions and behaviors of a group. Practices can usually be recorded, captured in picture and sound. Practices make up the interactions and operations of a relationship, family, organization, community, country, culture, and civilization.

2. Intake – What You Take In or Consume

What you consume or take in, your intake, also qualifies as a "practice." It is, after all, something that you do directly, and is a part of the social order. I list it separately due to its impact. Intake itself ranges from the most obvious essentials of air, water, food and light, all the way to the less obvious intake of stimuli such as sounds, noise, toxins, vibes, to even less obvious intake of ideas, energies, electro-magnetism, and radioactivity. Strictly speaking, intake is a subset of practices.

Food

Food intake has a direct and immediate effect on body chemistry and general well-being. The mix of foods you put into your system can either nourish you, effect an allergic reaction, nauseate, or even toxify you. Foods can enhance your thinking processes or gum up your receptors. Sugar can trigger mood swings. Many get dehydrated from insufficient fluid intake.

Sleep

Sleep is a major intake component. A large portion of the U.S. population is sleep deprived according to sleep experts. This is evidenced by prolonged yawning, dozing off in meetings, and dependence on coffee to stay awake. Catching an adequate amount of zzz's, sleep, is important to your smooth overall functioning.

Light

Lighting can also impact individuals in different, though major, ways. Vitamin D helps us to metabolize calcium. One source is sunlight. In the absence of full spectrum natural lighting from the sun, left brain students improve their reading scores under bright fluorescence, while soft lighting assists the global right brain reader.

Sound

Meanwhile, when comparing the empowering and steady rate of 60 tom-tom beats per minute, or the harmonic pace of Pachebel's *Canon*, to a typical rock-and-roll music beat, a definite debilitating effect from certain rock-and-roll beats is indicated by the reduction of deltoid muscle resistance in the listener. And Dr. Stephen Halpern contends that exposure to debilitating rhythms can weaken an individual for up to 10 times the length of exposure to the music.

Ideas

Ideas can empower or weaken as well. Note the "light bulb" over a cartoon character that universally indicates the dawning of an idea. Some of the impact of ideas comes from the method in which then are presented, the context in which they are received, while some is due objectively to the idea itself.

In her television interview that rocked Buckingham palace, the late Princess Diana was asked how she and Prince Charles told their children about their impending separation. Princess Di said, ***"I put it in very carefully. Of course, I don't know how it went in."*** Her statement indicates that the intention, clarity, and skill with which she transmitted the message had an impact on the outcome; but ultimately the receiver of the transmission is the final arbiter of the impact.

People who advise others on staying at their peak of high positive energy have recommended that participants in their training not listen to the news or read the newspaper due to the loading of negative content. Listening to messages of fatalities, felonies, foibles, and foolhardiness can take the air right out of some make them less energetic and positive in their daily lives.

Start to pay attention to the impact of everything you take in during the course of a day. This would constitute more intensive, focused, and disciplined journal work. And it could net you major insights and energy savings.

Avoiding Unintentional Intake

You might be standing in an underground parking garage waiting for your car without being aware that you are breathing in large amounts of the silent killer, carbon monoxide. You don't give it a thought. It does not register. Toxic intake can occur from unintentional, often unknown, exposure. You need to be aware of those circumstances that give rise to unintentional intake.

Images of Terror

For example, a major network television station in the Washington, D.C. market plays the previews of coming horror films on its 11:30 time slot. The preview comes with the usual gain in picture clarity and increase in volume.

With this slightly elevated signal, even if you are not consciously paying attention, the signal is registering in your subconscious. Standing there in your pajamas, flossing your teeth, seemingly paying no attention, you are taking the signal in unconsciously. And that ad will impact your peace of mind and your quality and depth of sleep for the night.

Other exposures may go unnoticed as well:

- **Radon gas seeps into your building from the foundation**
- **Mercury leaches from your old silver-colored dental fillings**
- **Effluents rise from carpeting, wallboard, and other building materials**
- **Mold, bacteria, and viral entities multiply in air and heating ducts**
- **Chemical contaminants come from cleaning liquids**
- **Utensils contaminate cooked foods**
- **Radioactivity emanates from seemingly benign smoke alarms**
- **Electromagnetic fields arise from your clock radio, electric blanket, wiring system, computer screen, cell phone, and micro wave oven when just plugged in.**

Some of these exposures can be detected just by being aware that they exist. Others require specific detection devices. For example, the electromagnetic field can be measured by a simple, inexpensive gauss meter. Check out your computer screen and the best distance to sit from it. Monitor the overlapping impact of phone, fax, computer, and other office equipment.

Check out your home. You may find that your clock radio is broadcasting over a larger field than any other appliance.

Mine was setting up a field four feet away, and I disconnected it immediately.

Stay Informed about Forces in Your Environment

Be informed about all the forces and factors that impinge on your body. Those can include such givens as gravity, atmospheric pressure, altitude, humidity. Some of these are natural, though changeable, and therefore can be monitored. It is a matter of measuring your personal intake, the impact on you, when possible. Or be aware of interaction effects, the context or environment in which they are occurring, or the timing. Even the best medicines, for example, can have a negative effect when mixed with certain foods, alcohol, sunlight, or other medications. Your pharmacist is an excellent source on these interaction effects.

The greatest discovery of my generation is
that human beings by changing
the inner attitudes of their minds
can change the outer aspects of their lives.
William James

3. Attitude – How You Approach Life

How you approach life is your choice. Your attitude impacts your mood and brain chemistry, as well as what you give off to those around you. You choose your attitude. How do you want to come across? How do you want to look at and approach life? What is your intention? The amount of positive spirit that you allow into your life is your choice.

At one point, the hard charging, striving, multi-tasking Type A personality was thought to be more prone to stroke and heart attack than the more garrulous, endomorphic, laidback Type B. Further research, however, has showed that one single factor accounted for this vulnerability of Type A's, the presence of hostility toward others.

Those who were hostile demanded that others behave in accordance with their express dictates. They would often become enraged toward them, vilify them, for not complying. These explosive tendencies can engender stroke and heart attack. So here is one example of how changing your attitude can change your vulnerability to a degenerative disease. Recognizing your own personal limits, as well as exercising a degree of optimism, can start you on the road to improved quality of outlook, and life.

Excess Positivity

Acting out of optimism alone does not mean that you mimic Shirley Temple in *The Good Ship Lollypop* – sweet, cute, and totally cheerful. That's a little too syrupy for daily life. And there are numerous recommended approaches to life that are also a bit excessive.

"Excess positivity" is the practice of viewing reality totally on the positive side. That means that no matter what is going on, everything is "great." There are no shadow sides, shortcomings, or negative aspects. The more accurate clinical term for this practice is "denial"!

When you require yourself to always be "up," "on," and "positive," you are adopting a reactive stance. Meanwhile, the denial required to adopt that stance is often covering up an undercurrent of fear marked by a refusal to see things as they are, lest negativity resurface. *The office manager for a motivational speaker decided to change the letters on his favorite coffee cup from "I'm terrific" to "I'm terrified." His wife walked into the office during the little prank and commented, "That might be true."*

The healthier balance, according to Dr. Martin Seligman, author of *Learned Optimism*, is an outlook that is weighted toward a positive perception of reality, yet leaves space for an acknowledgment of the negative, the shortfall. Just don't dwell on it, or you get caught up in the negativity.

Innertude®: Inflate Yourself to Proper Pressure

Innertude® is a comprehensive strategy for adopting a sustainable positive attitude. This key approach to resilience assists you in bouncing back from adversity, as well as in meeting challenges head on. Chapter 12 is devoted to this solid practice for living on the next best level.

4. Thinking: How You Focus Your Mental Energy

There are five modes identified so far to categorize how people occupy their minds. Not every one of them is healthy or helpful. The five modes are:

A. Meditation
B. Distracting With Frenetic Activity
C. Targeted, Focused Thought
D. Insight, Incubation, and Intuition
E. Rumination, or "Moody Mulling Over"

A. Meditation

Meditation is an active and healthy pursuit. You have to be discerning in holding out all thoughts. In its purest form, meditation is complete without thought. It flushes the brain of self-talk and distraction. Meditation provides a brain cleansing and a rest from the daily mental cacophony. Meditation requires practice and discipline to attain a level of calm and a contemplative state of mind. You have to be able to focus, to release your thoughts. You can still be conscious of your consciousness, or aware of your awareness.

There are numerous kinds and varieties of meditation, or practices that provide similar benefits. Reading and reflection on a spiritual reading or poem does not flush the mind, but rather seek clarity of thought and new realizations. Some may actively focus on a particular thought, vision, problem, plan, or lighted candle, and then simply see what arises in consciousness.

Meditation can be a "time out" for your mind, an inner silence, a restful opportunity to calm yourself and gain perspective. Once you gain this skill, you have a much easier time dealing with the distractive activity and rumination modes.

B. Distracting With Frenetic Activity:
"Avoiding the Devil's Workshop of an Idle Mind"

At some point, the phrase "an idle mind is the devil's workshop" made a very deep and scary impression on some individuals. Who would want to be taken over and possessed by a demon! Since hearing that comment, many dare not stop. They have non-stop frenetic activity. Being in motion is their form of "damnation avoidance."

A more benign perspective finds people being comfortable in being busy, busy, busy, as described by George Odiorne in *The Activity Trap*. They begin to know and value themselves as constantly on the go. It becomes the way they live.

Both can be very unhealthy and compulsive operational modes that drive a whirling dervish lifestyle, filled with non-stop activity. The endless activity serves to distract you from developing your inner self. Life is externalized, happening on the outside, where it is observable to all. This keeps the "actor" from getting close to his inner nature and self.

However, in some families, this may have been a necessary mode of operation for survival. So the message children got from parents was, this is a way to stay alive. Still, it marks a survival mode, especially as a diversion from coming to peace with your own inner nature.

One underlying fear may be a fear of being damned, not having a trustworthy nature, not being enough, of tending inevitably toward evil. To avoid that fate, constant action must be taken. This gets translated into the need to stay involved in a flurry of activity, and to be chronically distracted from self in the process. This pursuit is unhealthy, robotic, mechanical. It is also not fulfilling, not satisfying or replenishing. This mindless activity totally contradicts the degree of consciousness or awareness required for thriving. And meditation can be one remedy for it.

C. Targeted, Focused Thought

This use of your thinking function can cover everything from simply looking for your car keys to fulfilling a lifelong dream, project management, or mission. You seek a result and focus your mental energy on obtaining an outcome. You pursue it actively, and discern your progress and your arrival at the desired outcome.

Visioning would fit into this mode. Once you have the vision, you then need to establish a structure or format for guiding and following productive practices in realization of that vision.

D. Insight, Incubation, and Intuition

These are several ways in which insight, incubation, and intuition arise as a result of thought modes. All utilize the subconscious and have other similarities. You have utilized them if you have considered a problem, sought a novel response, speculated and wondered about how things would develop.

They happen on the inside. Little, if anything, is observable about the processes. Results arise more from your subconscious, if not from your unconscious. You can get results as a flash of recognition, a stream of consciousness, a sudden realization.

Even though insight, incubation, and intuition do not necessarily have a predictable schedule, the work they do can be initially focused on a specific problem or outcome. The results, then, are not just accepted wholesale. They are considered according to the criteria for the solution that was sought, or the level of creativity that was desired. You determine what, if anything, you ultimately will use of that particular insight, incubation, or intuition. You utilize discernment.

Of course, you have had unsolicited intuition. Suddenly thoughts arise from out of nowhere. They are spontaneous, emergent. But you still have the option to be discerning about the meaning and immediate relevance of that intuitive arrival.

Incubation draws on creativity for effective coping. Intuition is often naturally creative, streaming together thoughts in a new or unusual way. New input, or the prompting of the question, leads to new connections, synapses, combinations, and permutations. You gain insight from the synthesis of new elements.

E. Rumination, or "Moody Mulling Over"

The mental workings of rumination are much like the tornado scene in *The Wizard of Oz.* This use of mental energy involves the helter-skelter bombardment of seemingly out-of-control and chaotic elements. Some might describe rumination as an unending fantasy run amok, while others see it as the ever-changing, stimulating landscape in their vivid inner life.

Rumination arouses high emotionality. Here is the skunk works for most of our anxiety, depression, anger, panic. And, at first consideration, it seems to be out of our immediate control. But, is it?

Inner Paintball

The emotionality of rumination, or "moody mulling over," reminds me of "inner paintball." You may be aware of the military-games simulation of jungle fighting, using paintballs rather than bullets to mark kills and wounds. Dressed in army camouflage, teams of participants try to survive their encounter with the enemy.

Inner paintball takes place when an individual entertains just the right mix of provocative elements in thought to conjure up the brain chemistry and emotions that will keep him occupied, upset, or stirred up, yet having a vivid, stimulating experience.

Agnes was distraught as she related the situation. Her sister was going to get a cat now that her daughter was five years old. It would be "just awful." For when Agnes had lived in the guest bedroom in her sister's basement, she had two cats. But they were not allowed upstairs in the house at all and just barely tolerated to begin with. And now, her sister was going to get her daughter a cat! It would be catastrophic for the cat, cruel and unusual treatment, she wailed. When I backed off a bit to look at the situation, I mused that the situation could only currently exist in her mind since it did not yet exist in reality. It was Tuesday, and the kitty would not even be purchased until Saturday. I suggested that she had provoked her own mental state by what she was choosing to think about, and that she ought to" choose another thought."

Agnes was selectively choosing to upset herself. What is more, she expected me to get involved in the emotionality with her and play "Ain't It Awful!" Of the gazillion thoughts that she could have been using to occupy her mental energy, she chose and persisted in this one. What made it so ridiculous was that it had not even happened yet…and might not ever happen.

The Payoff from Rumination

One payoff to rumination is a sense of being a victim, together with the control of emotionality: a raw sense of pathos, the melodramatics of getting revenge, or righting wrongs. The client clearly demonstrated that she was in complete charge of what she chose to focus on so intensely. Then she could crank up the emotions to fever pitch. And that got her another payoff of internal stimuli.

Most who ruminate claim they are passive victims of the cacophonous thinking. They would have you believe that they take no active agency. In fact they may think that is true. The waves are being beamed in, they have no control. But they do, and so do you.

Change Your Thoughts. Change Your Emotions.

You can select your thoughts and the way you invest your mental energy. You can even select your reaction to your thoughts. If I max out my credit cards, I can sit at my desk and focus on how hopeless and futile life is. Pretty soon my stomach is oozing hydrochloric acid in keeping with all the anxiety I have generated within myself. By all rights, this is my dilemma. I am running out of resources, facing eventual bankruptcy. I can catastrophize with the best of them. It is my dilemma and I will be anxious and panicked if I want to. And, quite obviously, I want to. But I also have a tremendous range of alternatives. I can change my thoughts any time I choose, and bring on an entirely different mental set.

Should I choose more soothing thoughts, brain chemistry, level of energy, and focus, I may have to face the question of whether I am willing to give up the high soap opera and drama of being a victim. For one major payoff to producing all this seemingly out-of-control emotionality is the sense that I am in fact doomed and *have no choice*.

Yet, I am victimized by my own devices. And my payoff is twofold. I am in perfect control of the thoughts I choose. And I feed my addiction to stress by focusing on something that rattles my cage.

Victim: To Be or Not to Be?

Having become expert at being a victim, you may not want to give up your payoff. You can get a lot of sympathy for being a victim. You can maneuver people into position, honing victim-hood to a high art. You can whine over a four-octave range. And you get others to commiserate with you about how unfair life is.

So, as you sit there contemplating your approaching bankruptcy, confrontation from creditors, challenge, catastrophe, public humiliation, possible homelessness, you can continue to pour acid into your gut and harvest a range of emotions of pity. Or you can change your thoughts, and the commensurate emotions accompanying or resultant.

You will notice, I am not razzmatazzing you into thinking positive, getting out of the pit. I am simply advocating thinking differently, taking the live wire out of your brain.

Going beyond victim-hood is a major passage in maturity. It's a passage you are required to face if you wish to move on to the best next level for living.

The No-Whining Experiment
One experiment can clip victimization in the bud: You are not allowed to complain for 21 days in a row. Try it. See how far you get. If you complain just once, your 21 days begin all over again. See what it is like to go along and have to transform sources of whining into occasions for shining; glower into glowing; complaint into compliment. You have to change your perspective, look on the bright side, find the redeeming quality, appreciate specific aspects of your life.

Thinking Healthy
A major advance toward thriving is thinking healthy. The fifth thinking mode, rumination and resulting moodiness, consumes a tremendous amount of time and energy. Looking on the bright side can jumpstart your healthy thinking, put you in a more optimistic frame of mind, boost your spirits. But first, recognize that **you** are in charge of your rumination, and change your thoughts.

Meditate
Clear your head of debilitating thoughts, chatter, and disruptive self-talk. Focus and target your thinking toward productive ends. Release your creative abilities, your incubation and intuitive skills. Think funny. A humorous perspective lightens everyone's spirits, including yours. Humor also helps you transcend even the most difficult of circumstances. Finally, appreciate your own improvement in accepting responsibility for your thoughts, moods, emotions, and releasing your true feelings. This is a major advance on your part, one that you can celebrate, one that is essential to thriving.

5. Energy, Resonance – What You Emanate
Intake and practices both involve the structure or social order of what you do. Attitude and healthy thinking deal with your belief system. The way that you deal with all four of those items is what gives rise to your energy.

What you eat, how you breathe, whether you exercise, how you think, your attitude and resulting brain chemistry, each and all directly impact your energy level, how you resonate, and the emanations that proceed from you. This is what you give off. And it all carries a signal and has meaning and impact on others.

Your voice is one indicator of this resonance, as are skin tone, posture, the clarity of your eyes, relaxed muscle tone, gait and the bounce in your step and agility. Even handwriting has been shown to correlate highly with health and well-being.

Starting Your Day

If you start the day with a smile on your face, even before you get out of bed, as Valla Dana Fotiades advocates, you stand a better chance of following through with a more positive attitude. Well begun may be half done.

Eat a well-balanced breakfast, and your energy reserves are set for the day. Plan your drive time to work, and you are less likely to arrive frazzled and out of sorts. If you arrive with a low or dense level of resonance, fewer people will be drawn to you or want to do business with you.

The exercise you get will affect your energy level. Amazingly, when you come home from work tired, you get more energized by exercising than by taking a nap. Get your energy release by moving.

When you come to terms with yourself and your current reality, you stand a better chance of finding harmony within yourself and giving off good vibes. People get a sense of what you give off and will be attracted to you.

If you have a lot of baggage, are highly stressed, conflicted, or easily impacted, you are bound to have a lot of dense energy, low-frequency, heavy vibes. Like Joe Bltzflk from the *Lil Abner* comic strip, you will have the equivalent of a black cloud over your head daily. Your aura will be *schmutzig*. That will give you a dark visage.

Healthy people, unless they are helping or health care professionals, will steer clear of those who are dense and negative. If you don't have healthy interactions with people, then your journey will be a struggle.

So your task, should you choose to thrive more of the time, is to lighten up in all ways, resolve your internal and external conflicts, confront your fears, feel your feelings, deal with your reality, and find peace of mind and well-being through the way you carry yourself and act.

How Do You Resonate and Emanate Good Vibes?
There are numerous ways to lighten up. Most stress relief measures qualify. Deep muscle relaxation, massage, reflexology, yoga, stretch aerobics, Pilates method, acupuncture – all have gained credibility through the alternative health movement. They can reduce tension or static, and improve conditioning. They also reduce constriction in the circulatory system, increase blood flow, and free up energy. This constriction can also be affected by your intake, practices, attitude, and thoughts.

You have 100 percent of your energy all the time. The only issue is how to release the energy being consumed in internal resistance or constriction. Find and release your sources of constriction, and you invigorate yourself, rather than dulling and making your energy dense and self-consuming.

"Singing Is Seven Times Praying"

Chanting can be a great assist in freeing up energy, as well as in meditating. A repetitive chant, a long extended chant such as a requiem mass, or the Bhagavad-Gita. You get peaceful and harmonious effects from chanting, or even from listening to chant. But by participating and chanting yourself, you add the reverberation to your body, tissue, and cells. In vibrating your body, you can reduce the tension that you hold. And this clears the way for high positive energy.

Summary

In this world of turbocharged change, and the turbulence that results, you can find solace in knowing what five things in your life you can control, determine, choose: practices, intake, attitude, thought mode, and energy. You are encouraged to feel your feelings as part of the richest experience of your life. You are encouraged to craft your life in such a way that, by focusing on the elements you can control, you get an immediate gain from enhancing your energy, resonance, and what emanates from you.

The next chapter explains how to build a solid foundation for thriving within a balanced life, and how to reciprocate the energy that comes your way. It discusses meeting basic needs first so that you can then launch yourself forward on the path toward the thrival state.

It is circumstances which show what men are. Therefore when a difficulty falls upon you, remember that God, like a trainer of wrestlers, has matched you with a rough young man...so that you can become an Olympian conqueror. *Epictetus*

Chapter 10

Meet Your Essential Need for Life Balance

Build a Solid Foundation to Launch Into Thriving

There are certain fundamentals you need to have in place before you can hope to thrive on a regular and sustainable basis. You need to have balance in your life. The solid base required as a platform or launch pad to reach the best next step and thrival lifestyle is based on the six essentials of a well-balanced life. Family, career, community, personal, spiritual, and social aspects are all given serious consideration.

The emphasis here is building a basic foundation that consists of meeting your basic needs first and foremost. This is part of your responsibility to yourself. And only when some semblance of balance is in place would you have the basic platform from which to thrive on an ongoing basis. Maintaining this balance is a dynamic, ongoing effort, not unlike balancing on a log floating down a river.

Balance Is an On-Going Challenge

These six platform components for a balanced life contain the requisite practices and relationships that will provide you both support and challenge for the pursuit of thrival. They are all essential construction material for building and then maintaining an improved lifestyle.

Life Balance Areas

Family

I observe a number of career couples with their late-in-life infants out for coffee on Saturday morning in Old Town Alexandria, Virginia. The baby may be throwing a tantrum from his stroller while the parents sit ignoring him, that deer-in-the-headlights look in their eyes. That look says they are mystified about how to deal with the kid. The child has been with someone else all week, learning and growing. Now he is out with these people he lives with evenings and weekends. They are family, but are they familiar? They seem to lack a little.

The world of work and rapid change is pretty much stressing out everyone, demanding more time of already stretched parents. Getting home at 8 pm leaves no time for catching up with the kids' lives. And traveling 30-70 percent of the time makes it even more difficult to stay in touch and involved. One professional speaker said that as he headed out the door to the airport, his toddler asked, "Is Daddy going home now?" If you have a family, it has to be the major priority. Find the time. Make time. Time and presence are the two main things you offer your family.

Decide in advance of generating a family, whether you are really in this one for the long haul. Only then should you decide whether to make the commitment. Your "family" can be extended as well. There are those you are related to by blood, and there are those you are drawn to and attracted to. Choose and interact with both.

Career

One of my stress management participants blurted out, "Do you know why I'm a dentist?" It's because some seventeen-year-old kid thought it would be a neat thing to do. Now I'm thirty-five, and I hate it." Obviously he was ready for career counseling, if not a career change.

My first Washington, D.C. hair stylist was another example. He would give me a great cut one time, and the next time I would have to go in several days later to get my hair repaired. He was burnt out and performing erratically. So was my dentist, who sold his practice and went into commercial real estate. He got out shortly after claiming that my new crown was firmly mounted. Meanwhile, I continued to chew on the left side of my mouth for ten months until his hygienist confirmed my claim and the crown was secured.

These examples show the deterioration of professional performance when people no longer find their work satisfying. That is why filling out the life balance assessment that follows is important. You can track your own areas of joy and fulfillment as well as introduce new practices that you do find fulfilling.

What can you find in the work you do that is sheer joy? What would you volunteer to do, or seek out, or crave doing if it were not part of your job? What brings you the most enjoyment in your current work? From your past jobs? What is your passion? What have you done or observed being done that you find exquisitely meaningful? How can you do something of import, passion, and meaning to you?

While home offices and working at home are more and more commonplace, many entrepreneurs who work all by themselves soon find that social interaction carries a far higher reward than they ever would have guessed when they took it for granted every day when they worked for someone else. Now that they are on their own, they find themselves scheduling more meetings and lunches, and making social occasions at restaurants or coffee houses with their laptops just to be around people. We need solitude at times, but everyone needs social contact and interaction too. If your job does not provide enough, change it.

Within a job, you can continue to refine your skills. The best singers, musicians, and sports figures continue to receive coaching throughout their lives. They recognize that perfecting their craft is a lifelong quest. Fine-tune as you go. There is much to learn and take in, in the process. Learn to differentiate what is personal in your life and what is professional. The more clearly you demarcate the lines for your professional life, the more clearly you can improvise, stretch, and challenge yourself to grow even more. The best jazz combo requires a good percussive or bass beat against which to improvise. With that clear rhythm in place, there are structure and latitude for the improvisation to begin.

Community

How much community involvement is possible for you, given your family and professional responsibilities? Volunteer service is usually unlimited. You are typically greeted with open arms. And you can start your own categories of service or need fulfillment. If you do not live around extended family or close and supportive friends, the community may provide you with resource people and a support group for any number of life events. In this time of transient living, it is difficult to connect, get involved, and find acceptance within a community. You may have to be from an old family, or at least have lived there a long time to gain acceptance. Most places are experiencing unprecedented change. And you can always take a leadership role, rather than waiting for things to develop.

In larger cities, your community may consist of your neighborhood, your church, or even your child's school. It might be found in the people who rally around a particular political candidate or issue. Wherever you find community, embrace it and contribute to it. Reciprocity is the rule throughout. You have to give back as a member, as well as to partake in what the community has to offer.

Personal

We have already touched on finding private or alone time, time to yourself to pursue your own interests or just to find refuge. Many who drive to work get their alone time during the commute. They may not be aware of it, but this is their personal time.

For mothers especially, many of whom work outside the home, then come home to a second full time job, having a child is like being grounded for 18 years, with no time off for good behavior. And that can make child rearing a real drag. It was easier when there were extended family members nearby to provide respite from the children and to offer perspective when conflicts arose.

You need personal time, respite. Get a sitter. Have your spouse or a friend take the kids. Check them into a play gym. But get yourself time for yourself, without demands. You need to heal and replenish. You need time to be creative, to explore new aspects of your life. Give yourself time and space to grow.

I often hear that "A mother does X," as if there is some universal role prescription that harnesses them to rigidly fixed practices and unalterable obligations. Apparently each is buttressed by the potential of guilt if they don't do it. My response is that they are modeling parenthood in unfortunate terms. Their kids will get the message that they had better have fun now, because when they become adults with kids, it's all pretty joyless.

Draw boundaries. Cut out time for yourself. If it means trading off time taking care of others' children, do it. Take your time and feel good about it. This may be especially challenging for single mothers. But it is also part of being resourceful. Be a little more resourceful for your own sake, to get some relief, as part of your self-care. With luck, you will not have to wait for the kids to be asleep or finally to leave home, to get some private time.

Spiritual

Plato, Aristotle, and many ancients discuss the soul and the necessity of attending to it. Prior to the existence of modern religions, the soul was already an agreed-upon entity that needed attention and nourishing. Why should it be any less an issue for you? What do you do that is intrinsically soul nourishing? What could you add to your activities?

Religious practice is not necessarily spiritual, though much of it does have a spiritual component. But some is also more form than function. It is more what you do to nourish your spirit. And in the workshops I have done on "Bringing More Soul to Your Life, Work, and Career" everyone attending is working on issues of import to their deeper selves. All seem to have a personal take or understanding on what soul and spirit are to them, what it means to them. However, you may want to enrich your understanding by discussing these matters with theologians, ministers, priests, rabbis, mullahs, philosophers…those trained and practiced in this area. A spiritual adviser can provide guidance along the spiritual path and the spiritual dimension to life.

Social

This area may overlap with others. Generally, if you are moving around the country, or changing location within a city, you have to reach out, use connections, and be resourceful. Ingenious summer school students in Mexico City responded to classified ads for "furniture for sale" as a way of getting into local's homes without an introduction.

The way social life has evolved and careers have swallowed up the daylight, men often get so involved with their family and work that they have no other social life. They especially lack close male friends. And they seldom have a place to just hang out with their buddies, a place with no demands. Men should be able to congregate without intrusion, and without arousing a cacophony of suspicion. In most societies, up to the present, gathering has been part of the tradition and practices. Why not ours?

Relationship Testing

Relationships are essential to healthy living. Five considerations can revolutionize the conduct and appreciation for any relationship, whether that relationship is with another person, organization, job, or even with yourself. Here are the questions you can pose to open up these considerations:

1. *What is in this relationship for you?*

The emphasis is on what you will gain or get out of it, the self-centered incentive. How will this benefit me? What's my return on investment from the other elements?

2. *What is in you for this relationship?*

Sometimes you pick an activity based on the contribution you think you can make, such as in a volunteer role. You may have an expert or underutilized ability that you can offer.

On the other hand, you are often handed a situation with which you just have to deal. You would not have chosen it for anything, but you still got it all the same. Then once you have completed the process, passed through the trials and the fires, you are somehow changed in a way that you could not have realized. Or you have learned a valuable lesson. This consideration, then, deals more with discovery. For example, how are you different today as a result of having raised your children? What difference did that make in your life and development? How did that relationship mature you? What did you learn or realize from that?

3. What do you want?

This is "the" basic question throughout life, and one that most people have trouble answering easily, clearly, or accurately. This one takes work on an ongoing basis. For example, you may be considering buying a new car, but the car is really the secondary gain. What you are really after is the status and sense of power you will feel in being able to walk into a showroom and buy what you wish. So you could come to terms with your real desire, and know what you are really after. But this may require journal work first, to get a clear sense of what is at stake, what the issues are.

4. What do you want from this relationship?

This is a kind of specific second check. On second thought, once you figure out what you really want, you may not want this relationship at all. You may also have more finely honed your wants so that you understand precisely what you do want from this relationship.

5. Will you let yourself have what you want?

All the other questions are useless unless you consider this final question. This one colors all the others. Without it, you could continue your life and never quite get what you want. This question attempts to widen the context of your consideration, and put it in a more revealing light.

> *Journaling Note*
> *If you have difficulty admitting what you want, even in your confidential journal, try discussing this final consideration with someone whom you trust, someone supportive and encouraging, or a professional who can help you get an objective perspective on how you are denying yourself what you truly want.*

Do pay attention to how this question delves more deeply into what you do, indeed, want. And that may include specifics or whole new areas that you have not yet admitted to yourself.

Sheer Joy, Payoffs, and Tradeoffs
The balance, proportion, and dimension you want to attain have several gradients to increase your awareness and enjoyment. First, you will want to assess how much you currently do for:

1. The **sheer joy** of it -- you would need no pay to do it
2. The **payoff,** tangible return on your investment, e.g.,$.
3. The **tradeoff**, performing a given task to gain a benefit that exists separate and apart from that actual task.

"Sheer Joy" as the Basis for Your Activity
On getting enshrined in the Pro Football Hall of Fame in Canton, Ohio, Sam Huff said, "I can't believe that I have been paid to play this game, when I would have played it for free." I know what he means. I get paid for organizational consulting, thrival and executive coaching, and doing psychotherapy, yet I absolutely love doing them all. I could consult 27 hours a day. Each one is inherently rewarding with a lot of sheer joy built in for me.

"Payoff" as the Basis for Your Activity
Payoff means seeking something directly in exchange for what you put into it. The things I do for a payoff or fee compensate me for the effort that goes into my contribution. For example, when a speech involves blinding spotlights and I can barely see the audience, I do not get the face-to-face personal contact I prefer. I may seek my fee based on several criteria, such as size of the audience, level of participants in the organization, degree of customization, length of presentation, and whether it is a keynote/general session for thousands, or a smaller breakout session.

A multibillion-dollar incentive industry exists specifically to find payoffs in addition to base salary. An incentive will continue to interest, attract, and enhance employee performance when money is no longer a compelling incentive. An incentive is a payoff, a "what I do it for" kind of motive. But there are times when there is no known payoff sufficient to keep someone on the job. That is when a tradeoff comes in.

"Tradeoff" as the Basis for Activity

A tradeoff means that I choose to do "X" in order to support another unrelated activity. If you are ready to leave a job, and the only thing holding you there is one of the following situations, you are probably working on a tradeoff basis:

1. Your child is in middle school, and you do not want to upset her by removing her from her friends until she enters high school. So you decide to wait the two years and continue in your current job even though you find nothing particularly gratifying about it. That job may be the only thing available to you in this community.
2. Real estate prices right now are so low that you would sell at a loss. And since you are moving into a higher-priced area, you would take a tremendous financial hit. So you determine to stay put and wait for prices to appreciate or interest rates to come down.
3. Your spouse is completing an MBA program in 11 months, so you choose to stay in the area till he finishes.

In any case in which someone is choosing such a tradeoff, I suggest that person ***discreetly*** place a 3 x 5 card in his desk drawer at work, or in a safe place where she can readily refer to it. On the card I have them write the rough equivalent of:

I choose to continue in this job, recognizing fully that I find no reward in it, and that I will get out just as soon as Kim gets out of middle school.

That way, when the going gets tough, when the employee tends to forget the well-reasoned decision why she is still in this unfulfilling job, based on an outside considerations, the employee can pull open the desk drawer and remind herself why she is there. By taking full responsibility for her actions, and taking ownership for what she is doing in the long term, she can stay on in the job without feeling as if she is giving up her integrity.

Stop Re-deciding and Second Guessing

The 3x5 card works to spell out and remind you of the rationale behind your other life-shaking decisions as well, such as your decision to end an abusive relationship or to postpone a marriage. However, people tend to make a decision, then introduce doubt that it was the right one. Or, they tend to continue to make the decision by opening it up again and again. This leaves them with no stability whatsoever. That is where the 3x5 card can provide a point of reference. Write it out well. Review it. Keep it handy.

Gear Up to Assess Your Life Balance

On the following assessment sheet, determine what activities you have going in each area. Then determine what additional activities you can shift into the inherently rewarding/sheer joy column. You may find that on closer examination, several of your payoff activities can be reframed as inherently rewarding by looking at them more closely, or changing your attitude toward them.

Refer now to the Balance Assessment sheet that follows and fill it out.

Life Balance Assessment

What do you do for the sheer joy of it? Are there inherent rewards built into your current areas of life activity? The following format is designed to assist you in assessing your reward structure and in planning more intrinsic joy into what you do. There are three columns with which to assess your activities under each domain:

Intrinsic Reward – the activity is its own reward…you would do it even if you were not paid.
Payoff – this is a more tangible direct reward or consequence tied directly to performing specific services or producing. Salary, etc.
Tradeoff – this is a benefit which you acquire from a totally unrelated area, For example, you might stay in a job you hate so that your spouse can finish an MBA program. The benefit is peripheral to, not a direct consequence of that life area activity.

NOW, WORK SPECIFICALLY TO ASSESS AND PLAN TO FILL IN THE "SHEER JOY" COLUMNS AS WELL AS THE PAYOFF COLUMNS, AREAS OF HIGH REWARD. FIND NEW INCENTIVES FOR YOURSELF.

DOMAIN:	SHEER JOY	PAYOFF	TRADEOFF
Personal			
Work			
Social			
Family Community			
Spiritual			

Now review the assessment. See where the main imbalance is. Take extra time and do journal work on how to bring more sheer joy into your work and life. For many, increasing joy in work and life is a matter of adopting a new perspective or an attitude of gratitude, appreciating finally, what they had formerly taken for granted.

Move as many activities into the sheer joy column as you can realistically. You may find that you already have lemonade, when in fact you had always seen the activity as a sour lemon. For example, working at home might seem like a great idea, missing an horrendous daily commute. But you find you miss the social life in the office – including some of the individuals you formerly considered pains to be around.

Simple changes can be made in each area of your basic life balance platform such as changing to full-spectrum lighting in your office, getting a high-quality radio, getting a desk surface that elevates so you can do some of your work standing. And that is just the office environment. There is so much more that can be improved. You have unlimited opportunities to enhance your life.

Review the criteria that arise in posing those five questions about relationship. Does this put any of your life in a slightly different perspective? Are you getting an inkling of intentions you have not yet implemented? Even if this platform does not serve as a launching pad into your thrival state, you can enhance your life considerably by launching initiatives that come from your deeper purpose. You can also attain balance among your major life areas.

The Inner View: Perspective

The one choice you always have is how to view something from within. What perspective will you take? What is your attitude? With what frame of mind will you approach a task, spiritual, career, family crisis? You can always locate a second, third, and fourth wind of energy and tolerance in approaching tasks. It is all in how you look at them or frame them.

Maintaining the Balance

Revisit the assessment every six weeks to three months at first. Make sure that you are attending to all of your major life areas and that balance is a priority. This is your life. You want to have the basics in place and derive joy and satisfaction from all areas of your life.

Part III

Rules and Guidelines to Access Thriving

The following section lays out three rules and seven guidelines for getting into the thrival state.

Three Rules
The three rules set forth guidelines and a mode of orienting yourself in every given moment. They refer to behaviors you will want to establish as habits of living in order to thrive more frequently, and ultimately all the time.

Seven Guidelines
The seven guidelines that follow are directives or portals, any one of which may be adequate for you to gain full entry to the thriving state within yourself. Each guideline is associated with a distinct activity, skill, or practice found to be important in approaching the thriving state.

You may already have mastered these "portal practices." Hopefully your mastery will facilitate your transition into the thriving state. However, you may also encounter additional issues that impede your passage into thrival space. So, you may want to consider each guideline in turn, together with the rules.

Chapter 11

Three Rules for Thriving

Thriving Can Be Learned

Until now, you have accepted what you perceived as situational or circumstantial limitations. Once you hit a rough spot, you would have accepted it as an insurmountable limitation, and accepted it with disappointment or sense of resignation. After getting into a thriving space, no obstacle is perceived as a real or permanent limitation.

Accessing and recapturing the thriving state requires self-discipline, focus, and self-acceptance. Sustaining and extending that sweet spot in time requires an on-going persistence to initiate new practices, to stay focused and to weed out personal practices, assumptions, and beliefs that undermine thriving. Actually, once you are in the thriving state, you recognize that it is effortless. Regaining access through your own personal resistance, and then staying in this neutral space of your natural self, is tricky. To sustain your thriving feeling requires staying focused and maintaining an inner stability and connection.

Three Rules for Thriving on a Regular Basis

These three rules thread themselves throughout the weaving of the fabric of practices called for in developing your unique Thrival System®. The rules are undercurrents, present to and flowing through each moment as you explore the utility of each doorway, as well as other practices. The importance of each rule, in turn, will unfold as you proceed along the path toward thriving.

The rules are:

I. **Make a Present of the Present: Live in the Moment!**

II. **Accept Yourself and Take Full Responsibility for Your Life**

III. **Appreciate Yourself and Adopt an Attitude of Gratitude!**

Rule I
Make a Present of the Present: Live in the Moment!

Being in the Moment

Every now and then in your life there is a little oasis of total self-acceptance, satisfaction, and peace of mind. You are able to quiet nagging judgments and uncouple yourself from being ego driven. Questioning and self-doubt are boxed out. Forgiveness is quick. You find a peace from deep within. You live each moment to the fullest.

For those thriving moments there is **no need to do, or have, or be anything other than who you are**. You make space for yourself. The experience of truly being in that moment is inherently satisfying and precious. You feel complete, sufficient, "enough," fulfilled, and sourced from within. Life doesn't get any better than that. This is the richest experience of your life! This is being in the ***thriving state – a state of mind, not of external circumstances***.

You are focused without being self-absorbed, self-confident without being arrogant or overbearing. There is no need to look further, to clamor or strive, to be compelled or driven toward some distant goal. This is your life, right here, right now. The present moment is a gift to be absorbed and enjoyed.

Life just "is."
How you choose to deal with life,
How much of it you choose to access, is yours to determine.
You can anticipate life, ruminate over life experiences already past, or
Seize the moment and be vitally alive and involved right now.

"Now," this moment, is all there is to experience. Before this moment, all memory is perception; after this moment all there is, is hope, wishes, anticipation, speculation, and intention.

Yet a thread of life runs through us all. Everything you experience comes from a flowing together of events, stimuli, recollections, impressions, occurring in an ongoing now. And you are left to participate in them as you choose, right now, and you can access your life right now from moment to moment. You can also ignore it, be distracted by it, or be overwhelmed.

You have the capability to be truly present to yourself, feeling what you feel and aware of the inner glimmers even while you are recalling the past or anticipating the future. Ignoring the present while recalling the past can be as much of an escape, as anticipating the future, and as great a loss. You and I, we each end up missing "the experience of our life!" So, here is an exercise for being in the moment right now.

Time is so that everything doesn't happen at once!
The Flying Karamazov Brothers

Balance: Getting Focused and Grounded
One exercise that requires fierce focus, and also puts you squarely in the moment, is standing on one foot. This grounding exercise requires that you focus your energy down and into the ground. If you find that your ankle is wobbling, it could be just a muscular thing, or it could be that you are approaching this exercise a little high centered in your head, and the wobble indicates drama but not effective grounding.

In aikido, a soft martial art, this is referred to as weight underside. In ballet, it amounts to driving a spike by visualizing down into the center of the earth to stabilize your balance. This is represented in the symbol of thriving with a spike down into the earth's core. It signifies grounding, connecting to deeper sources, while centering is a matter of maintaining the integrity of one's core within one's body. The two, grounding and centering, are distinct and separate, although they do directly complement each other.

A leading Japanese batter, Sadaharu Oh 1., hit 868 career home runs and won 15 professional home-run titles in Japan during a 22-year career. As reported in *Psychology Today* May/June (1992, p.47.) he would swing from a one foot stance. He would also become conscious of his "one point," his spirit center located about two finger widths below the navel. He used this as a conscious point for both power and balance while swinging.

Application: Do this at your own risk !
You can practice getting grounded and balanced by putting on your socks or panty hose while you are standing. Do this only if you can maintain your balance or have support immediately available to steady yourself so you don't fall.

You will be required to stand on one foot at a time while putting on athletic socks. This process will get you

grounded early in the morning. You may have to practice and cheat a little at first by leaning against the wall or putting your foot back down on the floor.

The more you wobble, the more you are high centered in your head. You have to bring your consciousness down into your feet and below. You have the same challenge of gravity as every other human being. But you make yourself more conscious of it by concentrating your focus on the one-foot balance. You can learn a lot about your ability to focus, and expand your discipline in the privacy of your own home or office.

Anyone going into a situation in which he perceives a threat, or in which he wants to be better grounded, can use this exercise. Staying focused on the moment diminishes anxiety about the future, as well as reducing guilt, damaging self-talk, and admonishment from the past.

There is no limit to the moments available to you.
The limit may lie in how you experience the moment,
In how much you make yourself
available to the moment.

Moving ahead into the future, moment by moment, is an act of courage buoyed up with the excitement at the revelations of each breath. With each comes a clarity in many levels.

An "up" attitude is important. It helps you to lighten up, to skim and skip over the waves without sinking like a stone under the weight of self-doubt and disparagement.

You draw a bead on the future. Just as walking involves leaning and falling forward, thriving includes recognizing that you are in many respects out of control. You seldom think about it, let alone admit it. You surrender and live with not knowing. Meanwhile, you deal with all the currents and flow of both internal and external forces.

In surfing you look for a wave that will crest and carry you for a distance in its surge. Everyone wants the long ride, the perfect swell. You want to stay in the curl or the crest of the wave. To do so, you need balance, ability, perception, judgment, and release of control.

Yet, in thriving so much of the *ride* depends upon a kind of personal fulfillment, on breathing fully, and on a determination to stay connected within.

Riding the wave of breath in and out, finding the corresponding coordinates of rhythm, streaming, line, angle, and attitude will buoy you up and carry you through, then support you while thriving. It is this thriving place in yourself, this composite experience that you need to remember, so you can recapture that thriving space at any time.

Exercise: Listen and Feel Your Own Heartbeat
Quiet yourself sufficiently once a day to become aware of, and to hear, your own normal heartbeat. After-exercise aerobic heart beats that leap up in your mouth do not count. Nor does heart pounding from high-altitude adjustment. Return to this, your first awareness, once a day, to truly quiet yourself.

"Living in the moment" is a major mandate and key practice. It is supported by the practices that are part of following the next two rules for thriving.

Rule II
Accept Yourself and Take Full Ownership for Your Life

This rule deals with issues of personal initiative and responsibility. As such, it is somewhat more general than the more specific issues of acceptance and nurturance dealt with in Guideline #5.

It's Your Call

If you are serious about thriving, you have to get involved in your own life. Without the commitment or conviction to buy into, and use what you learn, your investment in a transition is an empty gesture. Ultimately, it may also diminish your desire to pursue meaningful growth any further. You alone determine whether you want to use the thrival guidelines and tools presented. You determine if you have time to implement them. Then you determine the degree to which you apply your new learning.

It's like the difference between shopping and buying, between trying and doing, between not making contact and having high traction. You can window-shop for a higher fashion of life without ever trying on the goods. Thriving requires a total immersion, taking full and complete ownership and responsibility for yourself and your life.

Use the following classifications to take a look at your current degree of commitment. If you wish, you can apply this to all your relationships: career, family, community, personal, and spiritual.

Levels of Involvement In Your Own Life

In your life you can work at several levels of involvement on a scale from passive to active.

1. **Passive**: Passivity usually refers to inertness or inactivity. However, you can be an active quarrelsome dolt, stonewalling and rejecting what comes your way, that is, passive-rejecting. And you can pick and choose from what comes your way, but it has to come your way for you to do anything with it or about it, that is, passive-receptive. But passivity does not require agency in your own life and initiative in your present or future.

2. **Interaction**: You can adopt a mild interchange with others and with your surroundings. You exhibit a mild interest but tend to be a bit reticent about getting your hopes up, taking initiative, or showing enthusiasm. Your stance is somewhat passive, waiting to be wooed by circumstances. If you wish, you can remain aloof and untouched. There is little sense of connection, or shared responsibility or interdependence. In a group situation, posing questions to the presenter, leader or manager would constitute interaction. It is up to you to participate.

3. **Participation:** You can engage actively with others, even take initiative and contribute. In a group situation, participation could run the gamut all the way from active, vigorous challenging of other participants and the main presenter of new materials or authority in charge; or it could be as little as your simply raising a hand to vote, sending non-verbal cues to others, such as in an auction. These are all degrees of participation. Degree and type of participation may be invited, allowed, or structured into a process. It is still your choice. You determine how much you want to dip your toe in the water, whether you are merely testing the waters of a transition, or going further. At this point, you begin

to hear from others and find common ground and a basis for interdependence.

4. **Involvement**: You jump in and use whatever you have to contribute and take an active role. Your focus is on proactively moving your life forward by productive exchange with others, as well as utilizing the resources you have and can develop. At this point, you are wading in with your opinion, acting less reticent and guarded, giving it your best shot. Your opinion is closer to your full truth. There is less jockeying for position, more straightforward commentary. The climate is such, or passions run high enough, that you come from your intention and speak from the heart. There is less pre-tense of hierarchy, of top-down relationships; more an exchange of equals, side-by-side relationships. While you may exercise discretion, you take full initiative and ownership for what you do. As a leader or manager, you recognize that you don't/can't know all the answers. You engage in inquiry, to find out the truth you do not know yet, clear and open discussion without resorting to gotcha's. You, almost exuberantly, admit to not knowing, but you will find out or outsource the research. A main point of involvement is that you are definitely in the fray, committed, leaving no question of your desire to execute. So you may be in the water but not getting your hair wet just yet. There is one more stage, a sort of baptism by total immersion.

5. **Immersion:** You are totally present, active, and cognizant of all the factors, variables, relationships, needs, and resources present to make this a viable situation. If this involves business, you go to the initial process source and to all the tributaries to

determine how to help your customer improve his supply line and productivity. If you are a down-stream supplier, you try to anticipate how to expand your contribution, facilitate the conveyance and value added aspects of your part in the process. Rather than sticking to narrow boundaries of appropriateness, you expand your contribution into the subtleties and nuances of the product or service. No holding back. This is your total life on the line. You are flat out there, committed totally, deeply, passionately. Your lines of communication with others are direct, unfettered, unrestrained. You provide direct, accurate, true data. And you expect, exhort, exact, and extract the same from others. There is a felt sense of mutual interdependence and reliance, of shared destiny and natural teamwork, of customer service, co-creation and co-crafting at its best. This broader swath of consideration expands perspective, and graphically depicts the reality of the situation, empirical data – not image, fantasy, speculation, or wishful thinking. Your emphasis is on being effective, resilient, and agile, rather than dramatic, torpid, and atrophied. You give up the pretense of control. You deal with the hand you are dealt.

At the same time immersion is not absorption. You do not give up your own boundaries, limits, balance, and proportion in the service of seamless interaction with the parties with whom you are immersed. If you do, you tend to lose the benefit. When immersion refers to your treatment of yourself, you begin to capture the fullest extent of what taking ownership for your own life truly means.

Ownership is a natural lead-in to the next rule and accompanying practices or applications of that rule – appreciation.

Rule III
Appreciate Yourself and Adopt an Attitude of Gratitude!

Appreciation means finding the value in others, oneself, or situations. In itself, it is a very healthy, enhancing, and maturing practice. For once you begin to look around at how much you have to appreciate, you may be bowled over by the sheer magnitude of gifts within and without that you have immediately available to you.

It has been said, "It's never too late to have a happy childhood." And the fact is that in looking back, you have a choice over what you focus on – no matter how horrendous your childhood experiences. And furthermore, you can continue to learn from your experience and the situations you are in. How you perceive your past is your choice.

In retrospect, from the standpoint of now being an adult, you bring new understanding to the pressures and responsibilities of parenthood. And you bring new tolerance in viewing your parents and siblings as fellow travelers on the journey, each with his own path to find, his own experiences to live out and learn from. In the process, you may drop your demands or regrets that they were not different.

Life is a gift God gives us every day.
And what you do with each day is
your gift back to God.

You now have years of empirical evidence that says they were not different. So, what can you learn from that? And what can you carry forward from that experience to help you in the future?

Write Your Appreciations in Your Journal

Zig Ziglar encourages people to "adopt an attitude of gratitude." His approach is that you should look continually for something to enjoy and do so with gratitude, thankfulness. It means appreciating what is there rather than complaining about what is not there.

It is not better to give than to receive.
It is better to give and to receive.

Use your journal to note what you celebrate and appreciate in your life, what you are grateful for. It is easy to determine payoffs or successes for which you are grateful, especially in situations you were attracted to specifically because of the benefit or payoff. But it takes looking more carefully to determine what you developed or realized of yourself by taking on certain responsibilities. For example, in most cases parents develop more patience and tolerance as a result of raising their own children. Looking at the relationship in retrospect, they can more fully appreciate that fact.

And, you may think you know what you want, but you may be realizing a whole different level of development just within yourself. Building a new house may result more in your becoming assertive, making reasoned compromises in light of time or cost factors, or recognizing that you typically plan out more than can be done and put yourself into a chronic state of exasperation.

There is the surface story. And you can find the good in that, and give thanks for it. And then there is the subtext, the "what's really going on." You may not fully realize the benefits you receive until you can check your rearview mirror. Only then do you see the clearly defined route over which you have traveled, and the residual gains you have made.

Gratitude Exercise
Wherever you are at any given moment, as long as you are not putting yourself in imminent peril, stop and take stock. Find something or someone to appreciate right where you are. Or, review your day briefly for the many things you missed on your way through it. There is always something to be grateful for. In fact, this appreciation meditation, this assessment of what you can be grateful for right this minute, can fully amplify and expand your mood for the moment.

For example, smog is not particularly appealing to me, but it may provide a fragrance that pointedly reminds me of a wonderful summers living in Pasadena, California, and Mexico City. And those memories bring a smile to my lips immediately.

So in addition to maintaining a positive, empowering attitude, you are encouraged to practice gratitude at all times. It amplifies your life and keeps you looking on the positive side.

The Guidelines That Follow
The seven guidelines that follow go beyond the restrained expectations and the gratuitous ignorance that prevail regarding the experience of thriving. These guidelines involve skills, information, and attitudes that make thriving much more possible and probable on a daily basis. Once you own your own determination and willingness to get into the thriving state, you can build on your first or entry level experience: happenstance, choice, or serendipity.

Where and How Have You Thrived?

You strive for these times. You wish you could have more of them. However, as long as you think that what happens when you are thriving is sheer happenstance, you do not focus on developing those capacities with which you could thrive more and more consistently.

When your circumstances change, just as when an arctic cold front blows all the blossoms off an apple tree early in spring, your feeling of "finally having it all together" may get shredded and blown. Epiphanies pass. One minute there was a surge of energy bursting forth in a fluorescence, and then, suddenly, there is a graceless decline, a gray deflation.

The apple tree will blossom again next year. Nature has its cycles that evoke the blossoms in springtime – same time next year. But you don't know when or how you can have your own personal epiphanies flowing forth again for this feeling and the thriving lifestyle. How do you get your vital sap flowing and create the conditions to give you repeated or continuing access to this thriving state?

You and you alone determine if you will allow yourself to get a lift in any given moment, to be living in that moment. Thriving can occur in any moment. A cool flame moves into the sternum and solar plexus. Suddenly, you are present in the moment and solidly real! You view what goes on around you from a personage grounded in the moment. If you used to be unstable, insubstantial, fragmented, and distracted; suddenly there is this gift of focus. You gain a feeling of substance. You feel complete, fulfilled, unshakably solid, and grounded. You have come home.

Chapter 12

Guideline #1: Establish a Thriving Attitude: Innertude®

There's nothing enlightened about
Shrinking so that other people
Won't feel insecure around you.
We were born to make manifest
The glory of God that is within us.

Marianne Williamson
A Return to Love

How Does Attitude Relate to Thriving?
Attitude is "a manner of acting, feeling, or thinking that demonstrates the individual's disposition, opinion, etc. *As a man thinketh, so he is.* Attitude is important in thriving because it comprises your approach, the way you organize and predispose yourself to meet life.

As in most cases, observing how someone acts, what he does, is the only way you have to assess his attitude, for attitude is held within. All that you can detect is an expression of it. And then you don't necessarily know if what you observe is a depiction of the attitude of that person.

No one can really know your attitude except through what you give off, do, or say. People can infer. But only you can know for sure. And you could be a little blurry on your own motives and intentions as well. You could carry on in a manner decidedly at odds with your true attitude and not be seen for who you are or how you truly are underneath. You could be in denial of what your true attitude is and solidly act in ways that match your self-image but not your inner self. So, you would be perceived as having "X" attitude.

Adopting an Attitude of Innertude®

If you have ever felt let down and deflated at falling short of your goals, mildly shriveled at the prospect of confronting a colleague, or hammered on by a particularly insistent individual, then this chapter has something to offer you even without moving into the thrival state.

This chapter introduces a major attitude shift that dovetails with the physical self-support practices that will be spelled out in the next chapter. You will learn to support yourself with a positive attitude and approach called Innertude®.

Those Less Fortunate

You know people who go through life cowering before others, ingratiating themselves, pleading for a place at the table. Not only does playing this undeserving, victim role deprive them of dignity, but dealing with them can be irritating as well. They live so crumpled up that you may feel a need to prop them up, lift them out of their own collapsed posture and psyche. They act pathetic, incapable of coping. They act as if they not only need a lift, but are also entitled to it. Of course all this entitlement comes at the expense of you and others, when they could be doing for themselves.

Even those who come from dented, deprived, diminished, deficient, and dysfunctional backgrounds can caulk their own leaks, hammer out the dents, and restore themselves to full height and presence. They can determine to re-establish their self-respect, dignity, energy, and presence through an attitude and practice called Innertude®.

What Is Innertude®?

Innertude® is a way of talking about an inner exercise that is both physical and mental. It is a generative practice designed to inspirit you and boost you in low times. You also gain inner support for all times that offsets stresses, pressures, and pronounced traumas. Innertude® requires strong resolve and internal monitoring along with discipline and focus.

Innertude® requires a specific increase in will power, personal awareness, and presence to support yourself from within. You have to be continually ready to rise to the occasion and fill out your entire stature. Innertude® carries a dignity and nobility all of its own. More than just posture, it is this generative attitude of pulling yourself up, inflating, and filling out your posture to your full, appropriate size.

Innertude® consists of:

1. the presence and maintenance of a highly positive mental attitude, together with
2. the commensurate physical practices required to maintain your full natural posture, height, and expansiveness. This takes conscious intention, support and containment of energy at a level sufficient to offset and to counter those external pressures that compress, diminish, deflate, and dispirit you. These practices include breath and posture, along with the mental aspect of the approach. You can control each one.

With Innertude® you gain an immediately applicable resilient approach toward life that incites you to move forward, confront challenges, and keep yourself open and flowing. ***You begin to establish and maintain an internal counter-pressure and buttressing that staves off collapses inside yourself.*** You maintain high mental health and high positive energy.

The Scientific Principle at Work Here: STP
Remember your seventh-grade physical sciences class? Your teacher placed an open one-gallon gas can over a Bunsen burner. When the air inside the can was heated up, she turned off the gas and capped the container. She went on lecturing, and several minutes later her talk was interrupted by the crunching sound of the gas can caving in to atmospheric pressure. This experiment demonstrates the effects of changes in standard temperature and pressure (STP) - the scientific fact that gases expand when heated, then contract when cooled.

That familiar experiment provides one basis for understanding Innertude® and what happens inside your body. When you are anticipating, thinking about, or being confronted with an unpleasant, traumatic, or new and challenging task, you may have the tendency to collapse even a small part of your self, like a ding on a fender or car door.

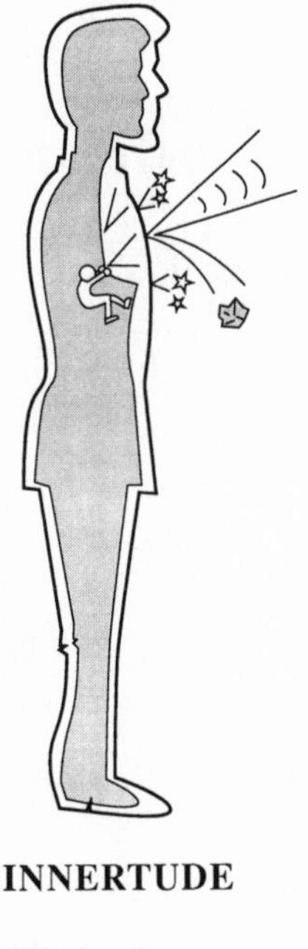

INNERTUDE

Thrival.com

Many actually report that they feel a little collapse in their chest, as illustrated in the Innertude® figure above. This literally translates into mentally and physically giving in to

- ***actual*** *external pressures*
- *the* ***anticipation*** *of external pressures, or*
- *the* ***perception*** *of external pressures.*

The Metaphor Behind Innertude®: The Inner Tube

This chapter presents several metaphors and concepts to convey the basic properties, qualities, and characteristics of Innertude®. The reasoning for these vivid approximations is to implant the details of the metaphor. Once it is impressed upon you, you can recall the metaphor more easily and draw from it the essentials you require to become self-supporting, elastic, and resilient. The following items grow out of the idea of Innertude® as an attitude.

Before 1962, when tubeless tires found wide use, an inner tube, was original standard equipment on all cars. Tubes are still in use in some driving lawn mower tires, bicycles, and motorcycle tires. An inner tube is made of rubber or a compound of similar elasticity. It has the ability to contain an air pressure that exceeds atmospheric pressure, to support much higher weight without collapse, and sufficient pressure to maintain its circular integrity. An inner tube that leaks or is low in pressure fails in each one of these functions.

The inner tube provides a pressure seal that keeps the tires leak proof and hard, helps the tire maintain efficient contact and traction with the road surface, buffers the load from the shock of impact with unevenness in the road, and protects the rim from imminent damage from major potholes.

See what parts of this analogy apply to you. Do you need more elasticity to generate a buildup of internal pressure, to improve your containment, or to widen boundaries in your approach to life on a day-to-day basis? Will that help you confront some of the sharper external objects you may run into interpersonally, physically, and emotionally? What about the sharp objects you run into within yourself?

The Observable Contrast: Winner v. Loser
Here is one easily observable example of Innertude®: Toward the end of any highly contested national or regional athletic rivalry, the television cameras scan the benches of each team. You can tell immediately which team is winning; which losing. Victor and vanquished are each distinguishable by their postures, facial expressions, and the look in their eyes.

Victory Stance
The winners are pumped. They stand erect, self-assured, big as life or bigger. They are smiling, jovial, joking with each other. They celebrate and congratulate each other with high five's, waving towels, and pouring Gatorade® over their coach. They are celebrating life, their team, and their performance. People are drawn to and identify with a winner's posture and energy: open, celebratory, beaming, positive.

The losers have baleful expressions on their faces and tears in their downcast, unbelieving eyes. They are caved in and low in spirits. If anything, they displace less volume than their bodies typically occupy. They have literally and "figuratively" shrunk. Their attitude is displayed directly in the posture they have assumed. They may sit with their heads hung and covered with towels. They act as if they would like to disappear, go away, or at least be alone in their embarrassment.

Reversal of Fortune from Totally Down to Euphoric
Sudden changes in the game's fortune can bring a major shift in feeling state, from dissatisfaction to bliss, from totally

down to totally euphoric. If there is a last-minute fumble recovery or the momentum of the game shifts to offer one final chance or last-gasp victory, the *down* team may already be so far gone, so off pace, that they have difficulty snapping out of it to create a turnaround.

Their brain chemistry from entertaining the high negative energy is debilitating and disabling. They forfeit the internal vitality required to sustain strength, stamina, and peak performance. When you coach yourself, you should not allow yourself to get down, to suffer the consequences of your own depressed mind chemicals. You have to be your own "personal motivator," one who does not get down, but who is continually keeping you in the game.

Realities of the Inner Game of Thriving

You carry around the rules to the game you are playing, the drama you are producing daily. And you measure yourself by your own expectations, your comparisons, your illusions of how things "should be." You then choose how you respond as a result of meeting your own standard, and how you stand in comparison with others.

You actually can manage every part of your inner game. If you require a specific achievement, goal attainment, accomplishment, or win in order to feel good about yourself, it is you yourself who put prerequisites on the joy you will allow yourself to experience in life.

You have to change your internal requirements so that you can win in every moment. At the very least you can allow yourself high positive energy with little or no negative tension.

Waiting until you have your own personally defined "winning season" in order to thrive is your personally inflicted condition of starvation, especially when you can have sheer joy right now at just being alive.

Proactively Turning Around What Life Hands You
Former UCLA basketball coach, John Wooden once observed that, "Things turn out best for those who make the best of the way things turn out." If you are determined to be a victim in life, you have picked up the wrong book. For, you cannot be a victim and thrive at the same time.

You now have the prospect not only of countering the pressures exerted on you by nature, others, and the environment, but of generating from within yourself, transforming your response to whatever you are handed by life.

Maintain Inner Pressure to Counter Pressures on You
Visualize a resilient inner tube within yourself – basically it is like a rubber bladder lining your entire profile just under the skin, from your toes to the top of your head. This inner tube requires an internal air pressure that will counter both constant and high-impact pressures from the environment. You have to maintain adequate inflation.

Maintaining adequate inflation means neither going flat nor reducing your internal pressure so much that you create a lot of resistance just to moving forward. Adequate inflation helps you to retain your natural shape, your basic proportions. It keeps you resilient, helps you to counter deflating rebuffs or put-downs.

Take Your Place and Occupy Your Own Space
Come up with personal examples of the effect of pressures that impact you and pressures that you put on yourself – pressures of which no one else is aware. For example, your expectation in approaching a confrontation weighs you

down. Or a personally debilitating belief, that you do not deserve a relationship, opportunity, or situation, can undermine your internal support system.

When you undergo a personal "cabin depressurization," collapse, cave-in, a loss of internal support in your daily life and dealings, in order to be able to thrive and to be available to others, you need to pay attention and take basic responsibility for confronting these pressures head on.

Your body is built to occupy a natural space. You are meant to displace a certain volume in measurable cubic feet. When you are constricted, deflated, having poor posture, you are not in position to occupy your own natural body space. Yet you alone can open yourself up and free the space up. Start within yourself.

You need to liberate yourself from whatever fears collapse you in the face of adversity from the environment, from others, or from yourself. Refuse to cave in. Insist on going forward at full space. To live shrunk, collapsed, constricted in less space is to deny yourself your own vitality and energy. To live in less space than you are allotted can also seriously impair your physical and mental functioning.

It's not just in some of us, it's in everyone.
And as we let our own light shine,
We unconsciously give other people
Permission to do the same.
As we are liberated from our own fears,
Our presence automatically liberates others.
Marianne Williamson

Initiating the Practice of Managing Your Innertude®
The first step in engaging the practices of Innertude® is to self-assess. Become aware of how you react internally to various pressures, thoughts, exchanges, individuals, encounters, and situations. One typical, and self-defeating, response to overwhelming circumstances is to hold your breath. Become aware of your personal sweeping or general practices first, then tune into specific cave-in or collapse circumstances or practices. Where and how do they occur in your body? How can you monitor them, then counter them when they occur?

Mentally recall or extend yourself into a problematic family, social, or business confrontation in which you have generally not fared well. See if you can determine specifically where in your body you collapse yourself, give in, reduce support. How did you organize your own collapse? How do you predispose yourself to fail? Or to feel failure?

Inner Exercise Promotes Aliveness
An older sibling makes a comment that freezes you in your tracks like a bunny in the headlights. You shrivel up inside. The "bladder" in a certain portion of your body deflates and you feel a collapse. You are "done in," depressed. So, fill yourself back up. Take a deep breath. Then another.

Anticipate and Rehearse Future Encounters
Project yourself forward in time and anticipate similar future encounters and undertakings. Tune into whichever part of your body seizes up, constricts, or caves in. How do you now reorganize yourself to create or meet that situation?

When you have time, you can also project yourself backward to heal your memories and even dissolve mild trauma. Breathe into that memory, dissolve the constriction with assurance of how you can now handle the situation well, and round out that part of your body.

Turn It Up a Notch

If you have difficulty getting a clear sense of how you seize up, then exaggerate the tension slightly in order to articulate it better to yourself. Blow it up large. Then step it down little by little, notch by notch.

You will start to discover how profoundly and totally you can take responsibility for your inner state for most of the situations you will encounter, whether meeting the world or yourself. You are capable of giving up your demand for payoffs for "bad" feelings and being a victim. You are the one who maintains them in the first place. You can let them go.

Approach for the Future

Your way of dealing with disappointment in the future may take on an entirely different approach. **You can counter your own collapse, patch your own leak. Once you pay attention to what takes the *wind out of your sails*, you can anticipate the emotional flat water and fill your own sails.**

Breathe fully and deeply. In the short term, keep your body exercised, nurtured, fulfilled, decompressed. In the longer term, continue to weed out and counter the effects of those internal and external circumstances that diminish your physical presence and spirit. You may be disappointing yourself by entertaining overblown expectations to begin with. Many people, for example, set realistic goals, then make them impossible to reach by setting too short a deadline.

You alone are responsible for generating your energy, maintaining it within a certain range, and releasing it in the service of yourself and others. As part of that *generativity*, you maintain your own physical space. Essentially, you have a right to that space and a fundamental responsibility to occupy it. This is a way of establishing your self-respect in the world.

No one can occupy that space for you. It is up to you. Do not confuse selfishness with taking basic ownership and responsibility for your own life. You have to assert your right to the space within you. And you have to claim it against any perceived external pressures or intrusions. That is your responsibility.

Sing

Singing is a highly generative activity. This may be one of the best single practices to help you to be self-supporting and to gain that sense of vitality that is the hallmark of thriving.

The basic mechanics and practice of singing have all the right components to catapult you into thriving. Getting a good instructor is most helpful. However, just singing in the shower is worthwhile for the benefits it brings. Singing includes standing straight, diaphragmatic breathing, internal muscular support for your singing, containment of breath and energy, vibrating your entire being, and inspiring yourself. There are probably brain chemistry changes as a result as well. In any case, there is so much to enjoy.

Do not confuse Selfishness with taking Basic Ownership and Responsibility for your own life.

Puncture-Proofing Yourself

When you depressurize your own internal cabin, you diminish your mood and stature in different ways. You give way by invoking or using certain biases, values, assumptions, emotions, predispositions, and attitudes you carry around those components of your belief system that set you up to being deflated.

You can "go flat" by your own interior devices in a totally benign environment by creating the puncture from the inside out. The needles that puncture your inner containment come from within. They may be a result of well-practiced fear, shame, self-doubt, or self-distrust. It is important to know the ways you puncture yourself and give up your own spirit and vitality. For those ways demonstrate a basic disbelief or self-distrust. Begin now to examine and change your basic belief in your worthiness.

If you carry yourself flat, thin, unprotected, slightly unconscious or in denial, you may get bashed, or you may experience extreme wear and tear. You need to maintain adequate defenses against the severe shock of potholes, speed bumps, and obstacles. The thin ribbon of a bicycle racing tire cannot protect the rim when it hits a curb. You also need thicker cushioning in order to meet the challenges of everyday living. You need to maintain adequate self-protection. You need continuing vigilance to see the big potholes coming, to buffer or avoid them.

Countering the Constant Pressures

It helps to know what wears on you constantly and continually, for it is so easy to lose sight of those chronic stressors. The pressures you are up against personally and professionally are not just social. They are measurable, quantifiable.

Innertude® is <u>not</u> a matter of blowing yourself up like the Michelin tire logo. That would be over-inflating, or puffery. That would exceed your own unique, appropriate human dimension.

Good Posture Counters Gravity

Gravity is one external invisible force that continually acts on you. And gravity most impacts your posture and the efficiency with which you carry yourself. Keep your spine straight. Stand erect, and practice good posture. Occupy the space you grew up and matured to occupy. That is one major way to reduce the effects of gravity on your posture and bone structure.

Atmospheric Pressure

Atmospheric pressure is another of the external, invisible factors that impinges on you. Few of us are conscious of the impact of atmospheric pressure. You become more aware when your plane descends from 35,000 feet to land, with the change of weather fronts, or taking a fast elevator to the 25th floor of a building. You experience the *atmospheres* of pressure while scuba diving in water 15 feet and deeper. One way you can begin to counter the effects of atmospheric pressure is to breathe fully and deeply.

Occupy the space God gave you
in this body at this time.

You want to be sufficiently present and at home with yourself so that you can determine to keep yourself filled. Direct and contain your own energy within from the continuing wellspring of life and passion that runs through you.

Have You Ever Had the Wind Knocked Out of You?

To elaborate on the quick access exercises to thriving beginning the first pages of the book, everyone will have had this physical experience of getting hit in the solar plexus sometime early in life. If you did not run into some-thing, then someone inadvertently hit you, and you had the wind knocked out of you.

You know that a quick jab in the solar plexus can have you doubled over and gasping for breath. It can feel like a near-death experience. As you buckle at the waist, you are stunned. You wonder silently if you can pull in another breath. Will your body work? Can you resume normal breathing? Even a verbal exchange can have the effect of deflating you, both literally and figuratively.

What About a "Near Life" Experience ?

Is there some way to deal with life's blows, potholes, and pressures without always being buckled over and done in by them? What about having the ***wind knocked into you***, a near life experience? How would you make that happen?

If you wanted to anticipate a blow to your *breadbasket* (diaphragm), recover from the blow, or deal with the chronic and occasional cave-ins that occur in your life; you can adopt an attitude that will provide a proactive, even preventive, approach to collapsing. Whatever hurts, scares, tightens, constricts, or diminishes you or the flow of energy and life force within you, you can counter with Innertude®. Develop it sufficiently and you could literally "knock the wind" into yourself.

You also need to know what resistance or perils lie in the way of establishing your Innertude®. What follows are the major obstacles that can overcome some of your best efforts.

Three Ways Innertude® Can Be Overthrown

Adopting Innertude® as your approach to life is not totally foolproof. Be warned that there are conditions and circumstances erase the benefits you would normally derive. The three items below are ones you can control:

1. **Outside-In Pressure** can overwhelm inside-out air pressure. You cannot necessarily foresee,

stop, or avoid this. You can make a quicker recovery through Innertude®.

2. **Puncture:** An internal puncture results in loss of air containment.
3. **De-containment:** Inside-out flagging of spirits, low stamina, and inattention lead to loss of internal air pressure.

The second defeating item, internal puncture, will take major work. It involves disarming your internal terrorist, who, through ineptness or intention, is out to pop your balloon. This is a major aspect of your transition to thrival from a survival mindset and mentality. It will be dealt with later.

A Bias toward Bouncing Back

Innertude® can provide the impetus for you to take on challenges that intimidate you, confront difficult situations, and bounce back from adversity. In a book titled *The Survivor Personality,* Dr. Al Siebert has a great deal to say about the ability of survivors to inculcate qualities, properties, and characteristics that help them to bounce back in the face of adversity. They have the ability to confront and deal effectively with challenges and confrontations. And at the core of the dissertation on what makes up the survivor personality is the single word that comprises most of the dimensions and characteristics of surviving: Resilience!

Innertude® tolerates a variety of assumptions, attitudes, and beliefs, but not negative energy or tension. You may still find yourself having negative emotions, but each pulverizes your internal support. If you have them, quickly release them, rather than using them for sympathy or cultivating and holding onto them for further payoff. Counter your negativity with a positive stance and spirit, i.e., with resilience.

Resilience

Resilience is one of the important qualities and outcomes of the practice of Innertude®, as well as in a thriving daily life. First a definition of resilience:

- *Bounding or springing back into shape or position after being stretched, bent, or compressed*
- *Quickly recovering strength, spirits, good humor, buoyancy*
- *Ability to recover from or adjust to misfortune or change*

Hardiness Criteria

Resilience fits with the research on hardiness-related personality characteristics, those that make you more bullet-proof in the face of the strain of change. To acquire the hardiness criteria and characteristics, you need to include in your repertoire the practices of being:

On Purpose: Purposive and committed. You create a sense of involvement & find meaning in what you do.

Efficacious: Effective in finding something that you can control about your job or environment, thereby over-coming helplessness and approaching mastery.

Choice Exercising: Challenged and opportunity- seeking in the face of change. Define problems as a learning opportunity. Be approach-oriented rather than avoid-ing situations. Be proactive.

Communal: Commonly bound. Feel respected, find value in friendships, and have a common ground or purpose with people around you, including social support.

Adopting a Puncture-Proof Innertude®

Adopting a puncture proof, non-deflatable Innertude® confronts the third item, de-containment. **This involves making the determination that you will breathe deeply and fill yourself up rather than allowing yourself to shrink or to operate under low pressure.** The choice is yours. It requires persistent focus, monitoring, and reminding yourself. This means that you maintain sufficient interior pressure to counter your felt and constant pressures, as well as to retain an ability to bounce back when impacted by the unknown and unexpected.

You establish and maintain the conditions within to support your own sustained high positive energy without tension. Meanwhile, you are self-injecting or catching your breath.

Getting the Benefits from Innertude®

Using Pain for Payoff

Who has not been gouged, wounded, traumatized in the course of living? Yet it is what we do with those circumstances and our attitude about them that determine the quality of our life. There are entrenched habits that establish how we deal with such things as pain in our lives. And unless we examine the role of pain and payoff in our lives, we cannot easily eradicate it or replace it.

When there is a deferred payoff to holding on to the pain, wound, or trauma, then any blow to you or any dent in your rim gives you a reason to stop in your tracks. And that only compounds the trauma. It can stop you on the spot. It is not unusual for someone to take off his most dented rim and blown tire when his life cycle becomes immobilized, then park himself on the side of the road. The difficulty becomes an excuse: "If it were not for "X," then I would be a fully functioning human being."

The difficulty becomes the "reason why not." Then it becomes a *trophy wound* that gets put up on the family mantle and venerated, rather than worked through as a matter of facing fear, dispensing with trauma, and rounding oneself out to move on with one's life.

I have counseled clients for chronic pain sustained as the result of a workplace injury. When they had a lawsuit for recovery in process under worker's compensation, typically the client would not experience relief from the pain or full recovery from the injury until the settlement was reached in the courts. Of course, not everyone recovered just because of the settlement. Some had sustained chronic pain and disabling injuries. But those who did recover did so only after they had extracted a payoff or had come to peace with the fact that they had lost the case.

Please know that this is not an indictment of those with legitimate challenges. It would take much more space to address those who have been injured on the job, and for lack of adequate resources and attention to their wounds, have been disabled for life.

Have you known anyone who was wronged by someone else years ago, and is still telling the story principally to gain sympathy or attention? When a wound earns such a payoff, it is pretty likely that healing will not occur until the payoff is exhausted.

Wound Worshiping

Holding onto the pain from these encounters amounts to wound worshiping. However, it is difficult for those who have been traumatized. They do need to talk through the pain and perpetrating circumstances to expel them from their system. Meanwhile, there are those who get such a payoff from telling their story that it long ago lost any value for de-traumatizing them from the initial shock to their system. The story is now an end in itself, getting them attention, sympathy, or another payoff they value.

Getting Payoff for Pain

You know people who have held onto the pain of their divorce, their latest illness, or a sliver in the finger, to get attention and milk it for all that it's worth. That is their payoff. This activity is often fostered in infancy by well-meaning parents who shower you with attention when you experience the normal hurts of growing pains and experiences. They lead you to believe that they, and they alone, will make it "all better." Hence, your solution lies outside yourself, in your circumstances and relationships. You have to give up the immediate payoff in order to release the pain.

You Can Retrain Yourself to Release the Pain

At age 8, I was cutting weeds with a butcher knife when one swipe continued on down and severed a small artery in my knee. I hadn't really felt a thing, but once I noticed the blood-soaked cuff of my trousers, I was able to not only

- *run the half block home, but then*
- *open the back door,*
- *find no one there, and then*
- *run to the front of the house where I knew someone could hear me.*
- *Only then did I begin to howl and cry.*

In retrospect, I was probably more scared at the sight of my blood than in pain.

I have retrained myself from my own lifelong practice of holding onto pain for payoff. And it is easy to let go now that I know I can release pain and get over it more quickly.

Now, when I stub my toe in the dark in an unfamiliar hotel room or step barefoot on one of my dog's partly chewed bones or a Lego under construction, I immediately say, "let it go, let it go." And it is amazing how quickly pain can be dispersed with this clear intention. It is also sobering to note how long pain, both emotional and physical, can linger when I think a payoff is due.

Blow the Dents Out

As an illustration to audiences of what has to be done to reverse the effects of pressures that impinge on you, I crush a soda can, and then blow it up. This demonstrates that you can "blow the dents out of" yourself as well.

Innertude® encourages you to blow the dents out, countering the crushing pressures before their effects get set in your metal. Seldom can you blow out all the dents completely, unless the can is really flimsy and you have terrific diaphragmatic pressure to exert. But you can make a huge difference in the major dents. Perhaps only an expert metal worker could get the can back to like-new status. And perhaps even years of therapy and personal work would not smooth out the dents and erase your personal traumas. But you can begin.

It may take expert and extended healing to get us to like-new status. Expecting more may be naïve and unrealistic. What we do by exercising Innertude® is to take responsibility for attaining a condition of physical resilience that *reduces the grip* of trauma, pain, self-pity, and the impact of change elements.

Forgiveness Helps You to Bounce Back

Forgiveness is part of the realm of resilience and Innertude®. Forgiveness will be discussed at length in Guideline #3, as part of becoming aware of your awareness and living in the present. If you hold onto the emotional wallops delivered in life so that you can gain sympathy for your pain and traumas, you will not bounce back. You tend to *bronze the dents*, and they become part of your trophy wound. You continue a dependency on others to patch your Innertude® and re-inflate yourself.

As you self-righteously attempt to blame and extract a price from others for the wrongs done to you, you hold anger and debt in the demand. You re-experience the pain and then wait for others to acknowledge and validate your pain, rather than taking command and relieving yourself of the pain immediately.

Forgiving is letting go of the stress and the pain, releasing it as quickly as possible in order to allow yourself to heal. If you *demand* an apology or sympathy, or still require someone else to *kiss it and make it better*, you leave yourself at the mercy of your own expectation or the response of others.

Waiting for a payoff for holding onto pain is like taking the valve stem out of your Innertude®. You lose control and containment. So give up your requirement of a payoff for your pain. Speed your recovery and maintain your resilience. Reestablish a counter-pressure in your Innertude®. Practice and learn to be both self-contained and self-satisfying.

Responsibility to Others

People don't intentionally drive around for long with their tires going flat. And, curiously enough, no one lets you drive around that way unnoticed. With just one tire low, someone will honk and point to your tire, indicating that it is low. Their concern is for your safety and the safety of everyone else on the road.

The motor oil commercial showed a race driver pulling in for a pit stop. His crew was questioning why he had motioned to his competitor that his tire was low. Why not let him go and find out on his own? He was, after all, the competition. The driver looked them in the eye and said, "Out there, if it goes bad for one of us, it can go bad for all of us."

That ad recognized our interdependence and need for collaboration, over competition and adversarial relations. So, why would you allow yourself, let alone others, to navigate life's highways deflated emotionally? Doing so ultimately wears you down, puts you at peril, even weakens you as well. Wouldn't it be useful to be reminded that our mood was going flat?

What if you accorded the same importance to the spirit and emotional well-being of others as you accord to their car tire pressure? That would involve giving them feedback about what they are emanating, what they are giving off, the effluents they are putting into the environment. They impact us as immediate witnesses and recipients of their moods.

Do you value the spirit of your fellow human beings? Do you see a value in expressing some level of concern about their well-being, as you would for their safety on the road? Do you see a value in supporting and inspiring others to boost them beyond their dispirited state? Then, even if you are reluctant to give feedback, you can be a role model of the liberated individual, emanating positive energy.

Half the poor world is starving to death, so live!

Auntie Mame

Summary

What is required to thrive over the long haul is your willingness to unburden, release, and lift your spirit. The approach, activity, and attitude for doing this are all rolled into the practice of Innertude®.

Innertude® asserts a unique approach to maintaining resilience through a commitment to an attitude of high positive energy in dealing with others, with life circumstances, and with oneself. In order to implement Innertude®, you have to move beyond the victim stance. That involves moving beyond the pain you hold to earn an emotional payoff and the cultivation of trophy wounds into a physical and mental posture that maintains you at full stature and has you primed to deal with whatever comes your way.

You have to learn to contain your own internal pressure, avoid puncture and leakage, and move forward determinedly and with focus. That may require assessing current assumptions, attitudes, beliefs, expectations, and practices that can deflate or shrink you. In this mental and physical state, you are predisposed to confront, respond, and master challenges that come your way.

The secret to success is constancy to purpose.

Benjamin Disraeli

Chapter 13

Guideline #2: Develop a Physical Foundation for Thriving

Most of the guidelines to thriving deal with perspectives, different ways of looking at things, mental shifts, reframing, rethinking, internal work, presentation, acceptance, and release. This second guideline builds the physical practices, the basic foundation. It also underscores and supports the practices required to sustain the high positive energy and thrival attitude, Innertude®. It all works together as part of building your Thrival System®.

Look at those specific physical elements and practices that you can affect, improve, pay attention to, and impact. They include:

breathing, posture,
grounding ,balance,
focus, centering,
traction, and voltage.

Caveat: ***Please exercise care and discretion in undertaking any of the following exercises. You assume full responsibility for any and all actions in which you choose to engage while in pursuit of your thrival state.***

Breathing

The Importance of Breath

If you are to move beyond a survival mode of living, you begin by improving your breathing so that you increase spirit and presence. And this is all part and parcel of moving toward a more highly positive mode of living.

Your first major autonomous act at birth is to breathe on your own. With that breath, you become a separate and viable organism. You inhale, metabolize, and exhale air on your own. How you continue to breathe impacts the richness of your life, experience, and your ability to thrive.

When you can't breathe, nothing else matters.•
American Lung Association

Breath is our physical basis of life. It is so elemental and essential, that without some attention to an increase in volume, any change of attitude could be undermined. All you have to do is to hold your breath for over 35 seconds in order to get a sense of just how important and immediate is your need for oxygen. You start to experience discomfort and a feeling of desperation for your next breath after only this short period of oxygen deprivation.

Breath Is Life

When your oxygen intake is down, there is not enough to supply your system requirements should you experience a surge of adrenaline in your bloodstream. You will feel like you cannot withstand these sudden changes. Surprises, interruptions, loud noises, energy-draining interactions with others can throw you off completely. You will find yourself clutched, grimacing, locked up, and gasping for breath. Deep breathing can help you maintain your mental and emotional equanimity in the face of major environmental stressors. It reduces the sense of being overwhelmed and the resulting strain.

You may have noticed on occasion when you are very uptight or anxious about a situation, that you get striations or streaks of yellow light before your eyes. That streaking means that you are near fainting for lack of oxygen.

Shallow Breath Reinforces the Survival Mentality
Dealing with fluctuations in emotional climate, change in physical activity, or variations in stimuli requires increased oxygen intake in order to deal with your internal physiological responses. A loud noise or unexpected confrontation while deprived of oxygen can startle you, find you floundering, needing to shift to a lower gear just to respond. Your system gets a wake-up call, and you have to pull in extra oxygen to meet your immediate physiological needs.

With a low oxygen supply in your bloodstream, you feel and are more vulnerable, less responsive. You are less conscious, less capable of coping by discerning and responding to what life throws you.

Self-Fulfilling Prophecy
Many people live right on the verge of oxygen deprivation, sheer and imminent demise, because of shallow breathing practices. Leaving yourself in shallow breath and on the edge of breathlessness engenders a sense of desperation, of fighting just to endure. You reinforce a survival attitude toward life fraught with fears and struggle by breathing shallowly, not robustly. Yet, last time I checked, air was still a free, unlimited resource

Startle Prevention
Specific benefits come with breathing deeply. When startled, you may find yourself with a racing heart and gasping for

breath. The instant excitement underscores your level of oxygen deprivation and perhaps your level of tension.

You need more breath to handle more life.

You can increase your ability to handle high stimulation such as loud noises, emotions, and heavy pressure by maintaining high oxygen intake with low tension, a positive attitude and high positive energy.

Breathing: 23,000+ Opportunities to Thrive Daily!
You are seldom any farther from thriving than your next breath. The difficulty in connecting comes from your inability to take the breath deeply within to find the deep fire in yourself and then to rekindle it.

On a physical level, the lower third of the lungs has the greatest oxygen-absorbing capacity. When you breathe only high up in the top third of your lungs, you metabolize at most .1 liter of air. The lower two-thirds of your lungs metabolizes a full liter. That is a difference of .9 liter per breath. So, only when you breathe deeply do you position your breath to benefit you optimally.

Since you breathe somewhere between 16,500 and 23,500 times per day, the depth of your breath determines how much oxygen you actually inhale during the course of a day. Simply multiply your total number of breaths times .1 liter or 1 liter. That .9 liter difference is a major difference in self-support, self-nourishment and well-being.

For example, 18,000 times .9 is 16,200 liters of air, a major difference for your vitality and clarity of thinking. Remember that air is still only about 10 percent oxygen, the majority of it being nitrogen. So, shallow breathing really shortchanges you.

The replenishing or restorative process takes place within, through deep, abundant, and generative breath. Conscious, focused, often fierce determination is required during highly challenging or distracting moments as well as in moments of low morale to keep the inner connection to yourself.

Nutrients for Your Brain

The brain requires 25-30 percent of your oxygen intake just to function normally. Lacking oxygen intake for four minutes or more, you can suffer irreversible brain damage. And breathing deeply can do more than ward off brain damage, it can also increase brain functioning, mental acuity, and clarity on a moment-to-moment basis.

While a few yogis have disciplined themselves to hold their breath for protracted periods of time, they are indeed the exception. They also learn to reduce their body's need for oxygen. Most of us do not have that developed ability or discipline. If you don't breathe, you don't survive.

Breathing is your most basic need. Undertake conscious improvement in breathing until you establish a more enhancing level of intake and energy. That means getting beyond acquired habits of shallow and controlled breathing. To make breathing more conscious, engage in breathing exercises. Several that follow in this chapter can provide basic inner relaxation and restore a vitality to your system that soon will become normal and natural to you.

Breathe to Thrive, Not Merely to Survive

The Importance of Quality Breathing

Thrival requires a quality of breathing that brings awareness, vitality, and relaxation. It also fosters your being centered grounded, and balanced. You want to go beyond the robotic and any sort of huffing and puffing into a calming and rhythmic, supportive and fulfilling replenishment of oxygen, together with the release of tension.

Live Your Life with Enthusiasm

How you choose to deal with your life experience, how much of it you choose to access is your decision. You can anticipate life, ruminate over your life experiences already past, or seize the moment and be vitally involved and alive right now. Live your life with enthusiasm!

Enthusiasm means,

"supernatural inspiration or possession;
a blazing forth of the spirit within."

Taken from the Greek, enthusiasm literally means breathing in the spirit, or inspiriting yourself. Think of the people whom you know that you consider to be enthusiastic. You are certainly thinking more of robust, energetic, erect postures than you are of sunken chests, drooping shoulders, and deflated postures.

Enthusiasm implies an increase or blazing forth of the spirit within. You are in charge. You can dull and restrict your experience of yourself as much as you wish. You can continue with limited contact.

If You Learn Nothing Else, Learn Your ABC's

Always
Breathe
Consciously,
Deeply,
Enthusiastically, and
Fiercely

This simple reminder alone can make a major difference in your life. It is important information. Your breathing consciously is required until you establish your basic habit of breathing deeply and become ***aware of your awareness.***

Encountering Resistance to Breathing Deeply

You may think that breathing is basic, obvious, and boring. Usually it is so obvious it is overlooked completely. However, deep breathing lays down the foundation for everything that is to follow. It serves marvelously to assist you to connect with your inner self, facing long ignored fears, shame, shadow, and denial and vitalizing your daily life and functions.

You will encounter points of internal resistance to your breathing consciously and deeply. Once you begin, you will start to dislodge and bring to the surface feelings and emotions.

Repressed feelings, ingrained trauma, or major fears might surface as your deep breathing breaks down internal constriction. If you are going to dust off your interior, you are going to set loose a lot of accumulated particles. You may encounter aspects of your shadow side that you had found easy to ignore. Then, suddenly there they are staring you in the face.

If you had a fear, concern, or rationale for suppressing feelings before, it will come back to haunt you, sometimes looming larger than it was originally. If what you dislodge surprises you or startles you, it may be more difficult to consciously continue to breathe deeply when these uncomfortable elements are released.

You will have to realize the value in quality deep breathing and sustain your intention to continue or start anew. Rather than reverting to shallow breathing to quell your inner uprising, you have to hold your focus and go through your breathing so that it dissolves once and for all without further entanglements. That is part of fiercely holding your focus, facing your fears, and working through them.

Fiercely Holding Focus

This is a discipline you would do well to learn: holding your focus no matter what is going on around you or within you. Recently, I was in a meditation class and found myself distracted by noises being made by a nearby participant. At each sniffle, I launched into blame: how if it were not for this person, I would be more deeply into my practice.

Then, I got the wake-up call. No one was responsible for my holding attention but me. And this person was providing the ideal challenge and teaching for me to increase my ability to focus in a world filled with distractions. My job was to learn from the situation.

About the Exercises

What follows is a series of exercises dealing with the most elemental and basic approaches to thriving. These exercises are offered to help you learn the physical practices that are basic and essential to thriving. You may choose from among these, or use those that you already know.

The effect of several of these practices is very subtle. There are seldom precise outcomes that will be identical to what someone else experiences. However, you will find similarities from time to time.

Judge the results of any and all exercises for yourself. Then stick with those that serve you best. Below are exercises designed to evoke the "deep breath" aspect of buoyancy, the deeply rooted feeling of grounded-ness, centering, and the like. Experiment to determine the value of these exercises for you.

Breathing Exercises and Practices

No gimmicks. Just be aware of yourself here and now. Recognize that you do not have to do anything gimmicky in order to thrive. You can be right where you are and simply become aware of yourself and your process of breathing. Focus on your breath as you inhale, then follow it out on the exhale.

> *Since you have the ability to be conscious of more than one thing at a time, you will find that your consciousness expands to encompass more of your immediate experience as you focus on being aware of what is going on around you.*

Opening to your immediate experience is one main outcome of most of these exercises. Several practices will emphasize awareness in specific areas to add to the overall sense and awareness of yourself.

Rib Cage Lift
Interlace your fingers and slowly and easily raise your hands over your head with your palms facing up toward the ceiling. You will feel a stretching in the muscles down the outer side of your rib cage. This exercise can be done sitting at your desk or standing. When standing, unlock your knees. Now, pull your navel in slightly toward your spine. Turn your pelvis under and forward. Now breathe into your solar plexus for a full, deep breath. This exercise literally lifts your rib cage and opens up a space within you for a fuller diaphragmatic breath.

Relaxing the Musculature Around Your Rib Cage
Imagine that you are inhaling through a straw. Put this imaginary tube up to your mouth and inhale as deeply as you can. Once you have taken in a full breath, add some

additional short inhalations to fill your lungs even more fully. Then hold your breath in for several counts before exhaling through your nose. This emphasis on filling your lungs can stretch the musculature on the inside of your rib cage.

When you relax with the exhalation, the tensed muscles relax. Become aware of the tension and relax them further. That leads to fuller breaths without resistance. A similar thing occurs when you overcome the resistance in the rib cage through rapid breathing. You can feel a release and ease of breathing toward the end of your exercise.

Breathing for Buoyancy

Inhale into your solar plexus. Feel the little appendage just below your breastbone in the middle where your rib cage divides in front. This is the zyphoid appendix. It looks like a little tailbone over your solar plexus. Just below this zyphoid appendix is the area you want to fill with abundant amounts of air. Expanding your solar plexus has the tendency to provide you with the feeling of buoyancy and lightness. Life doesn't have to weigh anything. And when you breathe into this area, you lighten your life considerably. In addition, you release hormones and oxygenate your system in a way that adds to the feeling of buoyancy or lightness of being. Use this exercise when you are feeling burdened, out of the loop, excluded, isolated.

Belly Up to the Bar for Buoyancy

One way to open up your solar plexus is to sit 1.5 to 2 inches back away from the side/edge of a table, or any object, that strikes at the height of the bottom of your sternum, immediately above the solar plexus. Begin to breathe in and expand your rib cage in front so that you literally extend forward toward and even touch the edge of the table with your solar plexus. If the expansion is done without much effort, you may want to push back a bit farther from the table's edge. This will extend your rib cage expansion even further. Each advance in extension will expand your ability to take in additional oxygen as well as to experience additional buoyancy.

The feeling of buoyancy is very similar to that of weightlessness, the "thrill" described earlier as the feeling of riding over the top on a Ferris wheel, or sitting in the "shotgun" seat of a car on a hilly road with sudden rises and drops. The car lifts off, floats momentarily, and glides over a bump in the highway.

There can be a feeling of giddiness. Since this is not considered a serious, adult feeling, you may not consider reaching deeper and focusing to extend it or build on it. But do extend it. This feeling can grow into a vibrating interior light show. Flames of the "deep fire" leap up.

The vibration from your center radiates out and enlivens your entire body. However, this does not happen automatically. You have to promote and focus on that feeling even while inhaling into your target area more deeply. If things go well so far, you may want to go deeper.

Posture

The Value of Good Posture

Your posture and alignment affect your balance all day long. If you are out of alignment, you must continually make adjustments to maintain balance against the pull of gravity. Conversely, the more you are in alignment, the more efficiently your body works in countering the pull of gravity.

There are several excellent ways to improve posture that I recommend. Structural Integration, or "Rolfing" as it is referred to popularly, and the Pilates Method® are two of those. The Alexander Technique is another.

Structural Integration works on the alignment of the body to provide optimal balance and efficiency in body mechanics for fluidity of movement, and in working with gravity.

Structural Integration works from the basic principle that the fascia tissue that surrounds the muscles is what gives the body shape. The muscles by themselves do not. Fascia tissue sheathes the muscle like the skin on a frankfurter. By separating fascia that are attached to other fascia, and to the bone, the body can be sculpted by fascia tissue manipulation into optimal alignment and energy efficiency. Make sure you select a practitioner that suits you.

The Pilates Method® is a blending of eastern and western techniques, utilizing yoga and other disciplines. The program maintains that if you take care of your core, your body will attain alignment and take care of itself. If you deal with the musculature in the solar plexus, it leads not only to improved posture but to straightening out the body.

There are individual sessions offered in Pilates centers with a series of mechanisms to fine-tune the learning. I advise that you take just one individual session with an instructor on the apparatus, to get a sense of whether it works for you. That was all I required to benefit. There are less expensive mat classes on exercises that do not require an apparatus, that you can practice anywhere, including your home or hotel room.

Good posture works not only for balance, but also for smooth, unobstructed internal functioning.

Grounding

How to "Get Down!" Breathing for Grounding

One additional function of breathing deeply is to provide you with centering and grounding. When you find yourself in hectic and chaotic circumstances, breathing into this area can restore your equanimity and perspective. This can "settle you down," or help you "get down" and stabilize yourself.

Now continue the breathing by lowering, dropping your breath just slightly below your navel, about l to 1.5 inches below your navel. This area is known as the "hara" in Japan. It is the spot that is considered to be a communication point with universal energy or chi. Breathe into this area. Feel the expanse of breath as your diaphragm pulls the breath in and down.

You can breathe in more than one place in your body at any one time. You can focus your breath to be both buoyant and grounded at the same time. Put together the previous two parts of this exercise and breathe into both your sternum and your solar plexus for buoyancy; and also into your hara for grounding **or** ***rooted-ness.***

To remain grounded requires a fierce determination to breathe deeply with flared nostrils, to keep your consciousness and balance down and centered.

Balance

Getting Focused and Grounded

One exercise that requires fierce focus, and also puts you squarely in the moment, is standing on one foot. This grounding exercise requires that you focus your energy down and into the ground. If you find that your ankle is wobbling, it could be just a muscular thing, or it could be that you are approaching this exercise a little high centered in your head, and the wobble indicates drama, but not effective grounding.

Getting Into the Moment

A friend who coaches football an east Los Angeles high school uses the one foot technique to keep his kids focused on the game, not on their last mistake. It keeps them focused and grounded in themselves.

Physically, driving a spike gets you planted firmly on the earth. It builds your base for being solidly present, conscious, ready to perform. Cut someone's feet out from under them and they have to start from scratch. So, this is a basic exercise for living in the moment, a natural offshoot of being grounded. It is the "get set" part of "ready, get set, go!" And it is one practice of body mind unity.

Application: Do this at your own risk.
You can practice getting grounded and balanced by putting on a pair of socks while standing up. This process will get you grounded early in the morning. To do this you have to maintain your balance or have support immediately available to steady yourself so you don't fall. Stand on one foot while you put a sock on the other foot. You may have to practice and cheat a little at first by leaning against the wall or putting your foot back down on the floor.

Use this exercise any time you are entering into a situation in which you perceive a threat, or in which you want to be better grounded. Staying focused on the moment can diminish your anxiety about the future, as well as reduce guilt, damaging negative self-talk, and admonishing yourself for past errors.

Centering

Grounding and Centering are Distinct

Until quite recently, I had equated grounding and centering. Now I consider them as distinct. In aikido, a soft martial art, grounding is referred to as "weight underside." In ballet, it amounts to driving a spike by visualizing down into the center of the earth to stabilize balance. This is represented in one symbol of thriving with a spike down into the earth's core. It signifies grounding, connecting to deeper sources. Centering, meanwhile, is a matter of maintaining the integrity of your core within your body. Grounding and centering, are distinct and separate, although, they do directly complement each other.

Centering is essential to maintaining one's center, dignity, and congruence in the world. Centering involves establishing and maintaining your limits, boundaries, and integrity.

Imagine a series of concentric oblongs, each hanging within an ever widening array of oblongs located within the center of the trunk of the body. When in balance and hanging freely, each oblong would be aligned with each other, and there would be equidistant space between each in ever widening oblongs.

The very center of the oblong houses a candle whose flame is right at the heart and sternum level. It burns efficiently and broadcasts light by standing tall within the inner oblong when one is centered.

However, there are times when you get out of alignment. The candle can be pulled toward the front of the rib cage in an attempt to answer the needs or demands of another person. Now you are off center, having given up your internal alignment.

This can happen if you are unable to exercise your own boundaries and limits, when you ingratiate yourself with others, depending upon them, seeking approval. A highly codependent relationship can result that tilts and sticks that candle right up against the sternum.

Presence Requires Centering

Like the other self-monitoring and self-managing operations that you are required to balance and regulate as part of thriving, centering requires determination and discipline.

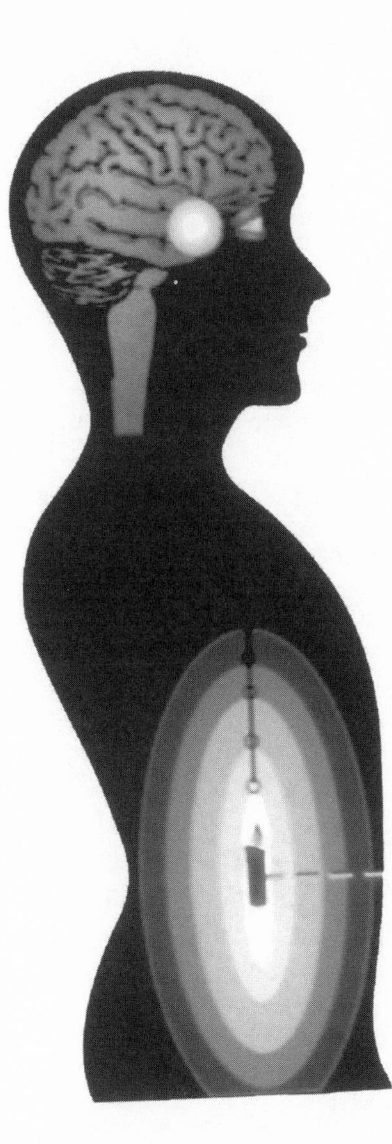

Make a true commitment to being centered within yourself. Make it a requirement that will eventually become a habit.

When you enter social situations or relationships, you have a priority of being truly present. You have to allow yourself the time and the space to get centered. Only then can you be present.

Consciously monitor your internal space as long as it takes to get a grip on yourself, to put yourself in perspective, and to maintain your integrity. Really be present and available with your inner alignment well in place before you take action. We will deal with this later on in Guideline # 5, as well.

Being truly centered and present is
a sacred trust and responsibility,
not an act of selfishness.

Extending Life Force

Chi, Qi, or key is a body energy that emanates from your power center. It can exist in varying degrees of purity and strength. You develop it through discipline and practices. When you are focused and deliberate in your actions, coming from your center with clear intention linked to your deeper purpose and passion, you are extending *chi.* This life force extension requires the developed ability and discipline of focusing. So, to be a conduit for this energy, and to act from your true self, you need first to be centered and grounded.

Traction

Getting a Grip!

Traction is the adhesive friction of a body on a surface on which it moves. In practice, traction is a relational term that involves friction, force, and balance. Your adherence to ground surfaces to facilitate walking, driving, or riding a bike is the traction you need in order to move about, and also to stabilize your balance to stand upright so that your feet do not slip out from under you.

The adhesion to a surface is the traction that allows you to overcome inertia, the friction or grip for you to push off in taking a step or to stop your movement. Your weight, center of gravity, and balance are important factors in obtaining and using traction effectively.

Traction: You Don't Miss It Till You Don't Have It

You have little sense of your traction or lack of it except when you lose it. Slippery surfaces from ice storms or leather heels on marble floors make you appreciate traction when you need it most. Too much adhesion, and you are glued to the floor like a deer frozen in the headlights.

We get a sense of personal security in walking, so traction impacts our sense of stability and mobility. Traction is a way of relating to the earth, a sense of focus that carries through our body-mind in terms of our ability to take ourselves seriously and to be taken seriously.

There are times when you will not be moved. Sheer resolve alone will not make that happen. Traction provides a steadfastness and a steadiness of purpose, giving your body a stable platform on which to stand, and from which to initiate movement. When friction or adhesion is excessive, it impedes our movement. When friction or adhesion is ineffective, you tend to slip, falter, or fall and you have to pay first attention to righting or stabilizing yourself.

How do you monitor your adhesion? This one is difficult, for if you are not experiencing any difficulty, you have to focus more consciously on the impact of maintaining adequate traction in situations where you would be more grounded or taken more seriously. It is a matter of being conscious of traction.

Building a Base: Providing Support and Getting a Grip
In many sports, traction is a major variable for stability. Golf shoes, football spikes, baseball cleats, gum rubber soles for hardwood games such as basketball and volleyball are each designed to provide maximum grip or traction on the playing surface of that sport. This translates in practice into quick starts, turns, and a firmer base when stopped, as well as less slippage.

Traction provides a base of operations. It is the stickiness for staying in place on a Teflon surface, or the step-off potential on a playing surface. Become more aware of how solidly you are planted when you walk.

In my sport, racquetball, a dusty floor can reduce traction and result in just the slightest slippage, leading to inaccurate and misfired shots. The difference between a slippage that allows slight movement and a clean grip is the difference between a ball that rolls straight out from the front wall, a winner, and one that will bounce high and stay in play. It is hard to aim from an unsteady carriage.

Exercise:
How your foot meets the ground has some bearing on your stability. Pay attention to how you walk. For example, walk barefoot. Do you cup your foot so that you roll around the outside rim when you walk? That would not give you relaxed

fluid movement or stability. Now, relax your foot. Let it settle into and spread out on the floor. Feel the improvement in how your foot meets the floor, providing padding, weight distribution, and direct contact with the floor.

The Centipede

Image that your feet have 100 tiny feet, like tire tracks, grooves running around the entire circumference of your foot. Now as you walk, rather than seeing your foot as heel-arch-ball and toes, see it as divided into dozens of individual sections, each with its own contact point. See your foot rolling onto the floor, one centipede's foot at a time. This can give you the flexibility to turn mid-step, with your first foot planted solidly enough to support your change of direction. Experiment with turning, stops, and starts using the concept of these 100 traction points. Consciously bring this into your walking whenever you can think of it, or whenever you need it to get better grounded.

Voltage

Increase Your Voltage: Strengthen Your Nervous System

What is your carrying capacity for stimuli? How much can you take before you are overwhelmed? At what point do you simply check out or leave mentally? You may want to increase your voltage, your carrying capacity.

There are various ways you can build toward maximum invigoration and the ability to enjoy it. In each case you are advised to check with your physician before beginning to stretch your limits. Several approaches you may want to explore include:

- **Work on your environmental limits**. In some clubs there is a cold-water immersion station right next to the sauna, whirlpool and steam room. This sudden change in exposure can be highly invigorating. It also rejuvenates and revitalizes your nervous system. Don't have a club? Turn your shower to cold after you have had a good hot shower. This snaps the pores shut and provides an eye opening change of temperature. Check with your physician first.

- **Work on your interpersonal limits.** Look people straight in the eye to a comfortable degree. Be aware of your truth when you are in their presence. Get into a sufficient number of social situations that you are no longer avoiding or overwhelmed by contact.

- **Work on your intra-personal limits.** Pay attention to your shadow side. As you uncover particular fears, face them, illuminate them, then embrace them and accept them as part of you. Any confrontation with your self-image may result in momentary disorientation. Learn to function with these temporary incongruities and disruptions.

In each case, you will be aware of a certain level of discomfort that is a necessary part of developing further carrying capacity and moving on. You want to be able to withstand normal to high levels of stimuli both within you and around you. That is the purpose of developing your nervous system. Breath, movement, and aerobic conditioning support neurological enhancement.

Summary

This chapter explores the physical under girding and requisites for a higher level of experience. The physical practices you have focused on include breath, posture, balance, and focus, centering, grounding, traction, and voltage. The main emphasis has been placed on specific body mind practices, the chief and most basic being breathing.

Mindfulness is part of this entire enterprise. Awareness is essential throughout to establishing these new practices, paying attention to what is important in the physical realm to support and engage the thriving state. Mindful determination to contain and stay fulfilled is the challenge of Guideline #1, Innertude®. Guideline #2 is a focused mindfulness that seeks ultimately to create physical habits and practices to support high states of being and consciousness.

Just ahead, the mindfulness of Guideline #3 is one of receptivity and openness to current reality. We go there next. After that, Guideline #4 will present opening yourself to have multiple perceptions, taking in a spherical panorama that comprehends and transcends your experience.

Chapter 14

Guideline #3: Accept Current Reality and Forgive to Live

As long as you don't forgive, who and whatever it is, will occupy rent-free space in your mind.

Isabelle Holland

What Is Current Reality?

A clear grasp of reality forms the basis for your experience. Your experience, in turn, is the basis for your authority. A clear grasp of reality forms a starting block from which to launch new initiatives, make choices, push off into new territory. Without traction or a grasp of current reality, there is no firm footing toward the next step. That is why a grasp of current reality is essential.

Reality never lets you down.
Only your demands, distortions,
expectations, illusions, and
ignorance of reality
let you down.

In *The Path of Least Resistance*, Robert Fritz provides directions for his visualization exercises in which he notes that it is important first to be clear about your present circumstances, your current reality. That provides a benchmark, the place in your mind, the basis, or starting point at which you establish the creative tension of your vision – how you foresee things, or how you want things to be.
As for your acceptance of your current reality, no one says you have to like it. You do, however, have to recognize, acknowledge, and accept it for what it is. To do less is destabilizing.

Fritz recommends placing your recognition and picture of *current reality* in a television-like screen in the lower left hand corner of your mind's eye. Then, he recommends placing the "best case scenario" of what you desire also in a television-like screen – this one in the upper right-hand corner of your mental screen as you look out and away. Next, you are to hold both pictures in your mind's eye at the same time.

Envision What "Could Be," Learn from "What Is."

Vision, Wish, Hope — What **Could Be**

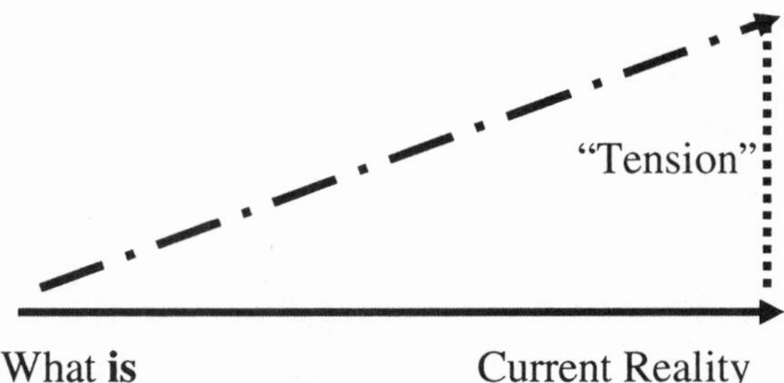

Baseline

Figure 14-1

Fritz contends that creative tension is involved in the creative process, i.e., holding your vision of *what is* together with *what you want to bring into being*. A tension exists between the two. Those who do not or cannot bear the tension of the juxtaposition of both scenes in their mind do not maintain the original pictures in their vision.

They may reduce the reach of their vision, what they want, excusing it by saying that they are shooting too high. Or they tend to overstate the circumstances they find in current reality, saying, "Oh, it's not so bad," or "It doesn't require improvement." In both cases the tension is reduced between the vision and the baseline current reality, the creative conjunction.

Numerous factors enter into your ability to determine an objective reality. You know the difficulty of doing so. Unfortunately, denial is a state that is easily maintained and most difficult to overcome. Denial provides an inaccurate reading of, intentional ignoring of, or obliviousness to aspects of current reality on either end of the vision stretch.

Acknowledging Doesn't Imply You Like Current Reality

Acknowledge that certain circumstances exist. ***Acknowledge*** means nothing more than *to recognize the existence of.* Recognize that this is the way it is, the state it is in. Acknowledgment is not an endorsement, or a matter of liking or disliking, but rather a matter of being aware of the existence of a situation and simply acknowledging that existence.

You do not create a reality by liking it or disliking it. And certainly our mere acknowledgment will do little to empower a situation. You serve yourself poorly if you admit into your reality only those things that you approve and like – as if your approval or liking had godlike implications for its existence.

Losing Sight of Your Initial Intent

One lawyer complained vehemently about the heartlessness of his law firm and the dryness of the work. Yet, he had chosen that firm specifically to learn the skills required in that "dry" work and to broaden his skills in one particularly arid area of the law.

His choice and conviction were clear during the first year but faded as the tedium of everyday routine wore on. He forgot how he got there in the first place and the basis for his choice. His initial intent and decision got overshadowed by every little setback and the boredom of the job.

You may have to remind yourself of how you chose or crafted your current reality as well. Have you lost sight of your initial intent? Your journal will give you a point of reference for getting in touch with prior intents, decisions, and desired outcomes.

The reality you find difficult to acknowledge came about partly as the result of your own choices. You may tend to forget that you made the choice and you may now feel slightly betrayed in having to deal with the consequences. Yet, when you can stand back from the minutiae and see the bigger picture, your perspective changes and reality no longer has the dragon's teeth it had before. Gaining a wider perspective can take the edge off the dragon's teeth.

Accept Current Reality

Acceptance means holding no provision for resistance or denial. It does include your being aware of what you recognize to exist. So a key element here is the scope of awareness that you bring to a situation. Your *take* on current reality comes from your distinct perspective, emphasizes specific facets, and may even overlook key elements of your reality or be particularly narrow or short sighted due to filters you have in place.

Forgive. Release Negativity. Move On with Your Life

Whoever wants to truly live in the present needs first to let go of intentions to change or redo the past. The past is gone. Nothing blocks living in the present like holding onto baggage from the past such as unresolved tensions or conflict. When you have suffered at the hands of someone else, there is a tendency to forsake peace of mind and seek revenge, rather than forgiving that person.

Past Is Perception

You see, what you have of the past is perception. It's your memories, perspective based on your filters, holdover emotions all wrapped up in the context of you living today. The statement "It's never too late to have a happy childhood" is in keeping with this ability to reframe, learn from, and move past your history. Living with an unchanged past is living in the past. Part of your work as a human being is to learn from your experience. So, if you have not done this consciously, it is time to begin. Use your journal.

Future Is Intention

Once freed from the ties of the past, you are free to plan your future. Like the illustration of a rabbit moving through a python in *The Little Prince* by Saint Exupery, your life is that little bubble of the present moment moving through the wind tunnel of time. Perceptions form the contrails of your past. Intentions form the angle with which you carve your way through to future experience. So begin to contact and surface your intentions, how you would have your life be. And use your journal.

Even regrets can keep you stuck in nether reality; retaliation even more so. Holding onto unresolved feelings about someone carries forward a residual tension that mars and cripples enjoyment of the present. By getting rid of negativity and streamlining emotionally, you forgo the resistance and residues of the past and pass through the continual rebirth of the present. Forgiveness releases and frees you to be fully in the currents of the present.

For example, a colleague "invades" the space behind your desk while you are on the phone. The problem is that you have some very personal papers lying on your desk face up, and you do not want to draw attention to them or act paranoid by flipping them over. So you take your chances on the papers not being seen, meanwhile seething at the colleague who has encroached on your space.

What you are not aware of is that your colleague is going on as three-week vacation and just stopped by to fill you in on a particular client. However, he could not spare the time to wait around, so he left your office before you got off the phone. That leaves you with the feeling of having been invaded, and a strong desire to let your colleague know how you feel. Only now, you will have to wait over three weeks to do so. If you hold on to that tension, you are likely to experience a number of outcomes, none of them particularly healthful.

Revenge Creates Tremendous Tension

The decision to exact a payback from, or to seek revenge on, the perpetrator results in direct tension to your body that, up until now, you experience as muscle tightness and constriction.

The Costs of Not Forgiving: The Chain of Events

It is not enough that you embody the killing negative tension of revenge. You also begin to act it out and groove it even further into your musculature. If you do not get satisfaction, or a chance to enact the revenge, the tension continues. In fact, when the perpetrator is not available for a time, or even leaves for good, you may hang onto the tension without dissolving, dissipating, or dispersing it. One literal grooving is through grinding teeth at night, clenching teeth during the day, and tightening jaw muscles.

If you are bent on retaliation or revenge, then you hang on to that tension until you mete out your own kind of justice. Only then do you release the tension, if it all. This constriction is often bound up in the jaw muscles. Now the damage begins in earnest.

> ***Revenge is like drinking poison and waiting for someone else to die.***
>
> *Jim Heslin*

The Downward Spiral of Revenge

- One immediate result of this tension can be **the onset of temporal mandibular joint problems,** or TMJ, with headaches, and clicking in the jaw when chewing.

- **Jaw imbalance**, if unrelieved, results from tooth grinding. (You notice luge riders in the Olympics, as well as football players, using mouthpieces to restore a balance in their bite so that they have a 15 percent increase in strength over an imbalanced jaw.) This triggers -

- **Chronic adrenal activity** due to the chronic alarm to fight or flee, that is sounded constantly by the clenching and the imbalance of the jaw, which leads over time to a

- **Loss of stamina and strength** as **the adrenal glands become exhausted** from the continuing alarm to which they are responding. The adrenal glands are the target organ, the recipient of your internal conflict. Adrenal glands tend to wear down and will no longer respond with secretion of adrenaline to arm you in the event of perceived personal danger.

- **Serious damage, major repairs and loss of teeth are likely to result.** Grinding down to the nerves can result in expensive root canals, crowns, and poor nourishment during the time the teeth are sensitive to touch.

As long as you carry forward the tension from an intolerable situation, or the tension of anger, holding a grudge, or seeking revenge against someone, or some entity, you are less likely to be truly present both physically and mentally to yourself and to others, to show up and live in the moment. The tension you hold on to keeps you anchored in the past due to a conflict that is unresolved in your own mind. It is all happening inside you. You are the cauldron for the conflict.

The so-called perpetrator may be totally out of the picture, unaware of having impacted anyone, and is not being impacted in the slightest. Meanwhile, the stimulus that triggered the revenge-seeking, your office invader, may very well have been vaporized or have moved away or died. And you, the revenge-seeker are determined and paying a high price to hold on to the tension and using it to drive your payback. The price in jaw and bodily tension alone is very dear.

Therapy clients are known to hold on to perceived slights, inequities, and injustices from dead parents years after their death. And some of them go to their graves with their gripes, without releasing or resolving their indignation and search for recompense, even though the perpetrator is long dead. The situation – and the pain that goes with it – is still on ***life support*** in the mind of the revenge seeker. This is another form of pain for gain, with all the immediate payoffs of potential sympathy and attention and built-in excuses for personal failures.

To Forgive Means….

Forgiving is more effective when you address with specificity and detail your intent and your release regarding your grievance. Make it directly to the perceived perpetrator, face to face or in your own mind. Your intent is the main factor in how effective you will be in gaining your release from the tension.

Even as you let go of blame and potential vengefulness, you may have difficulty forgiving yourself. For once you realize how much strain and negativity you have crafted and carried around, what you have done to yourself, you may have to release yourself from blame and further punishment.

No One Says You Have to Forget

Do you sense some conflict between forgiving and forgetting? Often when you are forgiving of another person, your trust of that person has already been sullied. You are not expected to forgive and forget, like nothing happened, to act naïve or ignorant around that person in the future. You are already forewarned he could repeat the behavior. The key word here is to "forgive," not forget. Learn from your experience. You are not expected to undergo electroshock to erase your memory.

Establish practices of skilled trust. That involves being open to the possibility that you were wrong in your judgment. Seek to understand the other person; or that he or she can change and be more trustworthy now and in the future. Be open to what the person actually does, and increase your trust accordingly. That is the practice of skilled trust.

If you are waiting for the person who "wronged you" to make "one false move" so you can nail him, please make no

If you are waiting for the person who "wronged you" to make "one false move" so you can nail him, please make no pretense of forgiving him. It is obvious that you have no intention to forgive.

However, this may be someone who is simply not trustworthy. You are not expected to parrot forgiveness and wipe your mind clear of any infractions. Learn from your experience. Forgetting would be a mistake on your part. But leave room for true forgiveness and rehabilitation on the other person's part.

Dealing with Personal Soap Operas

Melodrama 101, and the classic dramatic triangle, consists of a persecutor, a victim, and a rescuer. Typically, the persecutor sets this *Mighty Mouse to the Rescue* scenario in motion, although any victim, and even the rescuer, can initiate it as well.

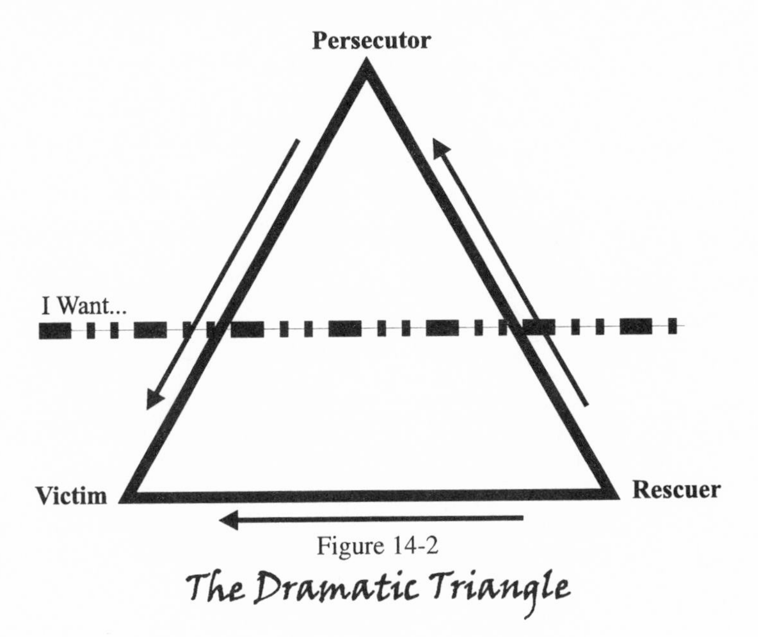

Figure 14-2

The Dramatic Triangle

In a classic scenario, one person may start the ball rolling by getting drunk. This victimizes the family. Then, once he returns to sobriety, he is contrite and may even sulk around playing the victim. And the family, once victim to his abuse, may take on the role of persecutor to make him pay for his transgressions. The cycle can go on and on.

One way to stop the unconscious dynamic of action/reaction, the cycle of behaviors and soap opera, is to simply ask the players, "What do you want?" This cross-cuts the dynamics. It can draw out the obscure dynamics, making them evident or obvious. That takes the players out of their habitual roles, and has them reexamine their intention and the choices they are making in relating with each other.

Releasing the Individual from Chronic Lockup

For an individual locked into her own personal soap opera, being confronted with a question about what she wants, the payoff she is seeking from this activity, can break her out of the trance. If the person who suffered pain or a slight wants to live at a level of high well-being, it is time to forgive and let go of the payback. Either forgive or forsake your entitlement to living in the moment and enjoying a thriving life.

Breaking that Chain of Resentment

Why is it when we hate what is being done to us, that we then turn around and do the same thing to others? Often this is generational. Children hated the way they were treated by their parents. They may have even vowed they would never do that to anyone. Then, when they themselves are parents, they find that they are doing many of the same things to their children. Most often they are reacting, rather than responding to the situation, their behavior having been imprinted by how they were treated.

How do we quit passing on the resentment? For in passing it on, we are setting up future generations to have to intercept these practices. Why don't we take the responsibility, intercept these resentment-filled behaviors, and end it now?

Resentment comes from a top-down system of relationships founded on status. "Kicking order" is one name for status and dominance among horses. The Alpha horse rules and can run off or reprimand all the other horses. Translated into family terms, this means that children are under parents, and usually the last one has no one but the family dog to kick on the power-status hierarchy in retaliation for the treatment he receives from other family members.

In addition to the forgiveness promoted here, there are systematic ways of working through lifelong resentments, inhibiting retaliation, and determining to treat others in a manner better than you were treated. Often this is done by going through counseling, parenting support groups, or group therapy. There is also individual counseling.

Summary

The third guideline to thriving mandates that you get a clear look at your current reality: at the context, the state things are in, and at what is going on. Acknowledge it, admit it, accept it, and continue from there. That is your current benchmark, the empirical base from which all visioning and imaging will proceed. To move forward you need to be clear about and appreciate where you are.

This entire chapter collaborates with the basic and overarching rule to live in the present. That means forgiving trespasses and certainly not retaliating against a perpetrator of harm. The only way you can do that is to forgive past grievances and release the negativity associated with them, so that you can release yourself and live in the present. You have to release yourself.

As you release yourself, use “skilled trust” in dealing with those whom you have forgiven. Trust and verify that they keep their agreements and do not intend or render harm. Stop passing on resentments from generation to generation. Making a better world involves taking steps that benefit everyone. Stopping resentments is just one of those actions, albeit an important one.

In Guideline #4, you will explore how the act of thriving is a *both/and* activity, not an *either/or* activity. You will have all the basic repertoire of knowledge, skills, and attitudes, plus practices and activities when you are thriving, as before. However, your every practice and perception can be made richer and more intense.

Chapter 15

Guideline #4: Multiple Awareness Transcends Circumstances

My therapy client felt like she was going to jump out of her skin. Acting visibly irritated, she thought she was the feeling, her irritation. And only when she could get some distance from that feeling by realizing that she could be conscious of it, did she calm down and go to work on what was bothering her so.

Many people think that they can at most focus well on only one thing at a time. So the prospect of thriving with expanded awareness to them means being unable to go on with their daily activities. In their mind it is an either-or choice: either thrive or go on with my surviving life pretty much as usual. That, however, is not the case.

But doesn't work take all your concentration? How can you continue to be responsible in your work and survive on the job while still being aware of what is going on within you? Up until now, that question alone has provided reason enough to sink, discard, or reject the possibility of feeling great on a sustainable basis. You are not introducing merely another activity into a schedule where activities compete for time.

Not only can you be aware of
more than one thing at a time,
You are right now aware of
more than one thing,
even though
Your attention might be locked onto
just one thing.

Multi-Awareness Is Not Multi-Tasking

Expanded awareness is about becoming aware of more of what you are already conscious of. If you were to stop dead in your tracks and pay attention to all that was going on within you, and your perceptions, you would be aware of much more than you are currently paying attention to.

Multi-tasking, meanwhile, takes pointed attention to a particular task. You may be able to choreograph a flow of activities, moving smoothly from one to the other. But each one in turn will require your attention at that moment. When you consider your range of consciousness, you can simply tune into that range and increase your awareness several times over.

Most people assume that thriving is a full-time, front-and-center full-attention awareness, mutually exclusive of and separate from any other aspect of living. Not true. Thriving does not consume total attention, leaving room for nothing else.

First off, it is a state of being, a condition you attain and maintain. Within that thriving condition, you have increased possibilities for attending to multiple aspects of your awareness.

You can transcend factors that formerly would have consumed your attention and impacted you deeply. You can both have multiple activities in your current life and conduct them in a thriving manner. You simply experience life and live it from higher ground.

Thriving Expands Your Awareness and Abilities
For this doorway, your multiple activities and awareness become more conscious, explicit, and intentional so that you can use them to your advantage.

Multi-perceptual awareness means that even though you focus on one thing at a time, you are actually able to be aware of several things going on at once. Reflect back on a recent party or meal in a restaurant. You may not have consciously noticed something occurring at the time. Yet it is possible for you to recall now additional awareness you did not note or specify in the first instance.

For example, even while you were deeply engrossed in conversation, you may have noticed a certain tension in the room every time the host walked through. You may not have paid particular attention to a couple talking in the corner, yet, on reflection, you picked up on a curious energy that came from that activity. Even though you did not specifically focus on it and observe it closely at the time, still it did not escape your awareness. For example, even though you are following and responding to one conversation, you might also be listening to pick up the weather forecast for the weekend.

One college president has the cultivated ability to listen in to the talk around him even while he is talking. And he can recount details from those other conversations. He can also describe in vivid detail what someone – usually an attractive woman – is wearing. Now, cultivate that ability to monitor multiple external activities and move it inside you. Then you will have valuable self-monitoring abilities.

Perspective

This fourth guideline to thriving is based on the fact that ***you can be aware of multiple goings on at the same time.*** You just might not be aware of all that you are conscious of. You become a kind of action central, the nerve center for your immediate circumstances. You pay attention to several things going on at the same time. You can rise above circumstances, and put yourself in perspective as well. Part of the richness of living at the next best level is being aware of your inner life while you are conscious of what is going on around you. You operate with a kind of 360-degree spherical awareness.

So, even while you can continue to think and act as if you are focused on and attending to one single point of concentration, you are taking in multiple stimuli from unlimited sources. One new twist is that you take this abundance of perceptions and handle them from a more intuitive base.

You could be attending a business meeting when you tune in to your own gut reaction to the environment in the room. What you are aware of seems to be at odds with what appears to be going on. As you consider that perception along with everything else, you get an entirely different reading on what is going on.

Multiple Awareness

Because thrival is a higher order of living does not mean that it consists of separate, exclusive, or as yet unattained practices. Thriving simply amplifies some awareness and intensifies others. It also stamps in new practices.

Your essential reality stays the same: Food will continue to stick to plates. You will still have to rinse your plate before putting it in the dishwasher. You will do that whether surviving or thriving. But the quality of the experience, the consciousness, awareness, and enthusiasm with which you do it, is what will differ. You can make washing a dish an aesthetic experience.

Thriving increases awareness and ability to utilize more parts of yourself. You do not have to choose between thriving and any other activity, any more than you have to choose between dancing and having a smile on your face. It is not an exclusive activity, but rather a quality of experience. The smile enhances what you are doing. It does not detract from or interfere with your dancing. It adds value. Thriving is easily added to and blended with your current daily practices.

Ordinarily, new practices take longer to learn and to put in place at first. Thriving is not only compatible with other activities, but it brings an efficiency to them that requires less effort.

Perceived Options

Often, your perception of a situation is colored by your own perception of your options and how to put them to work for you. How you cast a situation, your perception of it, often depends upon your role in it. If you are fearful, desperate, or prematurely set, you count on luck pulling you through, for you have severely limited your choices and your ability to adjust. You put yourself in the unnecessarily reactive stance of victim. That can happen for lack of clear data as well as lack of options or repertoire.

In racquet sports, if you plant your feet early, the ball may take an errant bounce and you are left swinging in the wind. You should set yourself only when you have sufficient information to guide your response. And often, the longer you gather information – rather than engaging in prejudgment – the more accurate you can be. Any early setup is done with full knowledge you will be better set to make adjustments to how the *ball bounces*.

Range of Choices

Knowing your situation helps you to realize the full spectrum of possibilities that fan out from that moment in time and from that circumstance. And knowing your choice points gives you freedom in any given moment.

At each moment in your life you have an unlimited expanse of choice points. Choice points are largely a matter of awareness, even though often the options are right under your nose. Until you become aware of them, you are stuck. So first be aware of the factors and variables in your environment and circumstances.

When you come to a fork in the road, take it.
Yogi Berra

Each choice or decision contains some uncertainty or risk. That is the essence of a decision. Without risk or uncertainty, no decision is needed; for choice becomes a forgone conclusion.

Choice Point Awareness

You are seldom painted into a corner with limited or destructive options. Even in the most limiting of jobs and relationships, there is always the possibility of doing something differently. You can exercise your choice point from any moment in time. Just as the spokes on a bicycle wheel radiate out from the hub in all directions, when you do something differently, you may well open up a full array of new options.

Reality Check on Options

As a person who has always wanted to keep his options open, I offer you the following reality check regarding options:

You do not finally have multiple options—
You do have multiple opportunities
from which to choose.
You have one choice.
And ultimately, you only truly have
those options that you exercise i.e.,
That one choice that you actually make, and
upon which you act and spend your time
is the only one you ultimately ever had.

Being Prepared

Basic career counseling advises people to always keep their resume updated and be proactive about staying alert to job opportunities. That way, irrespective of the situation, you always have choice points. The main thing is to be aware of them.

On occasion, you really do not have a sense of new options open to you. For example, when you lack control over another person's behavior, or over a situation. At that point, the main choice you may have is inside you, you can change your attitude regarding the situation or reframe the situation. You start to look at the situation differently, from a different assumption, value, or perspective.

Transcend Circumstances

The ability to transcend, to rise above, circumstances is the ability to actively maintain viable choices in even the most closed-off circumstances. And that is where multiple awareness is most valuable. Pull back and put yourself in perspective. Become a fly on the wall. See yourself in that situation. And from that vantage point, assess your options.

For example, someone in solitary confinement would be perceived to have very little freedom of choice or control over his own life. But no one controls that person's mind. One Japanese prisoner of war in WWII in the Pacific was placed in solitary in order to quell his rebellious spirit. However, the feisty major read the riot act to a guard who entered his cell uninvited.

His spirit, and his choice of actions, was undaunted by circumstances. Others might have been more circumspect and subdued. We can each continually find another angle or perspective on our reality.

The following exercise will give you an immediate check into your ability to have an awareness of more than one thing at a time. As you renew your awareness of this ability you have always had, you will also remember other situations with several simultaneous perceptions.

The "Six Eyes" Exercise

This exercise promotes multiple awareness, holding in consciousness more than one perception and perspective at a time. It is configured in terms of three pairs of eyes -- hence the name *six eyes*.

I. The First Pair of Eyes: A Soft-Eyes Focus for Stability

Begin by paying attention to the use of your own eyes for their day-to-day function of looking outward and seeing. The first pair of eyes is the one most people use to see what is going on around them.

Looking hard does not help you to see as well as soft focusing. A hard-focused, squinty-eyed, Clint Eastwood-type look may probe and derive specific information from a limited part of the picture. It does not provide a basis for stabilizing you in the environment.

A soft focus allows you a means of taking the situation all in, settling into it, and becoming content with it. Viewing with soft eyes provides a calming perspective. Not only are you more aware of yourself, but you are less stressed in the process.

A bug-eyed look of intensity and total focus may work against you. One result of overextending yourself, pressure eyes, is being off balance. In some cases, individuals tend to bug their eyes out, almost as a note of sincerity. For others, it is a sign of fear. It tends to push their eyeballs out just slightly and make that person look scared.

Bugging out the eyes causes them to move slightly out of their sockets. It gives that person a feeling of being exposed and unprotected. Thus, the fear is amplified and justified. In a sense, the pressured look is a little like dangling your eyes on strings out in front of your face, leaving them totally exposed to the elements and vulnerable.

Now try a soft focus. This focus allows you to become aware of a broader visual field around you, and to use the horizon as a point of stability. Sailors use this practice of focusing on the horizon to maintain inner stability in a rolling sea.

Soft focusing for stability can accomplish two things at once:

1. Give you a sense of having your eyes well contained and protected within your skull, and
2. Provide a conceptual space between your eye and your brain for discerning what you are seeing and giving yourself space to deliberate on what you will do.

You can then maintain your objectivity and equanimity in that experience. This reduces your being hot wired by your environment to ingest whatever you see.

1. Eyes Well Contained and Protected

Relax the way you are looking at your surroundings right now. Allow your eyes to relax and to recede slightly into their sockets. Now, become aware of your nose as a part of your visual field. You may even see your eyebrows brought into view to frame your field of vision. This visual framing can provide you with a sense of being contained, protected within your skull, not exposed. That is the first step: relax your eyes and put your eyes into their physical and framed context. Secure them and protect them naturally in your skull.

2. Create a Conceptual Space

Rather than having your iris pressed against the window-pane of reality, receiving whatever visual stimulus is there, then mainlining it into your cortex, this exercise lets you provide protective buffering. You do so by envisioning that space between the back of your eye socket and your brain. This is your "area of deliberation," your "I'll think it over" and "count to ten" spot.

The Nature Company has sold a little light that resembles a glowing ping pong ball. Try using this image to put a little space between your immediate experience of visual and other stimuli that come at you and what you do in response to them. Giving yourself this space can reduce the tension you feel and subdue any tendency to go out of control.

While the illustration below introduces an element that does not exist in us organically, the representation of the ping pong ball behind the eyes provides a space for discernment, for consideration of what that individual is taking in. And it is also a buffer and sign of emotional maturity to forestall mainlining input directly to the amygdala, a measure that promotes emotional maturity of deliberation before action.

Accompanying this exercise is a feeling of relaxation. However, by contrast, if you are accustomed to putting a lot of tension into your visual exploration or exchanges with others, you may want to increase the tension. By increasing the tension, you get a better sense of how much you have and how you organize it. Increasing the tension heightens awareness of the fact that you carry tension in your muscles all the time.

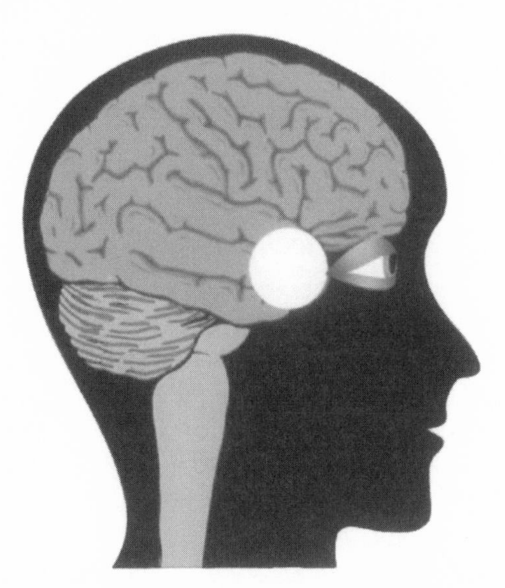

Now that you have increased the tension, take it up another notch, literally pressing your eyes out and leaving no space between brain and eye. Pay attention to what happens with the increased tension. Then begin to step down the tension little by little. At each reduced level, be aware of the difference in feeling and perception. Once you reach a physical point at which your eyes have receded back into their sockets and you are feeling well within yourself

feeling primed to observe, participate, and exchange with anyone on any issue – you have attained the relative peace of mind that can be accomplished with this more specific degree of soft focus.

You may find that your feeling of well-being gives rise to a pleasant, unforced smile. This is the natural result of the equanimity that you receive and enjoy in knowing or realizing that you are not a reactive organism. You have choices on how you will deal with what you see as your immediate environment and relationships. You introduce choice into your response once you recognize that you are contained, protected, and have the opportunity to process the visual stimuli coming in.

Creating the spatial buffer also seems to provide a time buffer. You become a more discerning, deliberative body, observing, absorbing, and then choosing your response. You have time to deliberate within yourself, to make sense of and decide what you will do about what you observe.

Now, allow your head to sit flexibly on your neck, something like the plaster dolls with the bobbing, waggling heads you occasionally see in the back windows of cars. Allow looseness in your spine, but keep it straight. Finally, find a clear horizontal line to observe so that you have your bearings.

II. The Second Pair of Eyes: Looking from Inside Out

The second pair of eyes bears what Deepak Chopra, M.D., calls the *silent witness* to what is going on inside. The focus of this pair of eyes stems from the same place as your physical eyes. But the direction is down and into yourself: *to watch, connect, and monitor your own inner feelings and process.*

Invoking this kind of awareness does not in any way limit your use of your first pair of eyes for vision. The chief difficulty you will have at first is in remembering that ***you are capable of maintaining each pair of eyes operating, at no loss to the functioning of the other.***

The Silent Witness

You can bear "silent witness" to what is happening within. The process of observation allows for a richer insperience, i.e., internally stimulated experience *exclusive of outside stimuli and experience overall.* Begin to think in terms of your own insperience and start to tune into it. At first this may seem like a gimmick, but it is the way you are emerging inside all the time, whether you choose to recognize your inner reality or not. Like discovering the beauty of a sunrise, you will develop a wonder at it all, for this is where your awareness resides like a treasure within you.

Insperience = Inside/In, compared to Experience = Outside/In Is internally stimulated experience exclusive of outside stimuli

Experience v. Insperience

Experience originates or is perceived as being stimulated from the outside. It is detected through your sense of sight, hearing, smell, touch, pressure, taste. It began as detectable, definable, discernible stimuli that originated from a source outside your body. It is then processed within you and dealt with on both a conscious and a subconscious level.

Until now there has been no distinction for internally derived and stimulated experience: what I call insperience. It all went under the rubric of experience. Insperience originates within. The source is your internal life. A welling up of feeling, energy, thought provides a pure internal experience.

Insperience may spring from the unconscious, the sub-conscious, or the conscious. It need not have any discernible provocation. What is important is that you connect with yourself inside and learn ***to locate and pay attention to your internally emerging phenomena***.

To avoid, ignore, or deny this aspect of your total life experience would be not to know yourself or the process of your life. Thriving taps into and is driven by the energy of the internal field, the joy that arises from the never-ending wellspring and flow of these insperiences that emerge within us.

Caveat on Insperience

An over commitment and focus to your insperience may result in your composing reality in your mind that is not indicative of objective reality. Insperience can result in a rich inner life, but also with the ignoring of external stimuli, even of empirical evidence. "Don't confuse me with the facts, my mind is already made up!"may reside in these quarters. Your mind can get carried away and create a virtual reality. You need a balance that includes empirical data along with your own integrity in action.

Monitor Your Insperience

Your first pair of eyes monitors externals and experience. This second pair monitors internals and insperience. By keeping an internal watch on what arises in the sphere of emotions and feelings, propensities, inklings, and glimmers, you gain an immediate sense of what is happening with and within you. Whether you act on the information or not, at least you are privy to how you feel and respond internally, moment by moment. This is a major part of the experience of your life. What you actually decide and do with that information is now your choice.

Using your congruent second pair of eyes ensures that your responses are more genuine, more authentic. It also reduces the chance that repressed feeling will come bounding out of left field in conversation or violent interaction. As you silently witness what is happening within, you can make choices to act on or to contain that insperience. Self-management requires the ability to monitor our internal life, and this second pair of eyes does just that.

The following exercise is designed to assist you in regaining internal connection with yourself.

The Silent Hum

The first exercise can be used to establish the internal connection, make you aware of your insides. It is also a powerful meditation exercise. ***To really get into this exercise it helps to hum out loud, to first feel the resonance through as much of your body as possible. Then when you are ready, hum silently, without making a sound. Close your eyes and hum in your mind's eye.***

You will find that many of the effects of humming and vibrating parts of your body occur even without making the actual sound. Maybe even better. The effect of "visualizing" is similar to the technique used by sports psychologist in getting athletes to visualize a run down a ski slope or a 10 meter diving competition. The athlete's body actually executes the same synapses he would if he were negotiating the ski run or high dive.

Recognition of insperience is an invitation to reconnect with your private spaces, and to recognize your uniqueness in the face of shared or common experiences. This is purely and totally your life as you reside here.

Imagine finding a radio in the wreckage of a plane on a Pacific atoll. Time and humidity have ravaged the guts of the radio. It has to be cleaned and restored; contact points cleaned, renewed, and reset; energy source renewed. There is a similar reinvigoration process required to restore ourselves to our original functioning state.

True differentiation and distinctiveness arise when you handle the full range of your experiences and your insperiences. For many of us, insperience and attention to impelling messages are unfamiliar new activities.

Insperience rounds out your experience. It completes the sphere of deliberation of events. Rather than your experience being defined strictly by your senses, you tune into the full concert of emerging messages. In order to have the richest experience of your life, you need not only to consider your experiences, but also to integrate them with your insperiences. The result is this spherical awareness from the core within you to the full field, realm, and area around you as if you were the core of a ball, and your field were the entire surrounding cover and core.

When you have overridden your own internal monitors and ignored your own deep-felt, significant messages, then you will have to restore the entire system of attention and sensibility with which you were born. You will have to activate it within yourself.

You have the internal instrumentation naturally. You begin by paying attention to the indicators. You can rebreathe life and resensitize those fragile tendrils by attending to them and encouraging yourself to stay tuned to them.

Engaging in this process is part of becoming more of who you are, consequently more human in general. You may find recall helpful. Others will simply have to relocate this aspect of their inner life. This may be the first time in your life you have worked on restoring your ability to seek out your insperience and use it to guide your thoughts and actions.

Not every insperience is one of sheer joy, but the mere fact of tuning into your internal world provides the moment-by-moment opportunity for new arrays, surges, and showers of sparks through the range of nooks, cranies, and ridges you can monitor with your internal sensors and spigots.

It is in this connection and attunement that we realize that our being in and of itself, has value. We need not have, do, or be anything more than we currently are, to have an inherent or intrinsic value.

Insperience and Containment

Becoming aware of your insperience will help immeasurably with your containment. ***Being connected and aware of these urges, responses, inklings, and glimmers emerging from within, you can take in the whole show, the vast array of internal indicators.*** With this increased awareness of what is truly going on inside, you can decide whether to express something, or to keep those matters to yourself, contained. That is the beginning of truly mature discernment in expression. And it requires a strong connection within.

Robert McNamara, former Secretary of Defense, in a memoir critical of his own performance in escalating the Vietnamese War, talked of his reaction to Norman Morrison's burning himself to death outside McNamara's Pentagon office.

"I reacted to the horror of his action by bottling up my emotions and avoiding talking about them with anyone, even my family...at moments like this I often turn inward instead – it is a grave weakness." W. Post, April 9, 1995, A. p.20.

McNamara's turning inward was a resort to denial, rather than a consultation with his inner witness.

Staying bottled up for years demonstrates an inability or lack of choice in expressing oneself. This is not the strong silent type in action. This is someone toughing it out, unable to be both strong and weak at times. This is not containment. This is a person in denial, emotionally unintelligent and incapable of dealing with his feelings.

A strong inner connection can lend breadth and depth to your perception of feelings and emotions. Rather than being driven by the effluents and residuals of feelings and emotions, you become more intimate with yourself. You participate consciously, guiding the process of realization and choice of the range of response open to you.

This allows you slight transcendence of feeling and emotion, to deal with as advisable and needed, not in retrospect some 20 years later in a memoir.

III. The Third Pair of Eyes: A Means of Transcending

Just as the second pair of eyes provides an internal connection, the third pair provides an expanded perspective and context in time, space, and humor

Humorists put a unique twist on situations with their perception. We tend to enjoy the varied ways they can flip flop a situation that was headed in a given certain direction. This perspective has a liberating aspect. We can unstick our perception by adopting a different approach, angle, or assumption. That is one of the functions of humor, the novel perspective that twists our brain. It unleashes a surprise by providing a direction or quick resolution, when our brain has already gone on ahead to what seemed the obvious conclusion. From it all, we gain a new or fresh perspective.

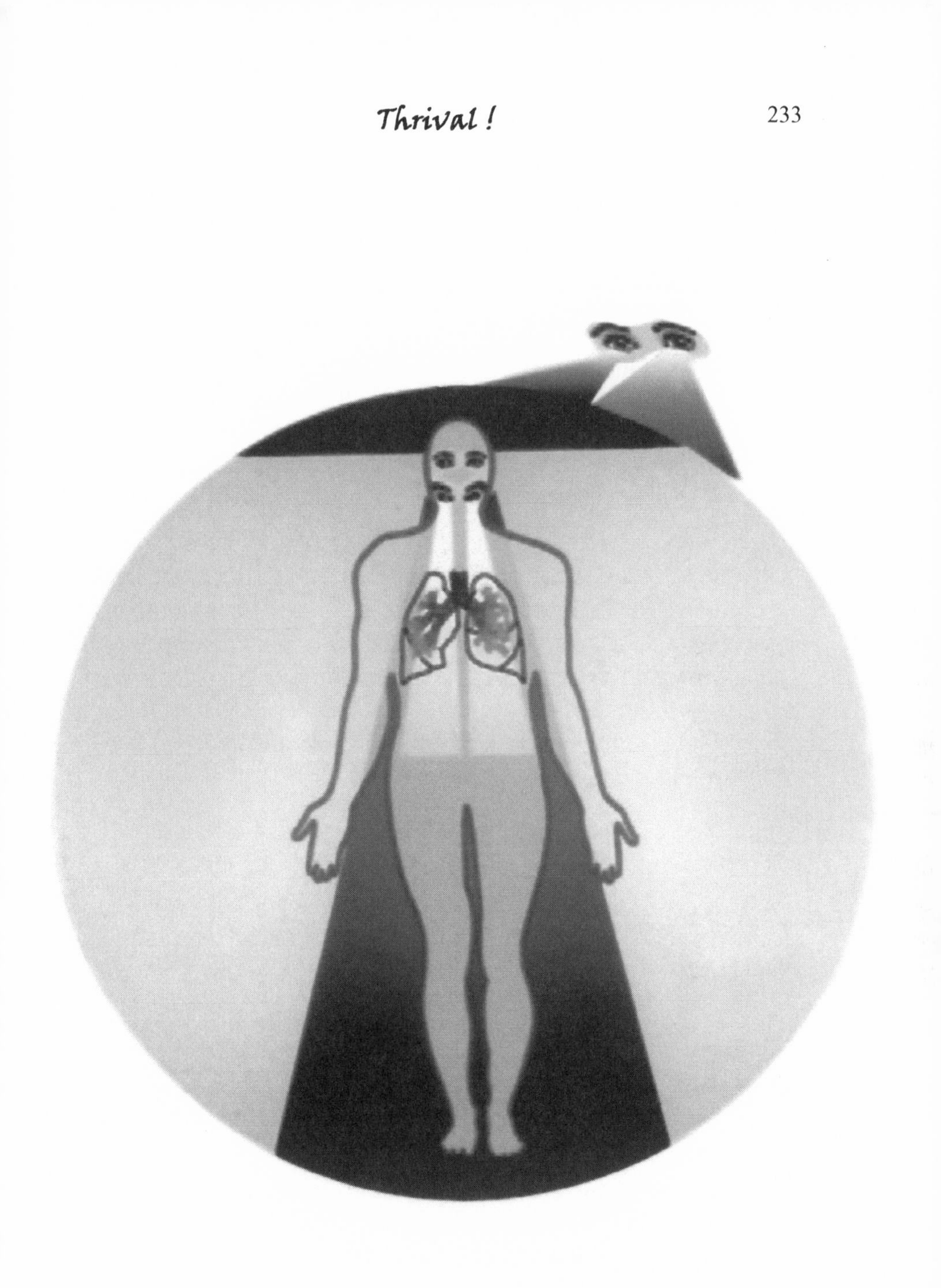

The third pair of eyes provides an overall and transcending perspective. Just as the first pair provided peripheral vision and the second provided internal vision, the third pair of eye provides a spherical perspective – above, below, front, back, and all sides – plus the ability to transcend or rise above immediate circumstances.

The third pair provides a larger picture against which to weigh the current situation. Imagine the third pair of eyes up over your right shoulder looking down. This is the proverbial *fly on the wall* perspective that you get on your own situation!

When you are nose to nose with someone, you may feel cornered, stuck, and helpless. When you hover over the scene, you can put yourself in perspective, put yourself in a little larger time/space context. That relieves you of the pinched feel of the face-to-face encounter. You can even find humor in it.

Seeing yourself in context provides you with an elasticity in circumstance, a resilience. If you limit yourself to the snapshot of any specific scene, your choices are restricted. However, if you allow yourself to assign the meaning to the situation, and adopt the perspective, you can assert some control and come up with new viewpoints.

Summary

You have reviewed a technique for putting yourself in perspective in a firm and total spherical context of personal consciousness by amplifying the range and spectrum of awareness.

- One major purpose of this fourth guideline is to reestablish an internal connection with your insperience. It is this connection that restores the flame to your deep fire, contacts your passion, and gives you the robust enthusiasm for everyday living.

- A second major purpose is to stabilize you and help you to transcend your experiences. And the major message of this chapter is that you can, in fact, be conscious of more than one thing at a time. Thriving is not an action separate and apart, an "either-or" proposition. It can be accomplished in most cases without focusing oneself down to multiple awareness.

Attending to your subtle and impelling messages is essential after a lifetime of attending to more overt, compelling messages, often ignoring your own emerging internal stimuli and the truth they carry.

Chapter 16

Guideline #5: Respect, Replenish, Accept, and Nurture Yourself

Most people seek after what they do not possess, and are thus enslaved by the very thing.

Anwar Sadat

Self-Respect: Fundamental to Your Internal Life Stance

Self-respect is essential to the enterprise of thriving. Self-respect is a quick-hitting term that strikes deep. It carries an innate value in and of itself that has a positive side for everyone. You can ask the most mush-mouthed individual with the most porous boundaries what he would be doing if he were more self-respecting and he will recognize and respond instantly with specific practices that carry a sense of value, worth, and dignity.

Self-respect is a basic underpinning, a foundation to self-esteem and self-acceptance. And even if self-esteem and self-acceptance are not your immediate objectives, self-respect itself carries a standard of decorum and dignity that is elevating and self-enhancing.

Self-respect is like a safety net in your own self-development and comportment. It is like having blocks under your tires on an incline, preventing you from backsliding. Once you have it in place, and act upon it, you will no longer engage in highly demeaning or self-negating activities.

Invoking self-respect seems to establish an internal pact within yourself. Once you establish it, you can draw upon an implicit intention to act in accordance with the higher standard implied by self-respect.

Respect Gets Immediate Recognition

I frequently ask my coaching clients, organizational consults, and therapy clients: "If you were acting on the basis of self-respect, what would you be doing?" There seems to be an immediate internal engagement (call it an ***ingagement***) by the client. His eyes often go upper right, as he envisions himself acting differently, sees himself acting in that same situation; this time with self-respect.

Every comparison my clients have mentioned so far demonstrates that when acting on the basis of self-respect, they immediately improve behavior or take a higher ground. An internal (dare I say "natural") standard has taken over without a suggestion of what that different action, behavior, or personal practice might be.

Self-respect carries its own value weighting, and tends to evoke a higher standard of behavior.

Recognize that self-respect is fundamental to enhanced lifestyle and behavior, whether you are inclined toward thriving or simply surviving better. Generally if you were acting on the basis of self-respect, you would be open to making the transition to thrival.

You may find an immediate impact of self-respect on your personal and professional practices. As you approach decisions, relationships, or choose your activities, ask yourself what and how you would be doing as a matter of self-respect. Self-respect is one criterion of judgment you will continue to value.

The conditions you impose upon yourself for self-acceptance are the very conditions that keep you from accepting yourself.

Self-Esteem: A Shaky Basis at Best

When self-esteem is dependent upon performance, reward, recognition, or the judgment of others, it makes the criteria that elevate self-esteem external to the person. If self-esteem can be earned or bestowed by others, then it can as easily be lost or taken away by others. It is out of your control.

The criteria for self-esteem need to be internal, personally held, owned, and controlled by you in order for that self-esteem to have sustainable value.

Once attained, self-esteem should be a constant. It should go to your core and not be dangled about you tauntingly as an incentive for performing well. Nor should it depend upon the judgement or evaluation of someone else. Hanging it out as something someone else gives to you just underlines the demeaning nature of having self-esteem bestowed by another, rather than realized by you.

Self-Esteem: Yes or No?

You either esteem yourself or you do not. If you esteem yourself because of something external to yourself, then you are truly off track and dependent. You are operating on the periphery of yourself. You need to establish the basis for your self-esteem from a deeper, more stable place in yourself. That is part of self-respect to begin with.

If you esteem yourself because of something external to yourself, then you are truly off track and dependent.

In order to truly regain your sense of self, you have to go deeper within than merely esteeming yourself. The next layer more central to your core and essence as a human being is **self-acceptance**. But unless self-respect is already established, you will not hold onto self-esteem for long. Self-acceptance rests first and foremost on self-respect.

Self-Acceptance

Self-acceptance, just like self-respect and self-esteem, comes with birth. I do not think that you need a certain number of years to qualify for or to earn a degree of self-acceptance. You are a totally intact organic entity when you are born. You are born with capability and potential to become a fully matured adult person. Any interruption in self-acceptance at any point in your life requires immediate repair and restoration to this natural state.

Self-acceptance, goes right to the core, piercing through the outer extremities that are lightly and momentarily impacted by affirmations, through the deeper level of self-esteem; it proceeds right down to the essence of what it means to accept yourself.

If you are successful in truly accepting yourself, then that one act can propel you into your thriving space. You can gain entry instantly. However, you do not adopt a mantra of self-acceptance. If you keep slipping out or backsliding, then you have not somehow accessed that thriving space. In fact, you can backslide and your regression goes unnoticed. Only with positive acts and practices can you fix your self-acceptance in place, and increase it.

Issues of Guilt-Shame-Fear
If dealing with issues of self-respect and self-acceptance do not challenge you adequately, you can also look over the bliss blockers™: guilt, shame, and fear.

- Guilt is from the past, the fear of punishment from oneself or from others. Often "having guilt" about something results in preemptive punishment of oneself in anticipation of punishment from others. It can also be remorse or regret for what you have done or failed to do.

- Meanwhile, fear is of the future, a problem of anticipation, worry, and fretting.

- Shame is in the present. Shame is a pervasive, yet obscure, theme in our culture and belief systems. It seldom surfaces directly as an explicit entity. Often it is confused with guilt. Yet it is a powerful motivator and major suppressor of vital energy in a majority of our population.

Shame means an underlying and pervasive sense of unworthiness, a deep sense of basically being defective and worthless as a human being.

Shame: Major Deterrent to Joy
Ultimately, our main focus is on the big one, shame. For not only is shame the least known of these big three, it is the most pervasive in our daily life and the most stifling.

Shame is a major deterrent to joy of any kind. It blocks self-acceptance and thriving. So, in order to move forward, you have to break the taboo that protects shame from open discussion and requires that it be secretly dealt with only by each individual in the privacy of his own thoughts.

You do not hear much about shame, because it is a taboo topic. Potter-Efron in their book *Letting Go of Shame* define shame as:

the painful belief
in one's basic defectiveness as a human being.

You Only See Their Surface

Covering up for a personally held sense of shame can be a major and lifelong compulsion for many extremely brilliant, compassionate, caring, and competent individuals. Many feel like impostors. Because of their shame, they never feel as if they are doing enough or well enough, even though they are doing what is humanly possible in their lives and relationships.

Many high achievers are motivated by shame. They are driven to avoid being exposed, being found out for the worthless creatures they believe/fear themselves to be. Always in motion, striving, and accomplishing, they use hyperactivity to "cover" for their suspected and deep-seated sense of inadequacy.

The internal dialogue of these seeming impostors includes such comments as, *"If people really knew me, they would certainly not entrust me with these responsibilities. I'm just pulling the wool over their eyes. I'm really a fake. But, if I were found out, it would be disastrous. So, I'd better work hard to keep from being found out."*

First: Confront Shame

Shame-busting is a prerequisite to thriving in the long run. In the short run, you might be able to sustain moments of joy. However, eventually, shame reasserts itself and corrodes your sense of self-acceptance, expansiveness, and celebration.

Facing the issue of shame is intense, both literally and figuratively. Direct confrontation with this taboo issue can be one of your major confrontations with yourself. It is best done with support.

As the major source of your tension, confronting shame is like looking into the blinding headlights of denial. At first, you have to get accustomed to the glare and over stimulation of facing it directly. You may have to look away, or take a break, then squint back indirectly such as through a reflection.

The same challenge awaits you with self-acceptance. The direct act of self-acceptance asks a lot of people whose acceptance and joy have been shrouded by a lifetime of shame. Build to it slowly by consciously establishing practices that demonstrate self-respect.

Going Public!

Thriving is enhanced, stamped in more deeply, by explicitly telling someone else that you know how to thrive and that you accept yourself. Telling, saying to just one other person, flies in the face of social norms.

> *And in order to get yourself back,*
> *to reaccept yourself totally and unconditionally,*
> *you need to tell at least one other person.*

Telling just one other person brings you out of the closet. It places you squarely in front of someone who represents your interpersonal realm, the realm in which you could potentially be ostracized, even banished. Since that is the worst fear for the human, the social animal, be aware of it and confront it early on. Telling just one other person helps you to do that.

By making the statement publicly, you confront your own catastrophic fear.

When you become at ease with your certitude about your feelings and perceptions, you no longer have to prove them to anyone or convince anyone of them. They just are. These inner feelings are inner facts, and you are the sole arbiter and authority that can monitor them and relate them for accuracy to anyone else. That will be the case with your self-acceptance, or lack of it. It is important to who you are and how you experience yourself.

Exercising Self-Acceptance

The following exercise is one direct approach to total and unconditional self-acceptance. Utilize the breathing exercises presented in Guideline #2 as needed. Especially pay attention to the exercise of taking deep diaphragmatic breaths in both your hara and your solar plexus.

Close your eyes and calm yourself down through controlled breathing. Get comfortable and settled. Alternate the breathing into your hara, just slightly below your navel, and up into your solar plexus. Then breathe into both places at once.

When you are at ease with breathing in both places at once, say to yourself silently:

> *"Now I accept myself directly and totally*
> *without qualification or condition.*
> *I am enough, no matter what, and*
> *I am emerging."*

On Already Being Enough

Many who first hear, "You are enough, no matter what," immediately hear a counterargument rising from their inner voice: "*No, you're not enough. You have to lose weight. You're not spending enough time with your kids. You have a very important project due and you haven't even begun yet.*" These are but a few of the typical arguments and forms of resistance you get to accepting yourself. That is why it is essential to immediately add, "and you are emerging."

"Enough" means that you are a complete and total organic entity, functioning fully right now. The mere fact of your existence has value and establishes that you are enough. There is nothing more required of you. There is no need for "when I do 'X,' then I will be worthy" proposals to establish you. Hence, your entitlement to be able to accept yourself.

You need not do, say, possess, or be anything more than you are right now. Just by the fact of your existence, of your essence, your being, you are enough. Your existence alone has worth.

You may think that withholding self-acceptance, depriving yourself of your own full-fledged support, motivates you to strive for more. Without that motivation, you fear that you would become smug, apathetic, torpid, a total couch potato without initiative. You would be a finished product, one stuffed sausage, just waiting for the grim reaper, enduring completion. A Polaroid snapshot could sum you up. Then you would be all over, finito, completed, kaput.

You say you want to do more with your life? How could you be enough when you have so much more you want to do

You have skills to refine, things to learn, a project to finish, words of kindness and love to express. Fine. You can do that. This is all possible with the emerging you. But why are you required to accomplish all those things before you will finally accept yourself?

Your next breath should be ample evidence that your life goes on joyfully when you accept yourself. Life is a process. Each breath brings new realizations, responses, choices. By virtue of being alive, you have a vitality that includes impressions, feelings, memories, desires developing within you moment by moment. This is part of emerging.

Thriving Is Active, Not Passive -- No Chronic Epiphany

The idea of *emerging* reflects the fact that just because you accept yourself, you are not suddenly going to be set in cement or bronzed in place. **You don't get thrivaled!** You should become more fluid, more alive while thriving. Yet, thriving is no chronic epiphany.

Emerging involves the simple realization that each of us is going to continue to grow and change and deal with new choices, feelings, and emotions. "I am enough, no matter what, and I am emerging," is a very clear statement of your reality and important to the act of totally, explicitly, and unconditionally accepting yourself, and then sustaining that acceptance.

Survival mentality individuals see this sense of emergence as **the threat of life**, life out of control, living without knowing how things are going to turn out. Since everything is couched in terms of survival and fear, control is always an issue. And control kills resilience. Emerging means emergency! Thrival mentality advocates see emerging and released flows of energy as **the thread of life**, a natural dynamic due to the convergence of multiple factors, integrated with their own ability to choose and respond.

Self-acceptance can occur at any age, although it may be more difficult the more self-negating or self-doubting habits you entertain. You can cultivate your own self-doubts as long as you wish, or you can end them.

Those who are addicted to stress find that self-doubt helps them to keep the pressure on themselves. They keep this burr under their saddle to keep moving. It's a little like keeping a shark in your tank to keep the rest of the fish moving.

The belief that you need that uncertainty cultivated by self-doubt keeps you under continual stress and drains your energy. You keep yourself in the grip of shame, disbelieving in your own self-worth. There is no confidence in this approach, no faith in yourself. The continuing felt reliance for a compelling, head-driven boost is basically a way to disown yourself, not accept. You also implicitly express distrust in yourself.

If you can't trust your trust,
how can you trust your distrust?
Alan Watts

Exposing yourself to the truth about your worthiness, your enough-ness, creates an internal crisis with the self-doubt you have spent a lifetime cultivating.

Spontaneous Self-Acceptance

Bill was a highly touted high school basketball player in a large eastern city. Great things were expected of him on the court, and the pressure had built steadily since his middle school days.

Then one day it happened. As he walked down the high school corridor between classes, Bill realized that he really did not have to perform any feats to accept himself. He could do that right now. There was no need to wait for the media reviews of his next game, no need to wait for all-city recognition, or for a championship trophy, or the inevitable college scholarship offers. He moved on somewhat lighter and more buoyant. From that moment on, he began to perform better as an athlete. He became his own man

Now he does not have to prove anything to anyone, although he does continue to do his best by competing against himself. That is his greatest challenge. But he does that without outside pressure. He has it ***in him to do****. He is self-motivating and self-managing. He recognizes and elicits his best without waiting for media headlines, pro scouts, the coach, or his teammates to tell him. He tells himself.*

It all happened so suddenly, his epiphany while walking down the hall. It was a silent rite of passage. He came into his own. To his teammates, he is now a little more self-possessed and self-assured, sometimes quieter. And there is a certain gleam in his eye that makes him look like he knows something no one else knows.

Bill provided his own unconditional self-acceptance. Accepting himself without qualification or condition, he moved to an entirely new level of living and performing. It was a spontaneous act. It just happened!

And as the meaning of it took hold, he removed himself from the major stresses that had surrounded him: expectations and pressure from the press, public, family, school, community, and friends. He also removed the pressure of his inner critic, the detractor who used to tell him that he would be banished if he goofed up or did not live up to expectations.

Transformational Moments

These moments of clarity and insight create such a brilliance that some who experience them are enlightened and transformed forever. They open up a new space in them-selves, find an energy and light to guide their way and propel them forward. Suddenly their vistas expand, narrow self-limiting perspectives broaden out, and their spirit takes on new depth, passion, and purpose.

Replenishing

Western sports tend to emphasize giving your all, "giving your last ounce of courage," and "leaving it all on the field." Only when the lactic acid has built up and exhaustion is obvious might you be able to hazard a rest and not be considered a slacker. In a brief and occasional athletic contest with plenty of time in between to recover, that is all well and good. But as a day-to-day operating mode, it has got to be taking a lot out of you.

In practices associated with eastern traditions, notably hatha yoga, with every major stretch or expenditure of muscular energy there is time devoted specifically and pointedly at recovery. Typically there is a replenishment of oxygen through deep breathing, as well as several moments for recuperation. You make a conscious effort to put back or restore what you just took out of your reserves. And that tends to lead to more sustainability in the long run.

Pro sports, corporations, and business operations in general are not catching on to the need for replenishment. Sports, for example, has wonderful examples of premium performance and extended careers by athletes who sought extra assistance in staying free of injuries and recovering from them.

Basketball great Kareem Abdul-Jabbar played well after colleagues his age had left the NBA. He attributed some of his agility and body resilience to his practice of yoga. Roger Craig, 49ers running back, would employ a masseur to do deep tissue massage of his bruises after each game. When Chicago quarterback Jim McMahon needed acupuncture for his hip, only a threatened strike by his teammates before the Super Bowl persuaded the coaching staff of the importance of having the acupuncturist on the bench.

Sleep experts now tell businesses they would be better served by following the natural sleep cycles of their employees and paying attention to these natural cycles throughout the day to improve performance. For example, a nap has been recommended in place of a coffee break mid-afternoon. And companies are now building nap facilities.

One sleep expert will not be scheduled for a speech during afternoon down time for sleep cycles. He doesn't want to fight the lethargy.

R & R

The act of replenishment requires that you follow through a kind of figure eight, or reciprocity figure. Rather than just expending, giving, you both give and receive, expend and restore. You internally monitor, or put yourself on a regular schedule to rest, recuperate, or replenish, much as you water a plant regularly to help to maintain the conditions under which it can thrive.

Dehydration results among those who expect and experience thirst before they replenish their fluids. Thirst is not the only indicator that you need fluids. You have to take the initiative to replenish yourself. A minimum of six glasses of water a day is recommended.

In terms of energy, replenishing is a little like keeping dry cell batteries from running down and staying down for a period of time. For once they are low for a time, it makes it more difficult to ever bring them back to optimal full power. Individually you are operating with many factors to consider in your overall energy scheme, so make replenishment an habitual part of your life.

Even when you are not in a position to top off your tank, it is important to be aware of the next way station down the highway. Attention to self-replenishment is a normal part of training, running, and recovering from a marathon. Extreme or highly intense activity for your body sends unmistakable messages to you in the form of thirst, muscle soreness, fatigue.

In lighter activity, or under chronic stress or denial, you might not get the message. That is why it is so important to begin to get in touch with, monitor, and fine-tune your awareness for your ongoing replenishment, self-nourishment and self-care in all areas of your life.

No matter how well you attend to your needs and maintain yourself, you will want to go further than merely replenishing, and become self-nourishing and self-nurturing.

Self-Nurturing

Visualize your very own self as a little baby in your arms. You have been entrusted with the care of this beautiful child your entire life. Proceed to keep the sensitivities, needs, and concerns of that vulnerable child aspect of yourself in mind as you conduct your daily business and pleasure. Now that you are more capable of taking care of all aspects of yourself than you ever have been before, are you ready to reverse some of the carelessness, denial, insensitivity, and even resentment that you have directed at yourself?

Nurturance goes far beyond replenishment as a standard of care, and as a manner of care. It can be expressed in the difference between a light glancing touch and a caress. Nurturing does not wait for expenditure to trigger its services. It may mean carbo-loading in anticipation of major run or hike, or getting extra sleep in anticipation of travel and a heavy schedule.

Here is a place to engage the journal, to learn from your experience. You may need to code or flag those area of discovery, question, or concern about specific aspects of your experience.

For example, I had been carrying at least five extra pounds above my usual weight and not dropping it. Then I remembered the very thing I had told thousands of participants in my Stress Management and Burnout Recovery workshops. *Exercising three times a week for one-half hour or more will keep you pretty much at your current level of burnout or fatigue. If you want to restore your balance and mood, you have to exercise four times a week for a minimum of one-half hour.* Once I stepped my exercise up to four times a week, the weight started coming off just as it had before.

You can be kind to yourself and take ownership for your own nurturing. That is something you can control. What you do to be self-nurturing may be as simple as taking a deep breath to calm or replenish yourself. Or, it may run the gamut of selecting your relationships wisely, going to a spa to pamper yourself, planning a schedule that gives you breathing space, and setting realistic time allotments for your weekend chores.

Take a Care Package

What would it take to provide for yourself when you go out on the road? You often need supplies that are not easily obtained. You arrive at a hotel after 10:00 pm without having had anything but an airline sandwich at noon. The selection is limited. So, begin carrying high-protein nutritional bars for quick pick-me-up, fruit to keep your system lubricated, or other high-nutrition, low-packing-requirement item. For day trips, you may want to carry your own water, or purchase it along the way.

Self-Care: Especially for Men
Self-care is frequently ignored by men. As youth, they feel immortal. Cultural and gender issues find them often neglectful in this arena of self-care. In fact, part of getting married is to find someone who will nurture them. The expectation is that it is their wives who are responsible for nurturance, preceded by their mothers. Men can get through a relationship like that without learning very much about taking care of themselves.

Women Fail to Self-Nurture As Well
Women are not that much better at self-nurturance, mind you. Many take care of and think of everyone but themselves because they were brought up to value service and self-sacrifice. In some cases their withholding from themselves is a way of expressing spite at their mother. You see, if their mother did not live up to their expectations for nurturing, they can and will complain beyond her death about their loss of the "good mother." They have a deficit that can't be filled. And since their mother is already dead, or inadequate, they will be darned if they will heal themselves. So, in a sense, they bite their nose to spite their face – and do not provide the self-nurturing they have longed for.

Many women treat themselves best when they are first pregnant. They do everything right. They take their responsibility to their child very consciously and seriously. But often those who act in the optimal service to the fetus do not continue to nurture themselves once the child is born. And then there are those who don't want to gain a lot of weight, or can't give up smoking and are fairly resentful about being pregnant in the first place. Self-nurturance is an act of maturity and an essential part of thriving.

In thriving, part of taking full responsibility for yourself is to accept your responsibility to yourself for maintenance and replenishment. The higher your resonance, the more you will have to attend to the fine points of self-care.

Is This Good for Me?

Anything bordering on neglect or abuse at this stage of your life – in your treatment of yourself – is testimony to habits you have gotten into. Some of these originate with your parents, family, community, or your culture, including the generation you were born into. Some may be a result of your rebellion, reaction, or resistance.

You are now in a position to evolve consciously beyond all that, to become who you alone were meant to be. Quit looking at molds, role models, and templates out there. They are a needless distraction. None of them is you or ever will be. None can ultimately guide you to who you really are. Begin to explore from within. This is inner work.

Begin with a determination to be good to yourself. Pose the question to yourself, when making choices, "Is this good for me?" Even better, "Is this really good for me?" For one main criterion for each of your choices should be its impact on your well-being and peace of mind, and ability to sustain the contact.

Replace Up-Down With Side-By-Side Relationships

Once you take responsibility for yourself you begin to develop more side-by-side relationships with others, in which both of you can be strong, responsible, and take initiative. This is the better relationship, whether at work, in a marriage, or on a team. It is the essence of partnership. It also blows right past parent-child relationships to establish more adult-to-adult relationships.

Summary

Direct self-acceptance along with the ongoing ownership for that acceptance, is the quintessential, the turnkey act required for thriving. It is, in fact, what elevates your experience slightly above the feeling that accompanies success. Directly and explicitly you are self-accepting. You have to like accepting yourself and back it up with self-nurturing.

All of your acts need to occur in the basic context of self-respect. You are enough, no matter what, and you are emerging. You may help yourself by stating publicly to another person that you know how to thrive and that you accept yourself. The most difficult barriers you need to overcome are mental, buttressed by a lifetime of shame that has been kept secret from everyone else and reinforced by your inner critic. Going public breaks past the prohibitions of shame, which rely on your conspiracy of silence.

Chapter 17

Guideline #6: Associate with Highly Positive People

In everyone's life, at some time,
our inner fire goes out.
It is then burst into flame by
an encounter with another human being.
We should all be thankful for
those people who rekindle the inner spirit.

Albert Schweitzer

Self-Igniting Activity

This book is based on the assumption that you are on your own with no support regarding thriving, and that you will have to attain and sustain the thriving state on your own in a culture geared against your thriving on your own.

This sixth guideline advises you to find role models of high positive energy and to resonate with them. Getting in sync with them may be one shortcut to thriving. But simply getting a hit from them will leave you dependent on them, on their being present for your future thriving. You need to learn how to do it for yourself, on your own.

Light Your Own Fire!

Buddha

Once you attain a higher level of energy and peace of mind in their presence, you are advised to tune into yourself. Learn from your good fortune. Replicate the thriving state on your own. They simply help to prep you for the experience and may provide the shoehorn to slide you through the portal.

Depending Upon an External Factor to Thrive
The main thrust of the entire book is to provide you with the basic insights and access to thriving that will allow you to sustain it irrespective of circumstances. If you can thrive on your own, then surely it should be easier for you to thrive with others who are supportive.

So far, the approach to thriving has consistently emphasized standing on your own two feet, locating, defining, and sourcing yourself from within. Guideline #6 is the only approach mode that focuses on something outside yourself, that is, on the value of personal contact with others as a portal to thriving. This occurs through resonance in relationship.

Thriving Goes Better with Others
Of course, thriving is much easier to sustain with the support or others and in the company of others who are thriving. Such support creates an environment in which you can hold onto the thrival state without the jostling, contention, and confrontation of those who are survival oriented. People who are thriving not only carry a higher resonance that you can tap into, they also have implicit respect for you. They are not intrusive or invasive. You do not have to expend energy being constantly vigilant around them.

Florists make corsages of orchids rather than dandelions because people like the delicacy, fragrances, soft texture, bright and subtle hues of the orchid. Most would agree that the orchid has a higher degree or refinement in the plant world than the dandelion. People, as well, can cultivate a higher degree of refinement, essence, and a resonance that is eminently attractive to others. It helps to be around those who model a higher essence. These are the people who truly have high positive energy.

Think about the people you enjoy. Who inspires you? Buoys you up? Chances are the first persons who come to mind are upbeat, inspiring, uplifting, positive individuals. Typically you feel loved, supported, safe, even energized around them. They have a lilt in their voice, a spring in their step, a gleam in their eye, and a positive "can do" attitude. They are optimists and "possibilists."

Physical Performance and Internal Energy States

The high positive energy referred to here is energy in high flow, without tension. That is the preferred performance state coached for and espoused by Dr. Jim Loehr in *Mental Toughness Training for Sports,* who has worked with Dan Jansen, and top tennis players. The introduction of tension throws off the free flow of energy, subjecting performance to uneven, jerky, or erratic movement. Rage and anger do not bring improved performance, because they cloud mental clarity and constrict physical movement. If anything, they work only in short term aggression, but leave costly residuals in the brain and body chemistry of that person.

Relating with a Highly Positive Person

Your day becomes special when you run into this highly positive person. Suddenly you experience a lift to your spirits. A day that was pretty fair to begin with, now has a zestful quality. But with this person there is an internal smile that finds its way out to play on your face. You find yourself at ease and inspired. Your pulse beats slightly stronger, and you are invigorated. You like yourself more and you like life. You are inspired and you may get a boost simply by thinking about this person. You are entrained to her spirit, expanding to encompass it.

Her enthusiasm may be contagious. You bask in the glow of her presence. You look forward to being with her. She provides an energy with which you gladly identify, resonate to, or get in rapport with. You gladly get in synch with the rhythm of her being, for you feel uplifted and expansive when you do.

There is something magnetic, charismatic, attractive, fascinating about the highly positive person. Not only are the lights on, but someone is really home. That person is interesting in herself. You may look to her as a role model. You may want to know how she makes the best of each situation the way she does. Hopefully you can learn how for yourself as well, or some of it will rub off. This person really floats your boat, lights your fire, and releases your spirit to its natural buoyancy.

When Another Lights Your Inner Fire

You may find that different people bring out different aspects in you. One person turns on your humor, another contacts a deep-seated conviction within you. When someone turns you on, it is natural to want whatever that person has. You want to get in sync with that person. But, what you may miss in focusing on that person is that the humor, or conviction, is within you. The other person may prime your pump, but you are the wellspring of that element within yourself. So, what you may want is to be around this person enough to get your pump primed so that you can draw up that part of yourself on your own.

You may very well be attributing to that person qualities, properties, and characteristics that you dearly prize in yourself, or desire for yourself. The person you enshrine in your mind and to whom you attribute a collage of characteristics, properties, and qualities may more closely resemble your higher self.

Beware of idolizing that person. You may be setting up a standard or comparison against which you would continually fare poorly, or deny yourself self-acceptance. And you are focusing outside yourself.

On Your Own

Thriving on your own gives you an opportunity to practice and get your skills down to sustain thriving without support. This is also important. You need to test your legs early in the process, to learn what you need to work on.

Meanwhile, you may wish that others would take the first step in thriving, in being congruent, getting their act together and living in their truth. You would then be able to step into a ready-made, low-risk community where thriving is the norm. Unfortunately, that is not what is required today. Today you have to pioneer in order to create that low-risk, thriving community.

You Are The New Frontier

Thrival requires a new frontier. And that new frontier is you. Should you choose to explore it, you become a lifelong pioneer. Your life becomes a quest, an inquiry rather than an answer, a journey, not a destination.

This new frontier requires a journey inward, a reconnection with and remembering of your innermost self. So you will be exploring mainly on your own. You will be out on your own cutting edge. So for right now, you choose whether to approach thriving or to avoid it.

Thriving requires an internal shift. With an internal frontier, the rules for exploration change from the conquest of America and other pioneering efforts with which we are familiar. When you deal with physical, geographical, visible frontiers, you have tangible measurable, documentable objects with other explorers to vouch for discoveries. There are objects that you bring back or witness as evidence from these new lands: gold, jewels, exotic foods, and spices. This does not hold true for inner frontiers.

With an internal frontier, the rules for exploration change to (are you ready for this?) "insploration." You have to dive deep within your own skin and psyche. Much of what you experience is in the realm of consciousness. You will find qualities such as peace of mind, ebullience, compassion, spaciousness, light. You will discover them as you begin your journey. And no two people will have identical journeys. However, they will be able to find commonalities.

Rich Life Experience Elicits a Full Range of Responses
Any outfitter for life would realize the variable conditions you might enter, the various circumstances, the things you have to be prepared for. Life is a journey. Be ready for it.

I am troubled by what comes across as **excess positivity**, a tendency to paint everything with a happy face with no acknowledgement of a very real downside or shadow side. Optimism does have definite health and attitude advantages, excess positivity is a state of denial. My preference is to make a realistic assessment of current reality, owning the good and the deficient. Take a basically positive approach, and also be open to the negative aspects that are present.

Denial Blocks Internal Self-Monitoring
Denial is the inability or unwillingness to face your feelings and internal reality. Denial puts you in a reactive mode in life. It takes you away from your own center and an authentic experience of your own life. If you are required to be "up" and stay "up," then you dare not look down or consider the alternative. Hence, you are constantly under

orders by the positivity police and have to act rigidly on command – a compelling requirement.

Your every thought and action must then be in support of the "appearance" of your "up" state, or of how you try to represent being up. In many cases it seems to be in emulation of someone else who was up. In the process of acting this way, you do not stay open to the full range or spectrum of possibilities with you. You deny your own ongoing life experience and your impelling energy that arises within from moment to moment.

I, personally, have a great love of reality with its many shades and nuances. I prefer to perceive it with balance and clarity. That is essential to my own understanding, and ultimately to my own sanity. When I deal with someone who cannot see shadow, I want to run. Initially it might be because of a flash of inadequacy that I am not as "up" as this person is. But that quickly settles into the unreality of his position, the strain of avoiding acknowledging what is so evident. I personally do not trust someone whose mood is "stuck" permanently on positive, with no recourse to concern or apprehension or caution on occasion.

I want to know that he can get his landing wheels down before he runs out of whatever currently fuels his seeming high altitude flight. I prefer someone who can see both sides, positive and negative, and come off with a balance in favor of the positive. That is someone whom I am more likely to find believable, and ultimately find more trustworthy.

Turn On Your Truth Detector

Someone who is living with his own truth will generally have a grounding, settling, accepting, validating effect on your deeper self. You will be more at home and at ease as the other person is at ease. He calls it like he sees it. Your spirit is elevated, assured, calmed, or made more peaceful in this person's presence. You feel a reverence for your true self from this person. You are not caught in an uneasy manipulation of an agenda that runs through you on its way to his goal.

You may sense a certain compassion from that person in recognition of the fact that you are not yet serving yourself well, not being true to yourself. And even then, **you are the final arbiter of what works for you.**

People with high positive energy will inspire you to be your own best person. They walk their talk. You get a real cool vibrational resonance from them. They will not distract you further from yourself, swat you away from your peace of mind, disconnecting you further. You become more focused, content with who you are, and find new levels of awe and reverence as you realize yourself. You move beyond discontent, desperation, and quick fixes of yourself, to the wonder of your life as an ever-arising experience.

The more I realize me, the more I peaceful me.

Beware Those Who Would Motivate You

When you are dealing with those who would motivate you, jump-start you, move you from here to there, you need to tune in to whether this serves you well. Someone can come at you with high energy and it is very seductive. Suddenly you are on your feet cheering and high-fiveing your neighbor. You heart rate is up. You feel a surge of emotion. You are ready to take the pledge, march off to war, or sell a thousand more of your product every day. But when it is all over, did you move in a direction that is in alignment with your purpose, passion, or agenda?

Buyer Beware

If you were moved where you did not want to go, then you were not being served. If you were compelled to set a goal without knowing your broader purpose, you may simply have been compliantly distracted or sidetracked. If you were moved and you do not know now how to move yourself farther by yourself, then you have become dependent on the motivator.

Author's Aside on Motivation
Motivational speeches, tapes, and programs are extremely popular. Motivational speakers are brought to pump up an audience. As a professional speaker, I am often asked if I am a motivational speaker. My stomach curdles a little at the question, for strictly speaking, I do not think that you can motivate anyone. The idea of motivating anyone seems demeaning. Inspire? Yes. But, motivate, no.

You Can't Motivate Anyone!
You can provide incentives. You can badger, cajole, intimidate, attract, provoke, collaborate, inspire, entice, pressure, nudge, compel, and a number of other actions to get another person to take more initiative in his own life, to be more self-igniting. But ultimately, ***only that individual can motivate himself****. Self-persuasion is more effective in the long run, more than persuasion from an outside source.*

Not everyone who shows up with a high level of energy is bringing highly positive energy. If you pay attention to your own response, as well as to what you see and hear, you can get a sense of where that person is coming from. He may be desperate. He may need for you to "move" just so he can think he made a difference.

He may fuel his major ego boost of getting you into action whether you want to or not. You may be his fix. And the buffeting you sense is his compelling demand for action, not for your welfare. You have to turn on your truth detector. The more that person needs to impress or move you, the less likely it is that he is truly responsive or acting in service to you.

Make Lemonade When They Hand You Lemons
High positive energy can transcend the most horrific of personal experiences. It truly is not just what happens to you, it is what you do with it that makes a difference in your life. The high positive energy you can maintain, is a result of your attitude toward life and how you want to live it. You can sweeten any situation by letting your energy flow, free of tension.

Give a man a fish, and you feed him for a day. Teach a man to fish, and he can feed his family for a lifetime.
Motto of the Chol-Chol Foundation

You need to learn the skills to be generative, and you will be less dependent on others, most likely becoming more self-supportive, even a boost to others.

Generativity v. Dependency
Even as we talk about the benefits of associating with highly positive people, we can also underline the importance of learning to generate your own energy and elevate your own life level.

Generativity is more than self-motivation. Generativity is the ability to develop more energy, or to release more, as the occasion requires. Generativity goes to the point of elevating your mood and energy beyond your usual level. It is a way of finding a new level of living.

The simple release of tension, driven-ness and striven-ness, constriction, and demands can float my boat effortlessly. Just by releasing personal inhibition and lightening up, I can float effortlessly out of the quagmire in which I have mentally mired myself or spent time wallowing. Having played the perfect victim, easing back into my natural state from all that internal compression is a relief and a better way to life. But generativity is even more than this.

Several of the skills of being generative dovetail with the breathing exercises in Guideline #2. Those that include relaxation begin the process by promoting release. You will recall that you have 100 percent of your energy all the time. The problem comes in converting and releasing that energy for purposes of improved quality of life and performance.

Insofar as your energy is impeded by inhibition, resistance, or constriction, then exercise, meditation, and relaxation can all promote release. Meanwhile, journaling about these chronic barriers to release, such as self-distrust, and resistance can begin the process of release by exploring where the tightness is being held.

With generativity, you can elevate your mood and energy, if not enter thriving directly. Among the solid practices for generating energy and energy release are bioenergetics, core energetics, kundalini yoga, and aerobics, and many of the cardiovascular and other exercises require increased respiratory functioning, blowing the cobwebs out, creating a resurgence of energy.

Learn to Lift Your Own Life

What is essential here is that you learn the generative skills to be able to lift yourself out of the psychological doldrums and put wind in your own sails. That takes skills, attitude, and determination.

When you have specific ways for knowing how to do it, you will be surprised by the fierce internal resistance you may encounter. How could you not want to feel better, when you in fact know how? This, of course, gives rise to dealing with your shadow side and to recognize the dangers of excess positivity.

Shadow Into Light

Dealing with your shadow side is part of the maturing process. To ignore or deny it is to live in perpetual fear. For, like the beach ball held under water, it is being driven to the surface by a natural force. To suppress it means expending energy uselessly.

Your dark side needs to be dredged up, embraced, and illuminated if you are truly to become a whole, self-accepting human being, and attain inner peace in life. To ignore your shadow side is to become brittle and reactive. You take on a porcelain-doll quality with the excess positivity you demand of yourself. You are unreal, partly because you emulated someone who appeared to be living well but was really in denial. Your own truth detector was malfunctioning. This person was not walking his talk.

Summary

Guideline #6 has dealt with accessing thriving using the role modeling. energy resonance, and company of others with high positive energy as a launching pad for your own thriving entry. But it is generativity that gives you the immediate possibility of recapturing high positive energy as needed and thereby making it easier to sustain thriving.

Being with balanced, non-intrusive, highly positive people is one method of self-love, care, and nurturing through association. Resonating with these individuals and having them as positive role models and support is helpful.

Meanwhile, be aware of the aspects of yourself, and of others, that are in balance, and not in denial – those who face life directly and live it to the fullest. And to maintain the theme of autonomy, you can learn specific techniques, attitudes, and skills to release and generate your energy. Your generativity ultimately can help you sustain high positive energy and the thriving state.

Chapter 18

Guideline #7: "Give In" and Thrive

Thriving is our natural state. Yet for most of us who have thrived infrequently, sporadically, or long ago, it does not seem possible it could be the effortless, easy natural way of being for us that it is. Certainly it is more difficult than that. As my friend Bill Scanlin put it so well, "When you don't get that feeling back, you tend to grow weary and lose your zest for it." Many just forget about the fact that they once experienced the thriving state.

Today the pace of life is undoubtedly quickening. Your acculturation, coupled with daily, high-strain practices can obstruct or wear down your natural flow of energy. You have become accustomed to paying personally in wear and tear, keeping up with what is swirling around you for fear of some imagined cost *of simply letting it go*. You are even reluctant to relax into the possibility of life being easier. What if you lose your edge? You continue to struggle unnecessarily, learning through sorrow rather than through joy.

You have just read the six preceding guidelines or portals to thriving. Any one of these entryways, or any combination may prove to be your opening connection to the thriving state. It depends upon you. There is no incremental build-up needed, no magic staircase to ascend, with entry by way of a mystical portal that you reach only after guideline #7.

Thriving Is Effortless
Since thriving is a natural state, striving or trying may be counterproductive. It's like the saying, *the hurrier I go the behinder I get*. The harder I try, the more I tighten and watch the thriving state slip further from my richest experience of myself. Letting go of the constriction means release from tension and ease of flow of energy throughout your system.

Your "Real Ease State"
All that you have to do to thrive is to "allow" yourself to experience your true original self. You have to release into the thriving state. That involves a letting go of fear, conflict, tension, and strain. It means loosening up a lifetime of residual tension and crimping. It means giving up imagined control where you have little or none to begin with. It means moving back inside yourself and trusting the impelling energy that rises within you.

"Giving In" Is Not "Giving Up"
Thriving requires a kind of *giving in*. But people are reluctant to let go in this way. Giving in easily gets confused with "giving up," surrender, or even with slacking off or shirking responsibility. Thriving may require surrendering the chronic state of tension that you believe keeps you on your toes. Few want to let go of that familiar and seeming guarantor of survival.

Giving in requires an acceptance that you already are at home within yourself. Self-doubts, tension, fear, and shame can sometimes interfere with your life force, taking you out of harmony with your own natural self. Only when you let go of all of that interference will you realize that you have been at home all along. You have had yourself "together" all along. You have simply been so distracted that you failed to notice and appreciate yourself. You had it all together all along. You simply did not realize it.

It takes so much to be a full human being that
There are very few who have the enlightenment
Or the courage to pay the price...
One has to abandon altogether the search for security, and
Reach out to the risk of living, with both arms.
One has to embrace the world like a lover.
One has to accept pain as a condition of existence.
One has to court doubt and darkness as the cost of knowing.
One needs a will stubborn in conflict, but apt always in
Total acceptance of every consequence of living and dying.

Morris L. West, The Shoes of a Fisherman

Few really understand this concept of giving in. Thriving is not an abandonment of responsibility for oneself. Thriving requires resilience, ongoing focus, concentration, and continuing adjustment to changing realities including your personal internal reality.

Thriving requires an efficient vigilance, a continuing self-monitoring to stay relatively balanced or to return to your central core connection. Even though the act of thriving is effortless, it requires maintaining your center, your grounding, balance, traction, awareness, equanimity, vitality. If your circumstances are like a hurricane with all the un-tracking and distraction that it implies, thriving requires on-going monitoring to let you find your stability within the eye of the hurricane.

Giving in is not meant to be glib, although it sounds something like the "Let go and let God" admonition from the twelve-step programs. But if none of the preceding doorways provided you access to thriving, it could be that you are pushing, striving, forcing, trying too hard. And a quick and sure remedy for trying hard and being ineffectual is to simply give in.

Give in to the reality of the moment. Call off the dogs. Give in to how you feel. Trust the context, reality, and yourself. Pay attention to your inner experience. Be aware of your awareness. Accept yourself within this reality right now. Allow your major conflicts to dissolve. You create your conflicts any-way. Sigh and release. Expand. Lighten up. Let your mind clear.

Exercise: Expressing Gratitude
In the easiest and most grateful way that you know how: Lift up your heart to whatever universal power and presence you revere! Place your palms in an upward offering toward the sky, at about a 60 degree angle with fingers up, palms forward and positioned directly up above and out from your head. Cleaning and jerking a barbell over your head would leave your hands in the same relative position. Bend slightly backwards from the waist. Mean what you do. Feel the result.

Thriving is your natural state. Joy is your birthright! Allow yourself to flow by removing your own internal conflicts.

Summary
At any one of the seven guidelines to thriving you could already have found your passageway into the thriving state. You do not necessarily have to go through each one in turn, in order to thrive. Your breathing alone, from the first guideline, might be sufficient to release you into thriving. However, to sustain the thriving state, you still need to consciously and fully accept and nurture yourself.

When you get to this point in the seven essential guidelines to access the thriving state, there are still further considerations, skills, and attitudes to learn. But at some point you simply let go and thrive, or go back and revisit the issues contained in guidelines one through six.

Chapter 19

Hints for Putting It All Together

The real test of learning is whether what is learned is applied!

Application Is What Counts
Now that you have read through the general rules, and the seven guidelines to thriving, what will you actually do? You have probably read your share of self-help books, and attended seminars, completing them with sound resolutions and written plans to do something differently. And your resolve stuck until the first distraction or old habits set in. What you actually do toward thriving is what is important here. Good intentions, wishes, desire, all fall on crusty ground. You have to do something, mostly internal, to break through the crust and cultivate your acceptance of new practices and your development of your own Thrival System®.

"Why are you here on the most beautiful day of the year?" I asked the participant in my World Bank seminar. She replied," I want to find the blue skies part of myself every day."

Here are several things to bear in mind as you make the adjustments that are part of your new thriving mode of life. In the items that follow, several address more sweeping issues such as setting a high positive attitude, while others address specific practices for particular situations or times of the day. You can implement them immediately.

- *Set aside the time to experiment with, practice, and blend new activities into your life. When you are short of time or tolerance, you tend to revert to business and behavior as usual and no change occurs.*

- *The more specific and detailed you are about what you are attempting to do, the greater the likelihood of your success. The details address how you envision your outcomes, in clarity of intent, or in specific picture-perfect detail.*

Once you are ready, trace through the pressures, pitfalls, and potholes of your typical day, utilizing the seven essential doorways to thriving, together with hints for putting together the thriving practices to either get you there (access), or keep you there (sustain).

Well Begun Is Half Done

Attitude (Plus Application) Is Just About Everything
Your attitude and predisposition are essential in initiating a positive inner game and the high positive energy that elevates your mood and spirits. Numerous activities relate directly with a high positive state. One is humor and smiling. Another is a sense of inner joy, delight, and expectation on facing the day.

Smile
Put a smile of contentment on your face before you open your eyes and your entire body can feel the contentment. This is the suggestion of Valla Dana Fotiades, sponsor of International Boost Self-Esteem Month, February. The smile already can put you in a good mood by generating good brain chemistry. Your attitude and actions trigger favorable brain chemistry. So you control your internal pharmacy, invironment, and internal climate every day.

Stretch
Stretch your body like a cat, elongating from head to foot, and loosen up your spinal column in bed, or on a floor mat as one of the first things you do upon arising.

Conscious Self-Acceptance
Throughout your transition, you will want to repeat your statement of self-acceptance to yourself the very first thing in the morning. That can set the tone for your entire day. You may want to put this on your bathroom mirror.

> *"I accept myself totally, right now,*
> *without qualification or condition.*
> *I am enough, no matter what.*
> *And I am emerging."*

Let yourself feel the results of that statement. If you are truly accepting of yourself, you can release so much energy that you can practically glide out of bed on the streaming and emanations. This can open up that tingling in the front of the sternum and solar plexus, and you are set for the day.

Follow a general regimen of self-care that includes special practices over and above routine teeth brushing.

Morning Rituals

Sun Salutation

Once you are up, go right into doing the basic *sun salutation*, a series of yoga postures to promote spinal flexibility and to stretch your entire body. This is one of the best daily exercises you can learn and provide for yourself. You need to maintain your flexibility and range of motion throughout life, or you lose it.

Detoxify

Cleanse your body of toxins first thing in the morning. Begin the day with a glass of purified water and a tablespoon of apple cider vinegar to counter calcification of arthritic joints. Dr. Joe Esposito, DCM, recommends an alternative, a tablespoon of olive oil for the same effect. If you do not want apple cider vinegar or olive oil, begin your day with deep breathing and a cup of warmed water to begin your digestive and eliminative processes. Green tea also provides a beneficial early morning drink.

Use a Tongue Cleaner

Use a tongue cleaner to get the Russian Army out of your mouth before you brush your teeth. A tongue cleaner will deep clean your tongue and reduce the colonization of bacteria that can become the source of infection, and mouth odor. Health, breath, and teeth benefit.

Self-Massage

Try giving yourself a sesame oil massage all over your body several days a week right before your morning shower. If you do not get touched or massaged frequently, this can provide the health benefits you are missing. More than a gesture, this is an act of self-nurturance.

If you do not have time for a full-body self-massage, focus your massage on the bottoms of your feet up to your ankles.

Then massage your face, ears, and neck. This stimulates circulation and internal connection.

Face the Day with a Plan

Anticipate and take on the day by planning and setting priorities for things you want to take care of. Some people do this before they get out of bed. Make your plan for the day as a guideline, not as a strict and compelling taskmaster. Make sure that you build in time for the unpredictable events that are sure to arise. And be flexible enough to be open to new opportunities or necessities during the course of the day. Be realistic with your goal setting so that goals are achievable within the time you allot or you create unnecessary stress.

Set Your Innertude®

Scan your plan. If you have not dealt with your concerns about the day's events by the time you get out of bed, find time before you begin your day's work to deal with any fear and resulting deflation of energy, breathing space, and mood. Any time you find yourself caving in or flagging in energy or spirit, locate the place in your body where this occurs and then breathe into and re-inflate that area in the manner outlined in the Chapter 12, discussing Innertude®. That way you can get the dents out without any further cave-ins. Then focus your energy directly specifically toward what you need to do, not on what you currently fear doing.

Elevate Your Energy

If you are facing a high-paced day, or a day with challenging meetings or confrontations, engage in a light workout in the morning in order to bring your energy level up to the challenges you have to face. That way you do not have to jump-start yourself, or hope for a resurgence of energy when you enter the situation that concerns you.

Elevate your energy level and heart rate upon arising so that you can envision yourself in your mind's eye comfortably and competently confronting these situations that arouse concern. Some travelers report that they walk fast in the corridors of their hotel. Still others will practice the breath of fire, for which instruction is advised, jump rope, swim laps, or run.

Mentally Rehearse

Envision yourself being totally present and looking all parties directly in the eye. Watch and listen to their responses. Speak in straightforward declarative sentences. See yourself being very clear about your agenda, as well as listening carefully and responding to them.

Quiet Your Mind

Quiet your mind through meditation, prayer, reflection, or mindfulness. Shut out all demands for approximately 20 minutes the very first thing in the morning, or during a commute to work in which someone else is at the controls. Cleanse your mind of agitation and static. Find your peacefullness inside. This fits right in with the meditation practice listed under the five thought modes in Chapter 9 on five things you can control.

Utilize your breath to calm mind and body and be aware of it through the day for both cleansing, restoration, and calming. ***Breathe in at a rate that is one-half of your exhalation rate. If you inhale to a count of 3, then you should exhale to a count of 6.***

Nurture Away From the Nitrates

Choose foods that are truly nutritious, calming, and healthy for you. Rather than combining bacon, coffee, and orange juice, together with sweetened cereal and milk, or a low-grade carbohydrate sweet roll – the combination from hell – consider what would be most beneficial to both body, mind, and spirit. Satchel Paige used to recommend avoiding french-fried foods because they *angry up the spirits*. And with fat, salt, sugar, and nitrates, you contaminate your insides until you can detoxify by excreting them out of your system.

Steer clear of sugar, salt, fat, and caffeine.

Sugar alone may put you through mood swings that leave you reeling within, then crashing, and finally seeking to satisfy your craving for something sweet again. Know the effect sugar has on you, whether taken in your coffee or as part of the prepared foods you consume.

Pay attention to the basics: rice, beans, grains, fruits, nuts, and vegetables. Also pay attention to food combining. Certain combinations of foods actually counter their positive nutritional effects by interfering with digestion. Nutritionist Wayne "Mango Man" Pickering of Daytona Beach, Florida, suggests that you pay attention to what you eat in order to optimize digestion and nutritional benefit rather than treating your stomach like a chemical dump, and a nutritional bypass due to bad food combining.

Getting Your Family Going in the Morning

Running a household is a matter of good organization and energy utilization. And thriving requires acting on the energies that arise within you and learning to trust that you will get done what is required, by following through. Being guided from within takes getting accustomed to.

You are not likely to engage your internal guidance full bore for life's major events without first testing it out to see if it works on the more routine and mundane choices during less pressured days. But you have to learn to trust your heart and gut sometime, so make it soon. And make your choices conscious.

Rather Than Build Up Negative Energy, Just Do It!
Getting the kids ready for school every day may require preparing lunches, having change in the right amounts, getting certain clothes or uniforms prepared. Whenever you think of doing something of short duration, just do it. It takes more energy and time to keep putting something off than it does to just go do it. You see, all the time you are holding it on the back burner, there is concern, strain, and energy draining out over whether you will forget, or won't find the time to do it. That accumulates as negative energy until you act effectively to overcome the resistance.

Drive Time: The Great Morning Commute
Give yourself sufficient time so that you avoid nail biters. Learn the traffic patterns coming out of your neighborhood. Anticipate alternative routes in case of traffic tie-ups or inclement weather. Take along books on tape, or music that you truly enjoy listening to.

Accept current reality each day so that you are not screaming at the slow-moving *turkeys* and rubberneckers who inevitably slow for an accident and any police lights.

Don't become your rage. Use your ability to be aware of your awareness to observe yourself. Once you become your rage, you are truly out of control and a danger to self and others.

If you really cannot move in traffic, then accept it. Don't damn yourself. Simply resolve to start earlier tomorrow. Late for a meeting? Call on your cell phone, or get someone to call for you.

If you are calm enough in the morning, and alert, you might try leaving all noise turned off and just tune into yourself. Release your breath and enjoy the rise and fall of your own breath and the realization and relaxation it brings. Make this your sanctuary, your private time.

Ongoing Everyday Practices

Develop Capacities

Use opportunities you have with kids, job, or household to fine-tune skills and become more adept every day. How you fare in daily events becomes an ongoing indication of how well you learn from experience.

Anticipate glitches and hazards in your daily activities. Become more efficient. Improve your choreographing of events, especially the repetitive, predictable ones. Smooth out the kinks. Buy time and you gain new options. For example, today get the kids up 10 minutes earlier to make their own sandwiches, rather than your having to stuff them in the van at the last moment to make it to the bus stop on time. Give them an appreciation of what it takes to maintain even the uncomplicated aspects of their lives.

Get That "Gleam in Your Eye"

You can put *a gleam in your eye* when you realize that you are openly, explicitly, directly capable of figuring out and coping capably with what is going on as well as everything you will face today. You get out ahead of the situation.

Rather than dulling your response and smothering it all inside, you anticipate and choose how you will respond. When you come out of your own self-styled closet to act and be as bright as you are, you will find that you are a lot more perceptive in knowing what is going on than you let on.

You also have to be willing to act on your truth, on what you perceive, detect, and know irrespective of how anyone else is acting or reacting. Putting that gleam in your own eye [It is definitely not a leer!] tends to open you up to being more savvy, clever, light, proactive, and on top of the situation, rather than thick, dense, torpid, stupid, plodding, and ultimately clobbered by events.

Respect Your Natural Rhythms and Cycles

Become familiar with your internal cycles. This level of inner self-knowledge is essential to understand what is happening with you at most times, what is influencing your mood, energy, or behavior. Several behaviors are cyclical.

Biorhythms are one example. Your physical, emotional, and intellectual fluctuations begin in regular cycles at birth, rising and falling in predictable measure. You can chart them and note high-performance days as well as "double' and "triple critical days."

Critical days occur when a physical, emotional, or intellectual cycle crosses over the mid-line from positive to negative, or vice versa. These are termed biorhythms and some people are convinced of their usefulness, while others consider biorhythms as bad science. See if yours portend important changes for you.

Other behaviors may simply be matters of personal tendency and sensitivity. For example, you may be especially sleepy in the early warming of spring as your blood begins to thin out. You can be blindsided every spring, or you can make note of it in your journal and know what is happening. If you have a protracted period for your seasonal changeover, try exercise, drinking extra water, or even acupuncture to move your through the energy changes. Better to take proactive steps, or simply admit that this happens in the spring…and take a nap. There is need for surprise, bewilderment, or to beat yourself up over it.

Note these personal realities in your journal, rather than learning about them again every time they come up.

The Case For The Siesta
Many employees have sighed that if only they could put their heads down for 10-15 minutes, they would be able to get through their energy down trough in the afternoon. When they fight off sleepiness, the trough may drag them down for hours. If they cannot rest, it may make sense to exercise lightly, to keep your blood stirring.

Dr. Jim Loehr states that research on people's cycles demonstrates that it is normal and natural for people to get sleepy and go into a recuperative mode in the afternoon. Business is now responding to sleep needs by granting employees a nap break rather than a coffee break, as a result of sleep research. And most savvy professionals will not attempt major business deals between 1:00 and 3:30 in the afternoon. That is when people tend to be drowsy.

Living With Yourself at Work
There are no hard-and-fast rules here. One of your main tasks at work is to transform your work style from the compelling, externally driven, exhausting approach most of us practice toward an impelling, internally resourced, replenishing activity.

All work requires a certain amount of structuring or organizing. Even a jazz combo requires a rhythm or beat against which everyone else can improvise. Lay down the basics that give you sufficient structure and mechanisms for advancing your work and performing your projects.

As you begin to work in a manner that demonstrates implicit trust in yourself, you can begin to quiet the nagging voices that have accompanied you most of your life like overzealous harpies and inner critics. Quit attributing Solomon-like qualities to others, putting them in a place of judgment over you. Accept yourself as enough. Feel the smile of contentment deep within and let it surface at the corners of your mouth as you take responsibility for your own care, decisions, and mood.

Slow Life Down with Enriching Experiences

By breathing slowly and deeply, you can actually expand your consciousness to take in what is going on. You can fill up your time by expanding your bandwidth so that you make time slow down. However, you have to consciously want and allow yourself to do so. By expanding your experience, you have more novel and unique experiences to pay attention to; fewer that are accustomed, or limited in scope. You can also transcend, rise above and gain a broader perspective on any situation you enter by using the "six eyes exercise" from guideline #4.

Maintain Presence in Any Situation

Conflicts and confrontations arise at any time. *If you carry yourself erect, level, and relaxed, and come on to people straight in posture, you portray an attitude that serves you well and presents you optimally. When you are tuned to yourself, you are more present and available to others.* In a major conflict, it is important that you maintain your own presence. Deep presence is a sign of emotional maturity, inner connection, peace, and equanimity.

Adopt the inner stance advised earlier in Figure 15-1 on page 225, by putting a "buffer zone" for consideration and discernment between your eye and brain. This is one way of maintaining an objective stance in any situation irrespective of the climate or passions being expressed.

Put Yourself in Perspective

Be able to see the bridge of your nose around to your eyebrows. These fixtures on your facet provide a frame around you whatever you look when you look out from your eyes. This gives you a physical context of presence and containment. See yourself in the perspective of your own body.

Express Your Intention

Review your awareness of your option to express yourself or to contain yourself. Become more intimately aware of your own intention. An awareness and consciously referring to your intention may take you in an entirely different direction from your usual habitual behavior. You become more available to yourself by making your intention conscious and then acting on it. Try it the next time you are in close discussion with a loved one. Say what you intend. And mean what you say.

When you are thriving you draw so much from your deep fire, that you fear no one's judgment. In fact, you can look upon judgment with some amusement, no matter how vile, intrusive, or unfair.

First of all, you have improved your sensors to read the basic tenor of the situation. If there is danger or outburst, you sense it in advance. Then you can look right at it and observe, rather than being pummeled to a pulp by whatever is sent your way. Your amusement comes with your continuing realization that you are acceptable to yourself. So all the caterwauling against you is really not going to impact you as it would most survival-oriented folks.

Even when someone is exercising judgement of you in a totally unjustified way, you need to exercise discretion. At no time should you put yourself in jeopardy. Be discreet. If their action and observations are unjustified, then you can let them glance off you or fly by. You can also counter them, or stop them.

If you hit your own personal limit, you need suffer no abuse from anyone – boss, colleague, employee, or spouse. Protect yourself. You need to know your rights and assert them for yourself. There are times to draw a wider boundary or limit around yourself as a defense against intrusion. As you begin to thrive, you will become more conscious of appropriate boundaries, and anticipate needed action before you are invaded.

Making Time for Yourself: In Defense of Respite

Private time is one of life's most precious commodities. And everyone needs it, especially introverts.

Most moms and dads no longer have a den or workshop for solitude. The kitchen traffic has four lanes through it with an off ramp to the refrigerator. So moms need to find private time and guard it jealously in order to have some balance in their lives with time out from, as well as quality time for, those they love.

Revise Your Rules For Being a Mother

Most mothers have hard-clad rules about what a mother does. Usually that does not include time to oneself. That is a foreign concept. Often moms see themselves totally at the service of others all day, every day. No limits. No boundaries. No rest. No respite. You can see where this is leading.

When you recognize your responsibility to take care of yourself first, then you can be more available to and give better attention to those who depend upon you.

In this formula of what a mother does, there is no room for taking care of oneself, no recuperation or restoration time. It is an exhausting role. So when I have introduced the need for private time during the day, most mothers have not considered it. Yet each one realizes that much quality contact gets lost when they are just getting through the evening ritual with the kids, rather than bringing their best rested self to the endeavor.

A real estate executive proposed to his family that he really needed to play tennis more, even though it would mean less time with his family. He explained that if he left his stress out on the court, he could be more present to the family. At first, every member of the family resisted and complained about his absence. But as they started to see the difference in him, there were times when they would say, "Dad, don't you think you ought to go play tennis?" And, at times, he took the kids along to participate.

Fast Times

These are times when nobody gets a break without setting aside time and holding to it. And there are the unplanned events of daily living: the kids are sick, a parent suffers a stroke in another city, and then the sewer backs up! These are times to put into effect Guidelines #3 and #7: Acknowledge reality, then give in and thrive.

Or there are the times you have a presentation to make at work the next day, and you find yourself up until 4 a.m. with food poisoning. Now you can roil against the fates, or you can assess the situation, get a clear reading on what you have to do, master your resources, and then set one foot in front of the other to get it done.

Self-Nurturance in Attitude and Practice

Self-nurturance is one practice that many adults find difficult to set in motion, let alone maintain. Yet this is basic taking care of oneself so that you can be present. The longer you have been self-abusive, in denial, or self-neglecting, the more practices, arguments, and habits you have built up in favor of proving your unworthiness to attend to your own needs.

Cheryl Austin-Brown, international consultant and seminar presenter, noted that when she traveled excessively, "Food had a critical impact on my ability to be successful with the people I interacted with, and I just don't forget that kind of a lesson."

*Cheryl was crippled when she was young and spent several years unable to walk, and with significant pain. When she was declared well after nine years, she found such joy in being able to walk and run, that she **cherishes** her mobility and pain-free existence. It is a joy she is conscious of daily. And she continues her ongoing intention to nurture herself and care for herself based upon her memories of those pain filled times. She has learned from her experience a lesson that she is not likely to forget. The value of such a lesson, of course, is in your application of it.*

The fine points of self-nurturing take time to become part of your self-care repertoire. First get the basics in place, then go for refinement. Of course it helps to be around someone who is self-nurturing and who can model it for you. There is so much to learn. Those who are self-nurturing can be written off as spoiled or self-indulgent by the envious who wait for someone else to take care of them. Being self-neglecting, self-abusive, and in denial serves no ones purposes. So at the very least take care of yourself.

Daily Practices

Water

Drink plenty of clean filtered, distilled, or spring water daily. Staying hydrated is one of the better things you can do for yourself. You do not always feel thirsty when you are dehydrated, so drink regularly and often. Keep your electrolytes up.

Vitamins
There is a great dispute over the usefulness and quality of vitamin supplements. I suspect that one of the finest things about vitamins, (even if they had no discernible nourishing effect) is that you take them with the conscious focus of improving your well-being. So even if the tablets and capsules don't work, the intention of self-care and self-nurturing does help. There are some vitamins that can be toxic when taken beyond the recommended dosage, so pay attention to how much you take.

Truth Telling: To Yourself and Others
Many self-nurturing practices are simple and second nature, like telling the truth, at least to yourself and getting closure in relationships and in dealings with others.

- Other practices may seem petty, like lowering food consumption three to five hours before bedtime so that digestion does not interfere with sleeping.
- Get a phone with a less rancorous bell.
- Put a night-light in the bathroom so you don't get fully awakened by bright lights.
- Get fluffy towels for your bath, flannel sheets for winter sleeping. As you love yourself more effectively, everyone around you benefits from the warmth, vibes, and good emanations. And you are the source of these good vibes. That puts you in the eye of the hurricane, the generative source.
- When you have time and the inclination, locate and visit a certified foot reflexologist. This health professional works on the pressure points in your feet with connections throughout your body to your vital organs. It is stimulating, refreshing, and relaxing all at the same time.

- Have a massage. Touch is essential to your health.

Summary

There are innumerable ways to express the way thriving can be implemented and maintained in your daily life. As you discover your favorites, I hope you will share them with other readers through Thrival.com. We touched on several points for putting into application practices from the seven doorways to thriving. These are simple starter applications. You can get even more by reviewing the earlier chapters on the rules, balance, and doorways.

In the last chapter we consider the more sweeping issue of making the transition from survival mentality and mindset to thrival mentality and mindset – an essential part of maintaining and sustaining thriving. This especially includes internal resistance points, stresses, conflicts, and energy drains on the path toward thriving: the place where your spirit soars.

Rule for Application: "Use Your Discretion!"

This is the main and underlying advisement with which you should consider anything you read here. You are still required to exercise discretion in what you do and in how you do it. You have to exercise skilled trust of yourself in utilizing intuition, gut feel, a strong sense of urgency, or an internal nudge as your prompt for action. After all, ultimately you are the one who has to live with the results. What you do, i.e., your application is your choice with your discretion.

Chapter 20

Where Do You Go from Here?

We can find examples of thriving everywhere around us. The following quote from Dennis Wholey is one example:

The happiness we are looking for...is already inside of us. Our mission is to discover our own individuality, uniqueness, and goodness, and to affirm the goodness and wonder of other people. We must love each other unconditionally without thinking: "What's in it for me?" We must love others for their own good and not ours. If we do good things for others unselfishly, they will love us in return, which will make us feel wonderful about ourselves – and that's happiness.

Parade Magazine, Oct. 26, 1986, p.9

You now know that the ***thrival state of exceptional well-being exists*** as a distinct, definable state of being. And you know that thrival is *attainable*, along with the new way of life it makes possible and portends. This introductory book has dwelt mainly on getting into the thrival state from a survival background, literally from endurance to resiliency.

Now that you have studied *how to access* the thriving state, what can you expect? You will now begin the process of ongoing behavior change that marks a transition. Few people can make a "once and for all" sweeping change of lifestyle. They get caught carrying baggage they brought with them, acting from old habits.

You will begin to run into snags in your life that will pose immediate impediments to sustaining the thrival state, and the commensurate feeling of success. That is all part of making a transition. You will need to monitor your own personal journey and manage yourself along the way. As you begin to fine-tune your guidance system toward the thrival state, you will want to learn the knowledge, skills, and attitudes that are part of sustaining thrival.

And you will want to study and overcome the impediments you will find in your way. You may find that you brought your own speed bumps, or are using your parking brake to slow your transition or to make sure it does not happen at all.

The Bliss Blockers™

The main resistance you will run into can be encapsulated in three main bliss blockers™, presented here to give you a bit of a head start in your transition to sustaining the thrival state more of the time. These are:

1. **The Survival Mentality, Mindset, and Practices**
The survival mentality is such a part of our daily lives that, up until now, it has not stood out as anything separate from the way life is. Pretty much everyone has lived their lives exercising only the options available under the survival mentality. As you begin to stretch out toward thrival, you will hit the end of the survival mentality bungee cord and be snapped back repeatedly. It is important that you know this in advance so that you can enter the transition forewarned and forearmed to move forward in spite of it.

It is essential to keep your journal regarding the resistance in yourself that you can attribute to the survival mentality. For then you can make your transition base it on the guidance you are getting on how you are being held back. After all, the survival mentality exists in your mind, so you can change it. However, it is ingrained in your tissues and habituated in your behavior. So you are in for a long-term weeding of your own soil. The root system of the survival mentality is complex and entrenched. You have to free the space in yourself to cultivate the thrival mentality and lifestyle.

In the meantime, shorten your learning curve for your own transition by harvesting all the vestiges of the survival mentality in your life and lifestyle, using your journal to note your discoveries.

2.Disbelief and Distrust of Human Nature

Underneath it all, this is the most damaging of the three bliss blockers, for it is the belief that gives rise to your attitudes, values, and sense of self. And that is what undermines what you then do in acting on that belief. As you keep your journal on this bliss blocker, note whether you are more trusting of others than you are of yourself. The disbelief in human nature, the overemphasis on our "broken-ness," sets the stage for distrust among all your relationships. But most damaging is the effect it has on how you think about yourself and the self-doubt it gives rise to.

3.Disbelief in Yourself: Shame

Your entire sense of entitlement, value, esteem, worthiness can be tied up in the way disbelief in yourself manifests in your daily life and actions. This sense of shame pervades and permeates everything you do and say. When you have yourself poised on the edge of banishment, with no redeeming value, how can you possibly consider yourself worthy of the joy of thriving? How will you face this, the most difficult personal bliss blocker?

As you keep your journal, you will find that shame is the greatest barrier to your thriving. How can you take steps toward the joy and pleasure in a thriving life when you consider yourself so undeserving? Such self-doubt will find you questioning yourself time and again, even from the very beginning, regarding your worthiness to pursue thriving. Write down your questions and your internal resistance.

4. Self-Sabotage

This bliss blocker is not as important as the other three. In fact, it is more of an example, the other three in practice. Self-sabotage does have several specific and definable characteristics. Notably, the very skills you use to undermine or sabotage your getting what you say you want can be easily transformed in a positive way to promote the task you set out to accomplish.

Among the readily identifiable types of self-sabotage, of "grasping defeat from the jaws of victory," are ***procrastination, being unable to say no, and doing too much,*** to name a few.

You will find that self-sabotaging practices have two qualities in common:

i. Control

Subtly couched in the activity of sabotaging yourself is a blatant attempt to wrest control from a situation in which you do not have control. For example, in procrastination, putting off what you eventually must do is a misguided attempt. You still have to do what you are postponing doing. And that conjures up negative energy toward the actual performance of the activity you are putting off.

ii. Stress Addiction

There is also a component of stress addiction in self-sabotage practices. The individual engaged in the activity is often taunting himself with the tension of the enterprise, e.g. putting off till the last possible moment something that absolutely must be done. This engenders stress under the surface and meets the needs of someone addicted to viewing life as a struggle and stress as the price you pay to live.

Write down your particular tactics for thwarting your own intentions, activities, objectives, and goals. Take a look at the skills required, plus the payoff for engaging in that practice. Look even at some of the clichés you are embroidering around your ineffectual activities.

Now that you are on your way to ***maintaining and sustaining*** the thriving lifestyle, you need to clear the trail for yourself as you run into the real and persistent blockage in yourself. For self-sabotage, that means looking at the skills you utilize to thwart yourself, and with a subtle correction in energy and the direction of your efforts, you can accomplish the task you set out to complete in the first place.

For procrastination, for example, you take the skills that allow you to

- **a. Prioritize:** prioritize everything ahead of what you eventually must do
- **b. Manage Time**: leave just the minimal amount of time to complete the task at the last moment, and
- **c. Focus**: know the status and precise details of the project throughout.

You also need to become aware of how a transition differs from change.

Change vs. Transition

The shape of change is a rather like a light switch that goes from off to on, a sudden straight-line motion from condition A to condition B. The new action is thrust into action and becomes the new operative approach. That does happen for shallow practices of minimal complexity and duration.

For the more complex and established practices, you will need to work your way out of the grasp of habitual prior practices and into the clear space of new and improved thriving practice. The shape of a transition is more like a roller coaster, with challenging ups and heart-in-your-throat downs. You have to be in it for the long haul…as long as it takes. Take the ride and you may be hitting new highs the rest of your life.

Life can be so much better. And it can start being that way for you as immediately as your next breath. So take a minute now to focus on thriving, and then continue to sustain it for the rest of your life to realize yourself more fully, and to have the richest experience of your life.

Take Root in

Your Own Soil

Joy Is Your Birthright!

Make Every Moment

Of Your Life

En-Joy-Meant

And Give Yourself

The Richest Experience of Your Life!

A great revolution of character
In just a single man
Will help achieve a change
In the destiny of a nation,
And further,
Will enable a change
In the destiny of all mankind.
Daisaku Ikeda

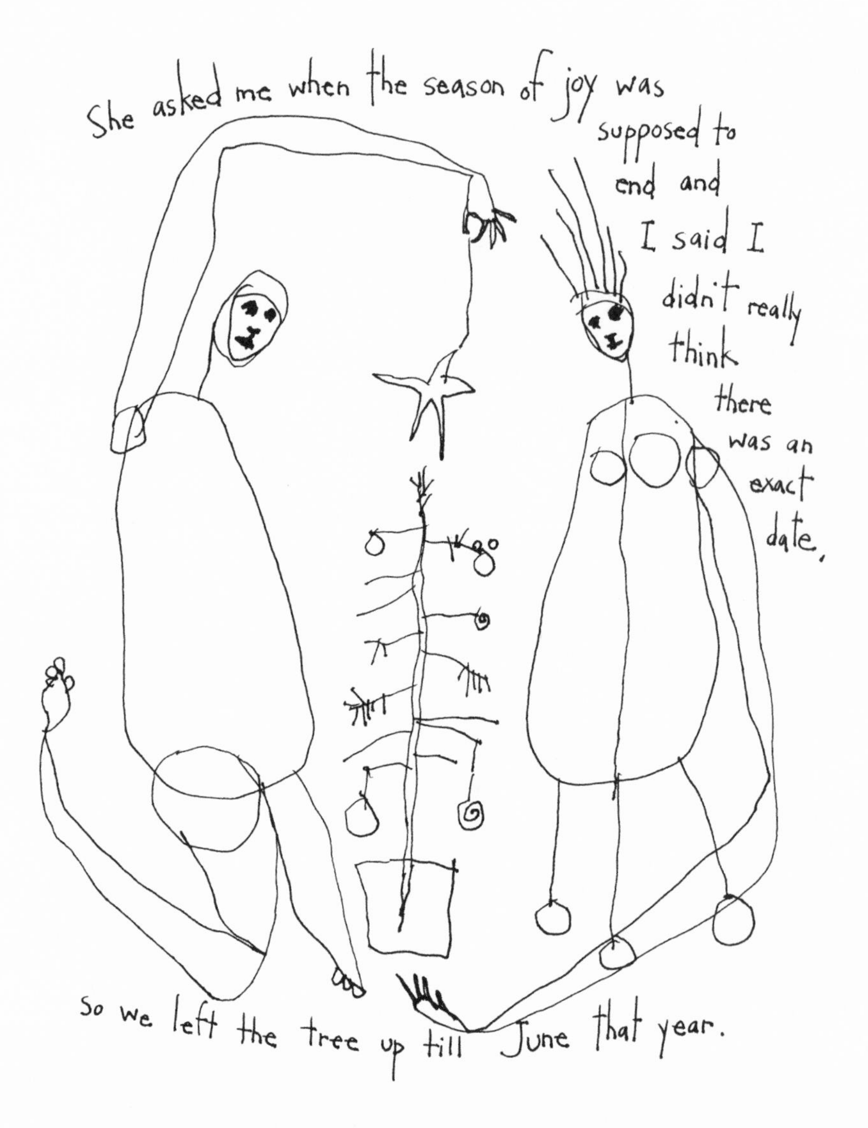
She asked me when the season of joy was supposed to end and I said I didn't really think there was an exact date,
so we left the tree up till June that year.

Recommended Reading

Aron, E. *The Highly Sensitive Person: How to Thrive When the World Overwhelms You.* New York: Broadway Books, 1997.

Chopra, D. *The Seven Spiritual Laws of Success.* San Rafael, CA.: New World Library, 1994.

Dahms, A. *Thriving: Beyond Adjustment,* Monterey, CA.: Brooks/Cole Publishing Co., 1980.

De Becker, G. *The Gift of Fear.* New York: Dell Publishing, 1997.

Ellyard, P. *Ideas for the New Millennium.* Victoria: Melbourne University Press, 1998.

Gallwey, T. *The Inner Game of Tennis.* (rev. ed.), NY: Random House, 1997.

Glickstein, L. Be Heard Now! *Tap Into Your Inner Speaker and Communicate with Ease.* New York:Broadway Books, 1998.

Hanh, T.N. Peace Is Every Step: The Path of Mindfulness in Everyday Life. New York: Bantam Books, 1991.

Ivker, R. *Thriving: The Complete Mind/Body Guide for Optimal Health and Fitness for Men.* New York: Crown Publishers, 1997.

Loehr, J. *Toughness Training for Life.* New York: Penguin, 1993.

Lowen, A. *Fear of Life.* New York: Collier Books, 1980.

Murphy, M. *The Future of the Body.* New York: Jeremy P. Tarcher/Perigee Books, 1993.

Myss, C. *Sacred Contracts. Awakening Your Divine Potential.* New York: Harmony Books, 2001.

Nelson, M. *Coming Home: The Return to True Self.* Novato, CA.: Nataraj Publishing, 1993.

Potter-Efron, R. and P. *Letting Go of Shame.* San Francisco: Harper and Row, 1989.

Putney, G. and S. *The Adjusted American: Normal Neurosis in the Individual and Society.* New York:Harper and Row, 1963.

Sams, J. *Dancing the Dream: The Seven Sacred Paths of Human Transformation.* New York: Harper Collins, 1998.

Siegel, R.S. *Six Seconds to True Calm.* Santa Monica, CA.: Little Sun Books, 1995.

Tolle, E. *The Power of Now: A Guide to Spiritual Enlightenment.* Novato, CA.: New World Library, 1999.

About the Author

Paul O. Radde arrived on earth during the Armistice Day blizzard, November 11, 1940, one of the worst in the Midwest. He likes to think of his life as a gentle counterbalance to the catastrophes of that day.

Through his engagements as a professional speaker, psychologist, executive and life coach, and organizational consultant, Paul works to bring out the best in people in all walks of life and at all levels of all types of organizations. His main keynote speech is on *Thrival!* He also presents seminars on leadership, management, influence, resilience, side-by-side relationships, and the highly sensitive person. He coaches executives to rise through the ranks through the use of thrival skills.

Raised in Wahpeton, North Dakota, Paul attended the University of Notre Dame for a B.A. in the Great Books program and earned a Ph.D. in Counseling and Community Psychology at the University of Texas in 1974. A fluent Spanish speaker, he spent two years in Chile as a volunteer and also worked in the U.S. State Department.

Paul conducted crisis interventions after 9/11 as part of his psychotherapy services in Washington, D.C., where he worked for over 25 years as a practicing psychologist.

He has also written two books on management and conducted training for thousands in first-line supervision, stress management, influencing decision makers, and leadership.

An avid racquetball player and skier, Paul also sings, plays trumpet, rides horseback, meditates, hikes, scuba dives, bicycles, and in-line skates. As a “P” on the Myers-Briggs, he had a wide variety of interests and projects. He lives in Austin, Texas.